PLAN
Z

PLAN Z

*The Nazi Bid for
Naval Dominance*

by

David Wragg

Pen & Sword
MARITIME

First published in Great Britain in 2008 by
Pen & Sword Maritime
an imprint of
Pen & Sword Books Ltd
47 Church Street
Barnsley
South Yorkshire
S70 2AS

ISBN 978 1 84415 727 3

A CIP catalogue record for this book is
available from the British Library

Typeset in Sabon by
Phoenix Typesetting, Auldgirth, Dumfriesshire

Printed and bound in England by
CPI UK

Pen & Sword Books Ltd incorporates the Imprints of Pen & Sword Aviation,
Pen & Sword Maritime, Pen & Sword Military, Wharncliffe Local History, Pen
& Sword Select, Pen & Sword Military Classics and Leo Cooper.

For a complete list of Pen & Sword titles please contact
PEN & SWORD BOOKS LIMITED
47 Church Street, Barnsley, South Yorkshire, S70 2AS, England
E-mail: enquiries@pen-and-sword.co.uk
Website: www.pen-and-sword.co.uk

Contents

Acknowledgements

In writing any book such as this, an author is always indebted to those who have left personal accounts of their experiences and those who safeguard the archives, whether they be of written records or of photographic material, including of course, to the Photographic Archive team at the Imperial War Museum in London. This is not an economic history, but economics and the often overlooked poor financial situation of Germany, in the days immediately before the Second World War had an impact on the plans for rearmament, so anyone interested in this aspect of Germany's preparations for war must be grateful to Adam Tooze for his work, *The Wages of Destruction – The Making and Breaking of the Nazi Economy*, a highly readable account that I can recommend without hesitation.

David Wragg
Edinburgh
October 2007

Introduction

If the outbreak of the Second World War found the United Kingdom and France ill-prepared, the German Navy, the Kriegsmarine, was also caught wrong-footed. In contrast to the period prior to the outbreak of the First World War, there had been no naval construction race during the 1930s that involved Germany, although there had been one between France and Italy. Germany undoubtedly wanted a far larger navy than that allowed by the Treaty of Versailles, or even by the Anglo-German Naval Agreement of 1935, but this was still some time away. The senior officers and planners of the Kriegsmarine did not expect war with the British Empire until 1944–45, Grossadmiral Raeder foresaw a major battle with the Royal Navy, one that would settle the issues left unresolved at Jutland, in 1948. This was not just wishful thinking, even Hitler had assured Raeder that there would be no war with England before 1943.

In September 1939, the Kriegsmarine had a number of major warships under construction, but only 59 submarines. It even included two elderly battleships of little use other than for coastal defence, the remnants of the small fleet permitted by the Treaty of Versailles.

At its best, this was a modern navy, but it lacked what was to prove to be essential for any blue water navy in the war that lay ahead, aircraft carriers and naval aviation. Priority had been given in the period immediately before the outbreak of war to the development of the air force, the Luftwaffe, and while the army had massively expanded, it also suffered weaknesses, with artillery and most supplies still depending upon horses. The Kriegsmarine was last in the queue for modernisation and expansion.

Looking ahead, the Germans had plans to create a navy that would be able to match that of the United Kingdom. These had started with Plan X, which had been followed by Plan Y, and finally emerged as Plan Z. This would have given Germany the balanced fleet essential for the war that lay ahead, albeit with more than 200 U-boats, later increased to 300.

Plan Z is often referred to by naval historians, but does not seem to have received serious consideration. Several have written it off on the grounds that Germany could not produce sufficient fuel for such a large fleet, but this was a problem that Hitler tried to address in his thrust eastwards. On the other hand, German aircraft carrier design was badly outdated, while operational questions over naval air power had not been resolved by the Germans. Plan Z also seemed to overlook the resumption of naval construction by the British, which would have rendered the proposed surface fleet as inadequate. The real questions over Plan Z have to be:

- How realistic would the plan have been given Germany's other military goals?

- How long could Britain and France have held back from war as Germany flexed her muscles?

- How would the ships have compared with those operated by the British and French navies?

- Could the Germans have made use of Japanese expertise?

- How long could Germany have afforded the manpower, materials and money that her massive arms build-up was already costing?

There are answers to some at least of these questions. There was a strong 'peace faction' in the UK that might have become more influential had Germany stalled over Poland for a year or two longer. The same effect could have been achieved had the League of Nations, or at least the UK and France, taken action against Italy when that country invaded Abyssinia in 1935 – closing the Suez Canal to Italian shipping would have been easy and highly effective, while plans for an attack on the Italian port of Taranto date from this time.

PLAN Z – GERMANY'S BID FOR MASTERY OF THE SEAS begins with a history of the Kriegsmarine and the impact of defeat in the First World War. This is followed by a look at the reconstruction of the navy and the rivalry between Raeder and Dönitz, and between these two and Goering, head of the Luftwaffe. The ships involved in Plan Z are then examined, along with the potential for a naval race between Germany, Britain and France in the late 1930s and early 1940s. The question over just how long Britain and France might have held off declaring war is also considered. An emergency alternative to Plan Z involving taking over units of the Vichy French and Italian fleets is also examined. Finally, a look at some of the major naval battles of the Second World War considers what might have happened at the River Plate, in Norway and in the hunt for the *Bismarck*, as well as the Battle of the Atlantic and the Arctic convoys, had Plan Z's fleet been in place. This, of course, begs the question of whether Germany could have become a maritime power, and of course the impact of such a large U-boat fleet on the convoys at the outset of the war.

Glossary

Allies – originally used for the Triple Entente during the First World War – the United Kingdom, France and Russia, but during the Second World War initially used for just the UK and France, and then later adding the Soviet Union and finally the United States of America.

Asdic – Derived from the initials for the Allied Submarine Detection Investigation Committee, and now known as sonar. Asdic or sonar equipment emits audible pings and then traces submerged objects through their echoes.

Auxiliary Cruiser – Merchant vessel taken up from trade and armed, with a naval crew. In British use, these ships were used as convoy escorts, while in German use, they were surface raiders. In neither case were they successful when confronted by purpose-built major warships.

Axis Powers – The alliance formed by Germany, Italy and Japan. Nevertheless, unlike the Allies, there was very little coordination at times, especially between Japan and Germany or Italy, or cross-fertilisation of ideas or technical developments.

Barbarossa – Code name given to Germany's invasion of the Soviet Union.

Battlecruiser – a warship generally with battleship calibre armament, but in which armour was sacrificed to give a greater speed. The German battlecruisers *Scharnhorst* and *Gneisenau* nevertheless had guns of just 11-in, and although these were supposed to have been replaced by 15-in guns, this never happened.

Battleship – designation given to large heavily armed and heavily armoured ship. Second World War battleships generally had guns of 15-in calibre, but some had 14-in or 16-in, and the Japanese had a class with 18-in calibre guns.

CAM-ship – Catapult armed merchantman, a merchant vessel with a fighter aircraft that could be catapulted off to shoot down enemy aircraft. The fighter pilot was usually from the RAF, but a number of Fleet Air Arm personnel also flew such aircraft. Problems were that the aircraft had to be sacrificed at the end of a single sortie, unless within range of land, and because of this, there was always reluctance to use the aircraft in case a more pressing need came later.

Case White – Code name given to the Invasion of Poland.

Coastal Command – A command within the Royal Air Force that provided maritime-reconnaissance and anti-submarine patrols and also search and rescue in the open seas, generally meant to be tasked by the Admiralty.

Corvette – During the Second World War, this referred to a warship designed for convoy escort duties, usually smaller than a frigate or destroyer, and also slower and of broader beam than the latter, as well as less heavily armed.

Cruiser – A warship smaller than a battleship or battlecruiser, but much larger than a destroyer. The Washington Naval Treaty of 1922 laid down that light cruisers had a main armament of 6-in guns and heavy cruisers a main armament of 8-in guns (displacement tonnage had nothing to do with it), but the British Town-class with up to twelve 6-in guns in four turrets were classified as 'heavy' by the Royal Navy. There were also merchant cruisers, although usually referred to as auxiliary cruisers (see above), and anti-aircraft cruisers, usually much older ships converted to allow their continued use.

Cruiser War – term also applied to commerce raiding.

Destroyer – Small warship, generally fast, and by the Second World War much larger than its First World War counterpart. Armament varied between 4-in and 4.5-in on British ships, but some German and French vessels were larger and the latter had armament in the *contre-torpilleur* classes of 5.5-in.

E-boat – enemy boat, usually a German fast motor gunboat or motor torpedo boat, but known to the Kriegsmarine as S-Boot, for *Schnellboot*, or 'fast boat'.

Electro-U-Boats – German U-boat development that appeared from 1943 onwards, with an enlarged hull to enable additional batteries to be fitted to give higher underwater speeds.

Enigma – The code used by all of the German armed forces, but broken once a machine and code-books fell into British hands. The breaking of the Enigma codes was a major factor in the Allied victory and especially in countering the U-boat threat to Atlantic and Arctic convoys.

Escort Carrier – Small aircraft carrier sometimes converted from a merchant vessel, but later increasingly using merchant vessel hulls to allow conversion to a merchant vessel post-war. Limited in the number of aircraft that could be carried, and in speed. Originally intended for convoy escort duties, but eventually also acted as aircraft transports and also acted in the combat role supporting invasion forces.

Felix – code name for a planned invasion of Gibraltar, abandoned when it became clear that Spain would not and could not cooperate.

Fleet Air Arm – Originally that part of the Royal Air Force that was deployed aboard Royal Navy warships, but it reverted to Admiralty control in May 1939, and naval airmen steadily took over from their RAF counterparts.

Frigate – Originally a general purpose sailing warship much smaller than the ships of the line, predecessors of the battleship, which disappeared from the world's navies during the late nineteenth century. These were reinvented during the Second World War as a convoy escort larger than a corvette and slower than a destroyer, and usually were dedicated anti-submarine or anti-aircraft ships. In more modern times, they have reverted to their general purpose function.

Kaiserliche Marine – official name for the Imperial German Navy.

Kriegsmarine – 'War Navy', the official name for the German Navy given by Hitler in 1935 to replace the old Reichsmarine or 'State Navy'.

Luftwaffe – German air force, which controlled all German service aviation after the outbreak of the Second World War. Although autonomous, it nevertheless developed as a primarily tactical air force without long-range strategic bombers until it was too late in the war, and therefore was hard pushed to maintain the attack on British targets.

MAC-ship – Merchant aircraft carrier, a ship that continued as a grain carrier or oil tanker, with a Merchant Navy crew, but had a wooden flight deck built over the cargo areas and the superstructure moved to starboard so that naval personnel could fly Fairey Swordfish on anti-submarine patrols around a convoy. Most were British manned, but two ships were manned by Dutch personnel, including aircrew and aircraft maintainers from the Royal Netherlands Navy.

Reich – The state.

Reichsmarine – official name for the German Navy after the abdication of the Kaiser and the creation of a republic or 'Reich'.

U-boat – strictly, in German, U-boot, or Untersee Boot, a submarine.

Wolf Pack – a group of submarines deployed against a convoy.

CHAPTER ONE

Germany Inherits Prussia's Ambitions

Germany has loomed as such a major presence politically, economically, industrially and, at times, militarily for so much of the twentieth century that it takes a moment's thought to recall that, like Italy, the country ranks amongst the younger European states. The country was originally a collection of independent kingdoms, with the strongest, Prussia, dating from 1618. Unification of Germany first came in 1806, when the Emperor Napoleon unified the country as the Confederation of the Rhine, but Prussia remained independent of this, situated to the east of the Confederation on the Baltic coast. This was part of the so-called Continental System, a type of enforced trading area and protection enforced by Napoleon and intended to exclude Great Britain from European trade. The Continental System was used as a form of economic warfare. Nevertheless, the reforms introduced by Napoleon were largely adopted in Prussia.

Prussia, or more correctly Brandenburg-Prussia, had begun its rise as the dominant military power during the seventeenth century, and under Frederick II, who reigned from 1740 to 1786, it reached an early peak. In 1740, Frederick attacked Austria and started the War of the Austrian Succession, one of the fruits of which was that his territory expanded to include Silesia under the peace agreed in 1745. Hostilities resumed with the Seven Years' War, which broke out in 1756 and lasted until 1763. In 1772, West Prussia was acquired and Poland partitioned for the first time. By the time he died, Frederick had established Prussia as the strongest German state militarily. Despite the seeming inability of his state to live in peace with its neighbours, Frederick's rule was no harsh dictatorship, and he was generally credited with being not only a just and enlightened ruler, but was also a patron of the arts, encouraged education and reformed the legal system, established religious tolerance and did much to encourage agriculture and industry.

1

BISMARCK – THE IRON CHANCELLOR

The collapse of the Continental System in 1813 and the end of French dominance in Western Europe created a vacuum, and in 1848, many German states were swept by revolutions aimed at establishing democracy and unifying the country. The revolutions were poorly coordinated and unsuccessful, with that in Prussia suppressed by Prince Otto von Bismarck, marking the start of his rise to increasing power. A step towards unity came with the establishment of the North German Confederation in 1867, in which the dominant state was Prussia. War with France followed in 1870–1871, which meant that France had to cede its provinces of Alsace and Lorraine to Prussia and then to Germany, which finally established itself as a single unified nation in 1871, under the leadership of the austere and authoritarian first Chancellor, Bismarck, with Wilhelm I of Prussia becoming the first German Emperor or *Kaiser*.

Born just two years after the collapse of the Continental System, Otto Bismarck pursued an aggressive and expansionist foreign policy. He went to war against Denmark in 1863–64, gaining the disputed state of Schleswig-Holstein and giving Germany a North Sea coast and ports for the first time, then with Austria in 1866, excluding the country from a future Germany, and in 1870–71 with France. It was the last conflict that led to the unification of Germany, while to the south, Austria and Hungary combined to form the Austro-Hungarian Empire, a political entity founded on weakness as Austria had lost the war with Prussia and ceded Venetia to Italy. Despite the fighting with Austria, in 1881 Bismarck attempted to embrace Austro-Hungary and Italy in a Triple Alliance, but failed. In 1890, he was forced to resign by Kaiser Wilhelm II.

Bismarck had ruled as a virtual dictator, not for nothing was he known as the 'Iron Chancellor'. His schemes for German unification and expansion were popular, but it took a strong and more liberal-minded Kaiser to keep him in check. His lack of tolerance brought him into conflict with the Roman Catholic Church and with the increasingly powerful socialists. Nevertheless, he was clear-headed and far-sighted, and amongst the first modern statesmen to appreciate the value of strategic alliances. He ensured that the new unified Germany was from the start a strong country able to withstand the pressures from neighbouring France and Poland, and the not so far distant but mighty Russia. It was not for nothing that a British cartoonist described his departure as 'Dropping the Pilot'.

MORE THAN A CONTINENTAL POWER

With Prussia as the foremost continental military power, a country able to challenge France even before unification, Germany inherited an enviable position in 1871. The new state was strong and viable from the start. It looked as if nothing could stop Germany from achieving whatever ambitions it might entertain. France had not only fallen from its powerful position during Napoleon's rule, it had been humbled during the Franco-Prussian War. Italy, united ten years earlier than Germany (although it had also been united by Napoleon, only for unity to end along with his rule), did not pose a serious military challenge. With characteristic energy and dedication, the Germans began to establish themselves as a major industrial power, and also sought colonial expansion. Even in the final three decades of the nineteenth century, possession of a colonial empire was held to be a good thing and an important status symbol for the European nations. Germany's plans were, of course, hampered by the fact that the British and French had taken the most appealing territories first, and the Dutch had also done well for themselves in the Far East, while even tiny Belgium had the Congo, rich in timber and mineral resources.

Prussia, and therefore Germany, differed from countries such as her future foe, Great Britain, for a number of reasons. Secure in her island isolation, Britain became a trading nation, and the merchant class effectively drove her constitutional development from the Tudor period onwards. Merchants needed freedom in order to function effectively, with minimal state interference, but they also valued the legality and enforcement of contract, and favoured the separation of power between the state and the judiciary. There was no need for a large standing army, which required conscription to meet its manpower needs, but there was a need for a strong navy to protect the trade routes and enforce colonial rule, although locally-raised troops provided much of the manpower ashore.

Prussia had developed without natural frontiers and saw herself as surrounded by enemies. Russia, for example, was ever expansive, and had the goal of a warm water port, and ideally not one that could have its access to the open seas blocked. The only guarantee of security for the Prussian state was force, maintaining a strong standing army in which conscripts predominated. The conscripts provided the basis of strong reserve forces, ready for mobilisation when war threatened. Wars were fought according to a strict timetable, starting after the harvest when manpower could be released from the farms and the storehouses were full. Force, or the threat of force, deception of the state's enemies and useful, if sometimes temporary, alliances, were all part of the mechanism for survival. Without natural frontiers, the state took all control to itself so that it could satisfy the needs of the soldiers and concentrate force wherever it was needed, to face threats that were either external or, on occasion, internal. Freedom and the interests of the individual were subservient to those of the state.

When Germany was created, as in most continental countries, the Army was the senior service, and indeed, for many years effectively the *only* service, which was almost the exact reverse of the situation on the other side of the North Sea. The German Navy in 1871 and for almost three decades afterwards, was little more than a coastal defence force, what would be described today as a 'brown water' navy. This is not to say that the Germans did not engage in international trade, for they had a merchant marine, and it was still the case that being an officer in the merchant service lacked the social cache of service in the navy.

All of this began to change when Wilhelm II ascended to the German throne in 1888 at the age of twenty-nine after his father, the liberal Frederick III, died after just three months on the throne. Frederick had often opposed Bismarck and it was no surprise that his son, Wilhelm II, sacked Bismarck in 1890, but Wilhelm was no liberal. His father and grandfather had placed great emphasis on the arts and industry, but Wilhelm was more interested in foreign affairs and defence. His mother, named after her mother, Queen Victoria of Great Britain, may have given him an interest in naval affairs, but whether she did or not, there was no doubt that the new Kaiser was jealous of Britain's naval supremacy. He wanted Germany to become a maritime power as well as a continental power, and for the German Navy, or *Kaiserliche Marine*, to rival the Royal Navy.

DEMONISING ENGLAND

The early years of the united Germany had been marked by a continuation of the earlier mutual admiration with England. Some German historians maintained that both countries showed a common 'Aryan' root in India, accounting for many of the similarities in the languages. Protestant England was admired as a role model by many Germans, as was the country's constitution and individual freedom. 'Admiration is the first feeling which the study of English history calls forth in everyone,' declared the historian

4

Heinrich von Treitschke in the 1850s. His views were to change. In 1874, he became professor of history at the University of Berlin, just three years after unification, with admiration replaced by jealousy and resentment. In this influential post, he began to demonise England, lecturing that England had been using Germany to implement her imperialist policies in Europe. As the years advanced his views became more extreme and not simply even more anti-British, but also anti-Semitic.

With the still young nation anxious to establish itself and possibly still unsure of itself, its Prussian military might notwithstanding, Treitschke's message found a willing audience amongst the senior civil servants, politicians and senior military officers in the capital. His rhetoric appealed to their Prussian upbringing and justified their recent wars.

'Unceasingly history builds and destroys; it never tires of salvaging the divine goods of mankind from the ruins of old worlds into a new one,' Treitschke lectured. 'Who believes in this infinite growth, in the eternal youth of our race, must acknowledge the unalterable necessity of war . . .'[1]

If this was strong stuff, worse was to follow.

> 'Amongst the thousands who march into battle and humbly obey the will of the whole, each one knows how beggarly little his life counts beside the glory of the State, he feels himself surrounded by the workings of inscrutable powers . . . Men kill each other who have great respect for each other as chivalrous foes. They sacrifice to duty not only their life, they sacrifice what matters more, their natural feelings, their instinctive love of mankind, their horror of blood. Their little ego with all its noble and evil impulses must disappear in the will of the whole . . .'[2]

When he died in 1896, the words of Treitschke and the ambitions of the young Kaiser had melded into what became popularly known in Germany as *Weltpolitik*, world policy. All of this coincided with the rise to power of a young German admiral, Rear Admiral Alfred von Tirpitz (1849–1930), who became State Secretary of the Naval Office in 1897. Tirpitz shared the Kaiser's naval ambitions.

The concept of *Weltpolitik* varied depending on one's viewpoint. It could mean creating a large fleet so that Germany became a maritime power as well as a continental power, and what is more the leading maritime power as well as being the leading continental power. It could mean adding colonies, or giving a boost to the overseas business of German manufacturers and merchants. It could also mean turning the minds of the German people away from Europe, and especially from the new country's own internal divisions, and towards a greater future, looking outwards rather than inwards. Such measures were attractive to the German leadership, struggling to absorb new states and create a single German identity, especially amongst those living in territories that had been forcibly absorbed into the Reich, such as Schleswig-Holstein, for example. There were also other problems, with the more liberal-minded middle classes needing to be swayed towards Prussian idealism, and the increased prosperity brought by trade and the acquisition of colonies being needed to sway the urban working class away from the Marxist ideals being propounded by the increasingly powerful and strident Social Democratic Party.

DIPLOMACY VERSUS A NAVAL RACE

Both Tirpitz and his counterpart as Foreign Minister, Bernhard von Bulow, were disciples of Treitschke. This team was handpicked to enable Germany to prepare a course that would lead at least to increasing confrontation with her European neighbours and the British Empire, and most probably to war. Bulow's role was to practise diplomacy to buy time for Tirpitz to create a fleet that could rival the Royal Navy, or, in his own words, in a letter to the Chancellor, Richthofen, 'in view of our naval inferiority, we must operate so carefully, like the caterpillar before it has grown into a butterfly'. This was the start of a naval race that neither side could afford to lose.

What the Germans feared most was a pre-emptive strike by the Royal Navy, and while this thought would have horrified the British Royal Family and the leading parliamentarians of the day, it would not be long before one British admiral, 'Jacky' Fisher, would advocate 'Copenhagening' the German fleet, a referral to the action taken by Nelson in 1801 when he discovered that the Danish fleet would not come out and fight, so he sent frigates into the harbour at Copenhagen. On paper, Germany was a democracy, with the structure if not the attitudes of a constitutional monarchy. The voting system in the Parliament favoured the upper house or *Bundestag* rather than the elected lower house or *Reichstag*. The Kaiser wielded far more real power than his British counterpart,

6

Queen Victoria, even though this was a period when monarchs still did have real power and their influence over those around them, including democratically-elected politicians, was considerable. Tirpitz had to steer the budget needed for this vast naval expansion through the *Reichstag*, or lower house, but first popular opinion had to be convinced that a great German Navy was needed, or even why colonies were needed. After all, many would question why Germany needed *Weltpolitik*.

Despite the ambitions of the ruling elite, the vast majority of Germans were not looking to seaward. Indeed, before unification, many of them lived in landlocked states. The notion of seafaring did not come naturally to them. A propaganda campaign had to be initiated to encourage the German people to support the new policies, even to adopt them as their natural right. It was from this time that the notions of racial purity and Germanic superiority began, and even the schools, perhaps particularly the schools, ensured that the Prussian Hohenzollern monarchy was exalted. They preached the need for patriotism and obedience. No longer were the universities and their professors above and beyond politics, for they too followed in the steps of Treitschke. The campaign even extended to the churches, with the Protestant Lutherian Church in particular joining the campaign; the Lutherians preached obedience and regard for the State and its authority, combined with a distrust of socialism and the individual's acceptance of his place in the social order. The campaign spawned pressure groups such as a German Navy League and a Defence League, a Colonial Society and a Pan-German League.

The campaign worked, and could even be said to have worked too well. Soon, many of the pressure groups and their members became something of an embarrassment for the regime, going further and faster than the ruling elite found comfortable. Such a public campaign also alerted many elsewhere to German ambitions, making the danger of a pre-emptive strike even more likely. Events began to assume a momentum of their own. Germany's neighbours became nervous. After all, it was less than thirty years since the Franco-Prussian War. Russia in particular, faced with growing social unrest and a country that was, away from the major cities in the west of the country, backward compared with the countries of central and Western Europe, could not afford a massive defence budget. Relationships were not eased when the German Naval Law, or *Flottenesetz*, of 1898 authorised the building of no less than nineteen battleships, as well as cruisers, destroyers and other small warships. This was a clear signal that German policy was to rival Britain on the high seas. That same year, pressure to ensure that a strong German Navy was created extended to the formation of the *Deutscher Flottenverein*, German Navy League.

THE FIRST PEACE CONFERENCE

The result of this unease was a first in international affairs, an international peace conference with its venue at The Hague. This was an early attempt at arms limitation, an abortive attempt to curtail the arms race, and especially the naval arms race, that was getting underway amongst the major powers. The Hague Peace Conference was met by widespread cynicism. As always, no one dared oppose it for fear of appearing to be a warmonger. In these days of nuclear weapons and the policy of MAD, Mutual Assured Destruction, it is instructive to note that then British Prime Minister, Lord Salisbury, believed that there was a danger that there would be a 'terrible effort of mutual destruction which will be fatal for Christian civilisation.'

Given that it was the first conference of its kind, and that many of the participants had been fighting each other within living memory, while they will still engaged in colonial rivalries, the aims of the conference were overly optimistic. Initially, the aim was for an international treaty outlawing war. If this would be unrealistic today, it was doubly so at the time. Fortunately, realism ensured that the objectives were watered down so that the agenda called for the banning of certain types of weapon, combined with a standstill in armaments procurement for a fixed period.

Starting on 18 May 1899, at The Hague, the conference was without precedence. At the time, such matters were normally only discussed between nations at the end of a war, when victors' justice prevailed and territory was divided. As always, the major powers eyed each other with suspicion. Despite war with France ending as long ago as 1815, and the two countries having collaborated, as in the Crimean War, Great Britain and France had come close to war several times, even as recently as 1898.

This is not to suggest that all of those attending did so from doubtful motives. Amongst those present were many who knew that war was wasteful and not an activity to be indulged in lightly and that the consequences could never be foreseen. These included the British admiral, 'Jacky' Fisher. Nevertheless, he was also amongst those with little time for those who tried to make war less

8

awful: 'You might as well talk of humanising Hell!' he declared.

The conference was in fact doomed from the start. The location was the *Huis ten Bosch*, House in the Wood, summer residence for the House of Orange. While Great Britain and her old foe France might have been content to see a standstill in armaments, and the Russians hoped desperately for reductions so that spending on social projects could be increased, the Germans were strongly opposed to any standstill and were determined to develop their armed forces so that the country was unchallengeable. Not only did Germany intend to retain its gains from the Franco-Prussian War of 1870–1871, it wished to show that a unified nation was stronger still. In addition, Germany did not at the time have the shipbuilding capacity of Great Britain, and did not wish to see any agreement that would inhibit the development of its shipbuilding industry, or indeed its armaments industries.

The British naval position was declared clearly by Fisher, who maintained that: 'The supremacy of the British Navy is the best security for the peace of the world.' He added later that if a nation was ready for instant war with every unit of its strength, peace was inevitable. Nevertheless, he also declared that it was his intention to be first into any conflict. A man of deep religious convictions, Fisher doubtless believed that the Almighty would scatter his enemies, but also expected his own fellow countrymen to take their share of the scattering.

'Suppose that war breaks out, and I am expecting to fight a new Trafalgar on the morrow,' Fisher responded in reference to a proposal that neutral colliers should be allowed to proceed un-molested. 'Some neutral colliers attempt to steam past us into the enemy's waters. If the enemy gets their coal into his bunkers, it may make all the difference in the coming fight. You tell me I must not seize these colliers. I tell you that nothing that you, or any power on earth, can say will stop me from sending them to the bottom, if I can in no other way keep their coal out of the enemy's hands; for tomorrow I am to fight the battle which will save or wreck the Empire. If I win it, I shall be far too big a man to be affected about protests about the neutral colliers; if I lose it, I shall go down with my ship into the deep and then protests will affect me still less.'

This stark realism was in complete contrast to the ideals of many of the delegates, diplomats with little or no experience of war. The British delegation made it clear that launching of projectiles from balloons, the use of submarines and of poison gas were the weapons

9

of the future – the first aeroplanes had still to fly – and that in a future conflict, civilians would be in the frontline. This last should not have come as a shock to the delegates. In Europe and Asia, civilians had always been in the front line as armies battled across the countryside, and the concept of civilians being spared the rigours and hardships of war was that of an island nation that had not been invaded for 800 years.

It seems that alone amongst the delegates, the Germans were the most realistic and open. They declared that the British fleet was useless and that they would sink it with their destroyers and torpedo boats. The warning was taken seriously. Just as in the late twentieth century, the major navies were concerned about the effect of fast missile-firing gunboats on their major warships, those of the late nineteenth and early twentieth century were worried about the torpedo-boat. In each case, the problem was that small navies and countries with relatively little money, could challenge the great fleets.

Over and above the propaganda efforts and the work of the pressure groups, the German body politic was soon swayed by British actions in searching German merchant vessels for contraband during the Boer War. This made it easier, in 1900, for Tirpitz, to get his Naval Act approved. The Kaiser, Wilhelm II, stated that he would make his Navy the equal in status of his Army.

The Anglo-French Arbitration Treaty of 8 April 1904, drew the line under many long-standing colonial disputes, and left the Royal Navy free to prepare to meet the pending challenge from Germany. In July 1905, Fisher ordered the Channel Fleet into the North Sea and then into the Baltic for manoeuvres, stating that 'Our drill ground should be our battle ground.' This was nothing less than sabre rattling and it rebounded on Britain as it created uproar in Germany and once again strengthened the hand of those pressing for ever greater naval expenditure.

Fisher was undoubtedly encouraged in his concerns over German naval expansion, influenced by the British Naval Attaché in Berlin, Captain Philip Dumas, who was able to visit the Schichau Yard at Elbing, where he learnt that the Germans would be laying down a new battleship in the autumn. He was remarkably successful in his ability to unearth intelligence, all of which was reported back to Fisher, and part of which was that the Germans planned to have a main armament of 11-in guns on the new ship. In contrast to the Cold War between the Soviet Bloc and the West, the Germans clearly did not restrict the movements of people like Dumas. Far from keeping the specifications secret, Soviet-style, they overloaded him with information, giving him too many details in the hope that he would be bewildered as their one concession to security was that they did not allow him to take any notes. Nevertheless, there were rumours that new ships were being built 'behind screens', and indeed, on one visit to Kiel, Dumas did discover two Dreadnought-type battleships under construction.

Neither Britain nor Germany could feed itself without imports, and for the Germans there was the added edge that the poor quality of much of the land meant that fertiliser also needed to be imported. Both countries had abundant fuel in the form of coal, but Germany was short on iron ore and most of that available in Great Britain had too high a sulphur content to be ideal for steelmaking.

In terms of industrial capacity, early in the twentieth century, the UK had the edge, especially in shipbuilding with the nation being the world's largest builder of ships of all kinds. Nevertheless, already there were signs that the nation's manufacturers were failing to modernise sufficiently and were losing their edge, while the newer German manufacturing sector was expanding rapidly.

On both sides of the North Sea, many pressed for an increase in the defence budgets, and especially in those for the navies. Yet, on neither side were such policies accepted by all, for there were those who felt that these policies were of themselves making the slide into open warfare more likely. In between, there were those who wanted strong, but affordable and effective, armed forces capable of defending the country. For the mass of both populations, mutual fear meant that the overwhelming need to be defended, to be secure, drove naval expansion.

While Fisher professed to hate war, he also wished, in his own words, 'to Copenhagen the German Fleet', starting a war without a declaration and hoping to inflict irreparable damage on the potential enemy. King Edward VII discouraged him, saying: 'My God, Fisher, you must be mad!' The Germans heard of this proposal, but regarded it as a rumour, while they also heard and circulated widely, the remark by the Admiralty Board's Civil Lord, Arthur Lee, on 3 February 1905, that Britain should 'get its blow in first, before the other side had time even to read in the papers that war had been declared.'

It soon became clear that the Kaiser and his ministers were convinced that there would be a surprise attack by the Royal Navy.

Indeed, a surprise attack on the Baltic coast at the onset of war was feared by many in the German armed forces. The main culprit was seen not as King Edward VII, but as the Admiral Sir John 'Jacky' Fisher, the First Sea Lord. In contrast, King Edward VII was seen by his own people as being a peacemaker, and a popular music hall song declared that there would be no war so long as good King Edward lives. It was remarkably prescient.

In the United Kingdom and in Germany, the press played up the scares, while fictional works were published, including the famous *The Riddle of the Sands* by Erskine Childers, while the German equivalent was *Der Weltkrieg: Deutsche Traume* (The World {or Wide} War: Germany Triumphant). The first book was one of espionage, the second, a futuristic novel in which a Franco-German-Russian alliance defeated the British, with Great Britain invaded after the Royal Navy was defeated. German journalists found irony in the use of the name 'Home Fleet' for the Royal Navy's newly-established main force.

Despite a state visit by the King to Kiel and Berlin in June 1905, and a visit by German warships to Plymouth in July of that year, the unease between the two nations was not dissipated. The British noted the professionalism aboard the German warships with considerable apprehension. Relations were civil and correct, but true warmth was conspicuous by its absence. The *Entente Cordiale* agreed in 1904 was seen, indeed presented by the German leadership, as an alliance against Germany. The Germans also recalled Fisher's belligerent attitude at The Hague Conference in 1899, just as much as he recalled vividly the threats made privately by German admirals. In German naval circles, the British First Sea Lord was known as 'Lord Fisher of Copenhagen.'

'England wanted war; not the King – nor perhaps the Government; but influential people like Sir John Fisher,' the Kaiser told Alfred Beit, the South African industrialist. 'He thinks it is the hour for the attack, and I am not blaming him. I quite understand his point of view; but we too are prepared, and if it comes to war the result will depend upon the weight you carry into action – namely a good conscience, and I have that.'

WIDENING THE KIEL CANAL FOR WAR

In preparing for war, there were many factors to consider. The Kattegat and Skagerrak were difficult and time-consuming to navigate, with a wandering route and too much shallow water. To provide easier access between the Baltic and the North Sea, between 1887 and 1895 the Germans had built the Kiel Canal, a ship canal sixty-one miles in length, through which ships could make the hitherto difficult journey in as little as ten hours, although there were a number of locks to pass through. This meant that the German Navy could move its entire fleet between the two seas, moving the ships to the North Sea for offensive operations, but bringing them back to the Baltic where they would be safer. Introduction of the Dreadnought-type battleships meant that the canal was inadequate as they were too wide to use it. Widening the canal, and the locks and their gates, was estimated by the British to cost £12 million at least. It provided a strong clue to German intentions when widening started in 1906. The British consul at Kiel passed the information on to Captain Dumas in Berlin. Not wanting to be caught out again, and finally recognising that warship sizes could only get bigger, the Germans doubled the width of the canal and also eased many of the bends. They also placed two new locks at each end to enable large ships to use the canal more easily at all states of the tide.

The work immediately alerted Fisher to the looming prospect of war and he used this information not just to calculate the cost of the work, which would be an additional drain on the German economy, but, far more important, also to estimate when it would finish. He concluded that it would take eight years to complete the work, taking the most likely date for the start of the First World War to 1914, and he also guessed that the Germans would want to complete harvesting before mobilising their largely conscript Army and going to war. This meant that war would break out in September or October 1914. The logic was impeccable. The work needed to be done, and continental countries had traditionally started fighting after the harvest was completed. On further consideration of the problem, he changed his mind and revised his estimate, deciding that war would break out during a bank holiday. He was right for his country declared war on Germany on 4 August 1914, the then date of the British August bank holiday.

The Director of Naval Intelligence, DNI, Prince Battenberg chaired a committee looking into possible threats to the United Kingdom. The 'two power standard' was taken as the minimum. This dated back to the wars with France that had ended in 1815, and essentially required the country to be able to match the combined fleets of France and Spain. Now, a new measure had to be calculated, based on the new enemy. The threat looked most likely from an alliance of Germany and Russia, or possibly France and Russia. Realism also dictated that having fought either of these combinations, and having been weakened in the process, the country might be attacked by an opportunistic power. The committee proposed that the Admiralty should plan on creating a fleet that was 'two power plus ten per cent', at least in capital ships. The fact that the standard started to be confined to capital ships showed an appreciation that the extra ships might mean reductions elsewhere because of financial and manpower constraints. It also reflected the fact that smaller ships were increasingly to play a subservient role and that, with their heavy calibre guns capable of firing accurately over longer ranges, naval warfare would be between battleships, aided by submarines. In February 1905, a second committee reported, and supported the findings of the earlier committee.

Meanwhile, the Germans continued to apply pressure on their neighbours. Stories about Germany increasing her shipbuilding programme were based on rumours, while the Germans deliberately planted stories about the German Dreadnoughts being bigger and more heavily armed than those of the Royal Navy.

Once again, the indefatigable Dumas, working hard in Germany, was a source of vital information. He wrote that while out playing golf: 'A German dirigible balloon [ie. a Zeppelin] came over our heads (one of the first journeys it has made) and I took copious notes . . .' It was to be another few years before the Zeppelin became more widely regarded as a threat. In October 1912, the Zeppelin *L-1*, under the command of Count Ferdinand von Zeppelin himself, made a record 1,000-mile flight, leaving its base at Friedrichshafen at 8.35 am on Sunday 13 October and landing at Johannisthal, near Berlin, the following day at 3.43 pm. The near round-trip caused a considerable outcry in England following a claim that it had been heard over Sheerness during the night, although no one had actually seen it. Questions were asked in Parliament, and the government proved unable to provide any answers. The German response that the airship had not approached the English coastline at any time did not convince anyone.

No less a person than Tirpitz himself met Dumas. Tirpitz referred to the 'nonsense about invasion lately written in England,' where people such as General Lord Roberts had argued that the Germans might land a force of up to 100,000 men on the East Coast of England. He went on to say that out 'of the 30,000 or so military officers in Germany one might expect that one or two sheep-headed lieutenants might write such rubbish.' Tirpitz found it incredible that someone with Roberts' reputation could advance such arguments. Napoleon had found an invasion of England impossible across a distance of just twenty miles. It would be impossible for Germany to embark 100,000 men, and, what was more, maintain their lines of communication. In short, landing an army would be difficult enough, but it ran the risk of being cut off. He concluded by mentioning that the figure of 100,000 men would be 'wholly useless in England even if we had no Army there to oppose them,' as it would be certain that a million semi-trained soldiers would volunteer immediately 'like magic'. He even reminded Dumas that the Prussians had halted before Paris in 1870.

Nevertheless, the Germans persevered with the build-up of their fleet. On 4 August 1914, Germany had sixteen battleships and three battlecruisers, while in home waters the Royal Navy had twenty battleships and five battlecruisers. These were the backbone of the fleet. In all, the Royal Navy had 68 capital ships, most of them pre-Dreadnoughts, scattered around the world, mainly in the Mediterranean, as well as 103 cruisers and 319 torpedo craft.

Within a few short years, less than two decades, Germany had built a fleet that could challenge the Royal Navy in its own home waters. This was as nothing, for Tirpitz, now ennobled with the 'von', ultimately planned no less than sixty battleships, each with a lifespan of twenty years actually enshrined in German law – a concept that was unthinkable in the United Kingdom – so that three ships could be built every year to keep the fleet up-to-date, regardless of the cost or the strain on the economy, or even of its manpower resources. Many historians now doubt Tirpitz's sanity.

It must not be forgotten that building this fleet was only part of the problem. A continental power with a relatively short coastline had also to build the manpower. Typical of the young men starting their naval careers at this time was one Karl Dönitz, the future admiral, head of the submarine service, later head of the German Navy and then, ultimately, Hitler's successor as Fuhrer. The cost of creating an officer corps was defrayed by passing it to the parents of the cadets and junior officers, even more so than in the Royal Navy. Over the four years of training and the following four years of service as a junior lieutenant, the total cost of the parental contribution was 7,000 marks, with 1,505 marks in the first year, some 200 marks above the average wage for a worker in industry. The initial training, equivalent to the four years at Osborne and Dartmouth in the Royal Navy, was just ten months, most of which was spent on a training ship and which included three weeks hard labour in the stokehold, in Dönitz's case in the heat of a Mediterranean summer. On completing the cruise aboard the training ship, the cadets were promoted to midshipman, *Fahnrich zur Zee*, and their specialised training started.

The officer cadets were drawn from the upper echelons of society, from the sons of impoverished nobility (despite the high costs), the sons of industrialists and academics, with almost half the intake being from this category, showing the extent to which academia had swung behind *Weltpolitik*, and of serving and retired officers. A few members of the lower middle and artisan classes, the *Kleine Leute*, were permitted to satisfy the social instincts of the politicians, and the odd baptized Jew, although this was the period during which anti-Semitism first reared its ugly head.

For the young cadet and officer, there was no doubt that they were in preparation for *der Tag*, the major battle with the Royal Navy in the North Sea that would finally establish Germany as the undisputed naval power. It was not only Tirpitz driving this expansion, but the Kaiser as well. Not for the last time, state expenditure on armaments rose alarmingly, well beyond what the nation could afford, and despite substantial rises in taxation, its debt levels rose dramatically. The newly important industrial class, and the traditional landowners, the *Junkers*, drifted apart. Industrial militancy rode on the back of the massive demands for labour of the armaments industry. The leader of the Social Democrats, August Bebel, was so alarmed at the direction his country was taking that as early as 1910, he started writing in secret to the British Foreign Office, saying: 'I am convinced we are on the eve of the most dreadful war Europe has ever seen . . .'

Notes
1 & 2   C. McClelland, *The German Historians and England*, Cambridge University Press, 1971.
3   *Review of Reviews*, Feb 1910.

CHAPTER TWO

The Great Naval War

As war loomed, in 1913 the young Karl Dönitz was a midshipman aboard the light cruiser *Breslau* in the Mediterranean, with the ship acting as the escort for the battlecruiser *Goeben*. Despite tension already rising in Europe, *Breslau* was allowed to coal at the main British Mediterranean Fleet base of Malta, on her way to the Balkans to join a British-led international naval squadron imposing a blockade on Montenegro.

While war was widely expected throughout Europe, and indeed many were anxious for a war that would achieve their territorial ambitions, none of the great powers was ready. Russia was dogged with social unrest and unable to meet the economic and materiel demands of war. Germany was bankrupting herself in an arms race, unable to afford both a large standing army and a navy that would rival the Royal Navy. Austria-Hungary was rent by internal divisions, a sprawling empire that included many different nationalities with many them anxious to break free. France was fearful of the consequences of another war with Germany, a factor behind the *Entente Cordiale* with the United Kingdom. The United Kingdom lacked the army that would be strong enough and well-equipped enough to engage in a continental war – it had not tried to emulate Germany by trying to have both the leading navy and the leading army. For the British, there was another problem, that of Ireland, where pressure for Home Rule was running at a high level.

The Kaiser wanted war, but not this war. As early as 1897, he had anticipated confrontation with the British, but not with the British, French and Russians at the same time. The British were bound to intervene, not only because of their links with France and Russia, but also if Germany was to attack France, the best route for the invading armies was through Belgium, and the United Kingdom was a guarantor of Belgian neutrality. In December 1912, the Chief of the German General Staff, General von Moltke, had called for war as soon as possible, before Russia and France were ready. This had been opposed by Tirpitz, who wanted to wait while the Kiel Canal widening was finished, a U-boat base in Heligoland was completed, and more of his battleships and battle-cruisers were ready.

For Germany, there was the absurd situation in which the two service ministries had been preparing for war, with the Army anxious that it should be as soon as possible, while the Foreign Ministry tried to contain the crisis that had erupted in the Balkans. The international naval squadron that had quickly formed to blockade the coast of Montenegro even sent landing parties in summer 1913, so that the Albanian port of Scutari could be freed from the occupying Montenegrin forces. All of this was under the command of Vice-Admiral Sir Cecil Burney, RN.

ASSASSINATION AT SARAJEVO

Germany, without a Mediterranean coastline or territories in or around the Mediterranean, at this time considered it necessary to maintain two major warships in the area. Some time earlier, she had played brinkmanship by maintaining that she had considerable 'interests' in Morocco, divided between France and Spain. The *Breslau* even refitted in Trieste, then Austrian territory, during the first quarter of 1914, before escorting the *Hohenzollern*, the Kaiser's yacht, to Corfu for a holiday visit. On her return to Trieste, she was ordered back to the new international naval squadron off the Balkans, and it was while she was lying alongside the British Minotaur-class armoured cruiser, *Defence*, on 28 June 1914, that news was received of the assassination of the heir to the throne of Austria-Hungary at Sarajevo.

Amidst the recriminations and counter-recriminations that led to first one declaration of war and then another, there were those in Germany working steadily towards a traditional continental war. A growing body of opinion wanted to put *Weltpolitik* aside for a while to allow Germany to secure her place in Europe, and also to stop the maritime enthusiasts taxing ever more heavily in a desperate bid to fund the growing *Kaiserliche Marine*. The traditional landowning classes wanted to retain power in the face of a growing Socialist menace, by this time the largest party in the *Reichstag*, although they retained power in the more influential upper house of *Bundestag*, while the Kaiser was almost an absolute monarch. In a very real sense, Germany needed a war to remove what it regarded as an external threat for good and establish itself as the leading continental power, and it also needed a war to unite its peoples and turn their energies away from revolution and radical ideas to external expansion and internal discipline.

The pro-war faction wanted a short, violent, Prussian-style war, smashing France so that she remained neither a threat nor a sponsor for the countries to the east of Germany, and then taking Belgium and the Netherlands to establish a satellite territory, a German *Mitteleuropa*, which would also include northern France, territories to the east and in the Balkans. This would also have the effect of keeping Russia contained. In effect, nothing less than a United States of Europe was planned. The *Weltpolitik* plan for colonial expansion would follow, aided by the occupation of the French, Belgian and Dutch territories that Germany so envied. Combined, these would provide a rival power base to the British Empire.

Meanwhile, with the great naval race with Great Britain having eased off and relations improved, there were many who hoped that she would remain out of a continental war. After all, did not the Liberal government contain a number of pacifists, and others who favoured social spending over defence? The Kaiser pressed Austria to take harsh measures against the Serbs, and the Austrians sought German support, and were assured that they would get it. Wilhelm II seems to have believed that neither Russia nor France would want to become involved, as neither was ready militarily, and neither could afford a major war. There was also the traditional view of a near-absolute monarch, that other monarchs, in this case the Tsar, would not wish to defend a regicide. This was despite Russia having earlier declared that any attack on Serbia would be a *casus belli*, and as it turned out, the liberation of the Slav communities within the Austria-Hungarian Empire became a Russian war aim.

The German armed forces were quickly moved to an alert, just short of being put on a full war footing, so as not to alarm or alert the other powers. In the Adriatic, the battlecruiser *Groeben*, suffering from boiler troubles, was ordered to Pola while workmen were sent from Germany to affect the necessary repairs.

Meanwhile, Serbia rejected an unrealistic ultimatum delivered by Austria, and on 28 July, Austria-Hungary declared war on Serbia. Over the next twenty-four hours, other nations declared war, with Russia declaring war on Austria-Hungary. The only questions that remained were over the side that would be chosen by Italy, a former member of the Triple Alliance with Germany and Austria-Hungary, and by Turkey, and whether or not Great Britain would join in. Whether or not she would, on the night of 29/30 July, the Admiralty sent a warning telegram to all ships, and HMS *Defence*, cast off her lines to *Breslau* and moved out of torpedo range, before disappearing into the darkness. Prepared for war, the *Breslau* was the sole operational German ship in the Mediterranean area, although the workmen from Germany aboard the *Goeben*, assisted by members of the ship's company, had already replaced 4,000 boiler tubes in just eighteen days. She left the dockyard, the work uncompleted, on 30 July, and the following day, Admiral Souchon, aboard the *Goeben*, radioed the order for *Breslau* to go to sea, sailing secretly but calling at Brindisi to organise colliers for a coaling session at sea.

Ideally, Souchon would have liked to take his ships into the Western Mediterranean, wreak havoc amongst the French troop convoys moving men and horses from North Africa to France, and then slip past Gibraltar for commerce raiding in the Atlantic, before heading back to Germany to join the scouting force of the High Seas Fleet. Instead, he took *Goeben* to Brindisi, where he rejoined *Breslau*, and was disappointed to find that neither at Brindisi nor at Taranto, would the Italians provide coal, initially claiming that the sea was too rough. Souchon correctly guessed that the Italians were intending to withdraw from the Triple Alliance, although it was not to be until 1915 that the break would finally occur and the country ally herself with Britain and France, the so-called *Entente* Powers. He moved on to Messina, where he could commandeer coal from German merchantmen. It was at Messina that he learned of Italian neutrality, and was refused coal once again. He requisitioned the German East Africa passenger liner *General* as a naval auxiliary, and seized the coal aboard other German ships in the harbour, gaining some 2,000 tons.

CHASED ACROSS THE MEDITERRANEAN
Souchon had counted on leading a combined German and Austro-Hungarian fleet to attack the French troop convoys running from North Africa to France, with just the possibility that Italian ships might also have joined. Now it was clear that he would have to operate without Italian support, and worse, the Austro-Hungarian fleet would also not be joining the two German ships. Never-

theless, he took the daring decision to press on with the plan. Leaving Messina on the night of 2/3 August, Souchon despatched *Breslau* to attack the French North African port of Bone, while he took *Goeben* to Philippeville, also in present day Algeria, and while on passage, he received the news that Germany was at war with France. From London, the First Lord of the Admiralty made it clear to Admiral Sir Archibald Berkeley Milne, commanding the British Mediterranean Fleet, that his first priority was to safeguard the passage of the French XIX Corps, but if possible he should use the opportunity to engage *Goeben*. Milne was not to engage superior forces unless he could do so with French support. Indeed, it was also made clear that Milne should husband his resources at the outset, with the promise of reinforcements later. Milne then received a succession of signals, demanding that *Goeben* be tailed by two battlecruisers, and that a watch be kept on the southern end of the Adriatic.

On 4 August, the battlecruisers *Indomitable* and *Indefatigable*, had *Goeben* in sight, but the damage had already been done. Souchon had arrived with *Goeben* at Philippeville on 4 August, flying a Russian flag, which was dropped immediately before the battlecruiser opened fire. Just fifteen shells were fired during a ten minute bombardment, blowing up a magazine, damaging the lighthouse and the railway station, but leaving the troopships undamaged. The bombardment was so brief because Souchon was delaying obeying his orders to reverse course and head for Constantinople, where it was hoped that the presence of his two ships would encourage the Turks to move beyond a simple anti-Russian defensive alliance with Germany and declare war.

In the case of war breaking out, the British and French had agreed that the French would have overall control of operations in the Mediterranean, but there were no joint exercises and, even worse, no arrangement was made for communications between the British and French Mediterranean commands. When the French decided to delay the sailing of the troopships from North Africa for a few days because of the danger presented by the German ships, Milne was not told. Despite the bombardment, when the British battlecruisers passed *Goeben*, steaming in the opposite direction at 10.34 on the morning of 4 August, they could do nothing as Britain and Germany were not yet at war, and could only turn and tail the German ship at a distance of some six miles. *Goeben* opened up to full speed, and the distance between the pursued and pursuers opened up, for although like *Goeben*, their hulls were also fouled, they had never been as fast. Despite being joined in the chase by a modern light cruiser, *Dublin*, by 21.00 the two German ships had given their pursuers the slip. Four hours later, the Mediterranean Fleet heard that it was at war.

On returning to Messina, the now officially neutral Italians finally allowed Souchon twenty-four hours in which to coal, despite war having broken out. After some delay to the Italian colliers, during which more coal was taken from German merchantmen, some 400 German merchant seamen and civilians from these ships were enlisted to speed up the heavy work of coaling in the summer heat. Once again, Souchon had to make do with less coal than he needed as men dropped from exhaustion and a rest had to be ordered before sailing at 17.00 on 6 August so that his men would be ready for battle. He needn't have worried. The British ships had gone west to act as guardians for the French troopships. A single light cruiser, *Gloucester*, was sent to keep track of the Germans and report their position, while other ships were guarding the entrance to the Adriatic. Souchon encouraged those aboard *Gloucester* to believe that he was heading for the Adriatic, but then changed course towards the Aegean.

To the north of the direct route the Germans were taking to their destination lay Rear Admiral Troubridge with his four armoured cruisers, who decided to try to cross their path, hoping that the 9.2-inch guns of his ships would give them some chance before they were pounded to destruction by the *Goeben*'s superior armament. His ships would have to come within ten miles of the enemy before they had any chance of striking back. Troubridge was dissuaded from taking this action by his flag captain, a gunnery expert, while his orders were in any case to avoid engaging a superior force. *Goeben* was indeed that, at 23,000 tons with ten 11-inch and twelve 5.9-inch guns, capable of 28 knots, the fastest and most powerful, and most modern, warship in the Mediterranean. Her escort, *Breslau*, 4,500 tons, had twelve 4.1-in guns and capable of 27 knots, making her also a significant fleet unit. Light cruisers of the day were far smaller than those of the Second World War, and indeed no larger than many modern destroyers and frigates.

The one obstacle to the Germans was the light cruiser *Gloucester*, and when *Breslau* was turned back to try to discourage her, the British ship opened fire, and a brief gunnery duel ensued until *Goeben* herself turned and started to fire. At this point *Gloucester*, reversed course, having already hit *Breslau* on the waterline, but without inflicting serious damage. When *Goeben* resumed her eastward dash, *Gloucester* resumed the chase until ordered by Milne not to go east of Cape Matapan, at the tip of the Pelopponese. Nevertheless, the voyage eastwards had not been without pain for the Germans, as the work on her boilers cut short by the outbreak of war soon began to tell, with some boiler tubes bursting leaving four men to be scalded to death.

Despite Milne eventually sending a strong force eastwards, Souchon took on coal at Piraeus before entering the Dardanelles and heading for his destination. The Turks were still sufficiently undecided that no one knew how they would react to two German ships arriving. The situation was resolved by the German ambassador suggesting that the ships be 'sold' to Turkey, which appealed to the Turks as the Royal Navy had requisitioned two battleships being built in British yards for Turkey. On 16 August, the ships were transferred to Turkey, but complete with their German crews, who even adopted the Turkish fez as headgear. *Goeben* became the *Sultan Selim* and *Breslau* became the *Midilli*.

The failure to stop the *Goeben* and the *Breslau* from reaching Turkey was one of the earliest failings of the Royal Navy, and it was keenly felt. At the end of October 1914, Souchon took his two ships supported by Turkish ships and entered the Black Sea to begin a bombardment of Russian forts

THE NAVAL WAR

Despite the popular belief that it would 'all be over by Christmas', it soon became clear that this was to be no short war, at sea or on land, or indeed in the air. The Germans had placed much faith in their ability to use surface raiders against Allied shipping, but the German surface raiders were soon penned up or sunk, and the attack on Allied lines of supply had to be left to the U-boats. This new form of naval warfare soon proved that they were perfectly capable of the task. Annual totals of merchant shipping tonnage in the North Sea and the Atlantic sunk by U-boats rose from a meagre and sustainable 3,369 tons in 1914 to 700,782 tons in 1915, 508,745 tons in 1916, 2,895,983 tons in 1917 and were still at 1,044, 822 in 1918. To these could be added the 350,853 tons lost in the Mediterranean and the 44,520 lost to U-boats based at Constantinople in 1915. Indeed, in 1916, losses in the

Mediterranean reached 1,045,058 tons, much higher than the Atlantic figures, while in 1917, the Mediterranean figure was 1,514,501 tons, and it was still slightly more than half this rate in 1918.

In London, Fisher, who would have crippled the German Navy before it had a chance to enter the war, returned to the Admiralty as First Sea Lord in October 1914, but walked out frustrated and angry with the politicians, including the First Lord, Winston Churchill, in mid-May, and spent the rest of the war on the sidelines. His departure more or less coincided with Italy joining the war on the side of the Allies against Austria-Hungary.

That this was a 'World War' could not be doubted with the Battles of Coronel and then the Falklands, and fighting in East Africa and in Mesopotamia. In East Africa, two monitors attacked and sank the commerce-raider *Konigsberg* in the Rufiji River. It was also the start of operations by British submarines in the Sea of Marmara and in the Baltic, while a Turkish cargo ship became the first nautical victim to aeroplane attack in the Dardanelles. It was not only at sea that the *Kaiserliche Marine* and the Royal Navy clashed, with operations on Lake Tanganyika in late 1915 and early 1916.

Yet, despite these actions, with British defeat at Coronel being followed by victory in the Falklands, a major naval battle eluded both sides.

NEW YEAR LOSSES

For the Royal Navy, 1916 started badly, however, with the pre-Dreadnought *King Edward VII* striking a mine on 6 January, and sinking off Cape Wrath on the far north of Scotland. On 8 February, the British government formally sought naval assistance from Japan, which sent two destroyer flotillas to the Mediterranean during April. Looking at the monthly losses of merchant ships during the First World War shows fluctuations in the figures. This was due to the 'on-off' nature of the U-boat campaign. At first, operations were limited to attacking warships without notice, while merchant vessels had to be stopped and those aboard given a chance to take to the lifeboats before the ship was sunk. A combination of factors, including losses of U-boats to the Q-ships, merchantmen fitted with concealed guns and manned by naval personnel, which the Germans thought to be treacherous, and the sheer need to make an impact on the steady stream of ships carrying cargo for the

British war effort, meant that unrestricted U-boat warfare followed. This was stopped in the North Atlantic after provoking protests from the United States, but continued in the Mediterranean where the U-boats were less likely to find ships carrying US citizens. Nevertheless, unrestricted U-boat attacks were authorised in British waters on 23 February 1916, although suspended again on 24 April following fresh American protests. Throughout this period, the Royal Navy attempted to keep the German fleet in its bases. On 7 March, the first British mine-laying submarine, *E24*, laid mines in the mouth of the River Elbe. By 1 May, the Germans not only returned to unrestricted U-boat warfare, they took the battle into the western Atlantic for the first time.

The U-boat was not the only example of new weaponry that appeared in the war. On 1 April 1916, towns on the East Coast of England were bombed by German Zeppelin airships, but further south, over the Thames Estuary, another Zeppelin, *L-15* became the first to be brought down by AA fire and crash-landed in the Thames Estuary, where its crew surrendered to a passing warship. Towns on the East Coast also suffered shelling from German battlecruisers, which bombarded Lowestoft and Yarmouth on 23 April. It was not just over England that the Zeppelins were at risk, for on 4 May, *L-7* was brought down south of the Horn Reefs on the eastern side of the North Sea by fire from the light cruisers *Galatea* and *Phaeton*. These large craft were difficult to destroy completely, unless the hydrogen gas caught fire, and so *L-7* was able to ditch in the North Sea where she was destroyed by the submarine *E31*, which also rescued seven survivors.

When the long awaited clash between the two navies finally came at the Battle of Jutland on 31 May, the Royal Navy lost the battlecruisers *Indefatigable*, *Invincible*, one of the victors of the Falklands, and *Queen Mary*, as well as three armoured cruisers and five smaller warships, while many other ships were damaged. In all, 155,000 tons of British warships lost compared to 61,000 tons of German warships, while 6,090 British sailors and marines were lost compared with 2,550 Germans.

The truth was that for all of their speed, the battlecruisers were vulnerable. Perhaps the losses could have been lower had the Royal Navy learnt the lessons about the dangers of flashback from the turrets and into the magazines, already discovered the hard way by the Germans, but this is pure speculation. The German battle-cruisers were better armoured.

AFTER JUTLAND

The world could never be quite the same again after Jutland. Everyone in Great Britain had waited for this battle, assuming that the Royal Navy would be victorious and that victory would shorten the war. Even if there had been a British victory, it would not necessarily have been decisive. Nevertheless, Jutland did at least discourage the Germans from seeking another major battle, but only after a further excursion into the open sea. On 18 and 19 August, when Scheer took the High Seas Fleet out into the North Sea again, his reconnaissance force of eight Zeppelins mistakenly reported that the Grand Fleet was approaching, mistaking light cruisers and destroyers for battleships. Scheer took his ships south hoping for a major naval engagement, but in so doing he took them away from Jellicoe and the Grand Fleet, who were actually at sea again, but returned to base rather than risk his ships in the heavily mined southern waters of the North Sea. Both sides suffered losses, with the submarine *E23* torpedoing the German battleship *Westfalen* north of Terschelling, forcing her to return to base, while the British lost the light cruiser *Falmouth* to a U-boat's torpedo as she crossed the U-boat line. Not surprisingly, the light cruisers and destroyers spotted by the Zeppelins, were not allowed to attack the High Seas Fleet as it would have been suicidal.

U-boats apart, the High Seas Fleet spent most of the rest of the war on hit and run operations. In October, two of these were mounted. The first was a second bombardment from the sea of Lowestoft on 26 October, while that night, German destroyers were sent against Dover. The latter operation was probably not worth the effort, as most of the seven vessels sunk by the destroyers were British fishing vessels, small drifters, adapted to handle the barrage. This type of operation was to continue in early 1917. The Germans did not always find themselves unopposed, and on the night of 23/24 January 1917, the German 6th Destroyer Flotilla found itself facing the two Harwich destroyer flotillas off the Schouwen light vessel. In the frantic battle that ensued, both sides lost a destroyer.

GAINS AND LOSSES

As far as the Royal Navy was concerned, another bad start to the year also came in 1917, with the pre-Dreadnought HMS *Cornwallis* was torpedoed and sunk 62 miles off Malta by *U-32* on 9 January. Two days later, the seaplane carrier, *Ben-my-Chree*, a converted Isle of Man packet steamer, was sunk off Kastelorizo by fire from Turkish shore batteries.

The first real good news came on 6 April, when the United States finally declared war on Germany. Within a month, on 4 May, the first USN destroyers arrived at the Royal Navy's base at Queenstown, in Southern Ireland, ready for convoy escort duties. Nevertheless, two German light cruisers, *Bremse* and *Brummer*, found a British convoy between Bergen and Scotland and sank the two destroyer escorts and nine out of twelve merchant vessels. Two destroyers made an entirely unsatisfactory escort, but even if there had been twice the number, they would have been outgunned by the light cruisers.

The submarine remained the main menace. It was probably exactly what the Admiralty wanted when *UB-8* sank a dummy vessel designed to look like the battlecruiser HMS *Tiger* in the Aegean Sea, as such dummy ships were intended to deceive the Germans and even draw their fire, or their torpedoes. Far less welcome news was the sinking of the armoured cruiser *Drake* by *U-79* in the North Channel off Rathlin Island, between Scotland and Ireland.

On 17 November 1917, German battleships and light cruisers put to sea to protect minesweeping forces which were being harassed by British light cruisers and destroyers. Instead of frightening the crews of light cruisers and destroyers, however, they suddenly found themselves facing three battlecruisers, *Courageous*, *Glorious* and *Repulse*, off Heligoland Bight. The weather was worsening at the time and after an inconclusive initial exchange of fire, the Germans mistook the battlecruisers for the approach of British battleships and broke off the engagement. This was a case of poor ship recognition as *Courageous* and her sister *Glorious* were what were known as 'light battlecruisers'. The following year, on 20 January 1918, the German-manned battle-cruiser *Sultan Selim* and light cruiser *Midilli*, ventured into the Aegean to attack British shipping, finding two British monitors, and in a one-sided engagement, sunk both of them. Nevertheless, it was a pyrrhic victory for, on their return to Constantinople, *Midilli* struck a mine and sank, while *Sultan Selim* ran aground.

By this time, Karl Dönitz had left the *Breslau*, or *Midilli*, and after training had switched to the U-boat arm. His experience there was to influence his future opinions on naval warfare.

On 15 February, German destroyers attacked the barrage

between Folkestone and Cape Gris Nez, but to little effect, while a destroyer action on 21 March off Dunkirk saw eleven British destroyers and four French engage eighteen German destroyers, of which two were sunk by the Allies.

Meanwhile, the long-feared Bolshevik Revolution was taking place in Russia. Nevertheless, with a successful naval blockade of Germany established, there was sufficient confidence to move the Grand Fleet from its forward wartime base at Scapa Flow in Orkney to the new naval base and dockyard at Rosyth on the Firth of Forth on 12 April. There was also a partially successful amphibious operation to block the entrances to the German-held naval bases at Zeebrugge and Ostend, to close the entrances to U-boat and torpedo-boats using blockships while harbour installations were also destroyed. Fisher would most definitely have approved, and might even have demanded such action much earlier.

While the first offensive operation from an aircraft carrier, HMS *Furious*, a converted light battlecruiser, against Tondern on 19 July marked a change in naval warfare, the situation was changing in other ways as well. On 8 August, the Royal Navy laid the first magnetic mines off the French coast at Dunkirk. This was a bold step, not least because at the time, and for many years afterwards, no one knew how to sweep magnetic mines.

Even so, the more traditional ways of stopping shipping also remained, and it was on 1 October that the net barrage across the Straits of Otranto was completed.

As fuel supplies in Germany began to run low due to the blockade of Germany, the U-boats ceased commerce raiding on 21 October. There was just one last blow for the U-boats left at sea, looking for British warships, when on 9 November, the pre-Dreadnought *Britannia* was torpedoed and sunk by *U-50*, off Cape Trafalgar. This was not the way that everyone saw it. Faced with mutinies within the fleet and an overwhelming sense of looming defeat, many senior officers saw one last blow as a way of the *Kaiserliche Marine* going to a glorious ending, with many senior officers proposing that all available surface units should be sent to sea in a 'death ride' against the Royal Navy, now reinforced with US battleships.

The Armistice on 11 November 1918 was no doubt a welcome relief to both the *Kaiserliche Marine* and the Royal Navy. The German fleet had suffered a series of mutinies starting in late 1917, and at Kiel the port admiral, none other than Souchon, the man who had given the British the slip in the Mediterranean and the Turks a battlecruiser and a light cruiser, surrendered his command when the 3rd Battle Squadron steamed into port flying the red flag. Nevertheless, order was regained and on 21 November, most modern German warships and all of the surviving U-boats obeyed the Allied order to proceed to Scapa Flow. Although a few also reached the United States, including the Dreadnought *Ostfriesland*, those at Scapa were all scuttled without warning on 21 June 1919.

CHAPTER THREE

The Treaties – Versailles and Washington

While the skeleton crews of the German warships effectively interned by the British at Scapa Flow remained aboard, those from other ships around the world became prisoners of war. Many found themselves aboard British warships which took them to Southampton, where they disembarked and went to a prisoner of war camp near Sheffield. This must have been an uncomfortable time for the Germans, and especially for those who had been U-boat commanders, such as Dönitz. They discovered that the British newspapers were calling them war criminals and demanding their execution, as well as that of their senior officers and the Kaiser himself.

This was a traumatic period for Germany, and for a while it seemed that the revolution in Russia would spread to the country. Amongst the prisoners of war, disillusionment set in and many rejected the Kaiser, blaming him for the war and German defeat, and professed themselves republicans. Dönitz was not amongst them.

Despite the fears over their future, repatriation of the naval prisoners started in early summer 1919, and Dönitz was amongst the first. He returned to Kiel to find the great naval base empty, while the only work in progress was the destruction under the Allied Control Commission of those U-boats that had not been sent to Scapa Flow.

While post-First World War Germany was occupied by the Allies and there was even a British Army of the Rhine, as after the Second World War, and reparations were set in hand, the damage to the country was far less than in the later conflict. Not only had there not been the heavy bombing raids of the Second World War, for the technology was still in its infancy, but the Allies had not had to fight their way to the capital, a process which inevitably resulted in massive destruction in late 1944 and the first half of 1945. While many officers in the Navy and the Army planned to join the

30

Socialists, others planned to bide their time until a reaction came against the Socialists and they could then topple the post-war government and reinstate the monarchy. Nevertheless, those senior officers still at their posts and not held as prisoners of war, had other plans, longer term plans. The officer corps was to remain in being ready to rebuild the armed forces.

The thinking behind this was not so much an acceptance of defeat and of the new German state, but in fact a reaction to it and a definite rejection of the new order. For many senior officers, world power, or *Weltpolitik*, had not been rejected, but delayed. Even amongst the losses and the overwhelming sense of defeat, a powerful German Navy was being planned once again. There was a new head of the Navy, Admiral von Trotha, who had been one of those planning the all or nothing 'death ride' as the war drew to its weary end. Trotha was a strong proponent of the policies espoused by Tirpitz, and foresaw the resurrection of the German Navy as the primary instrument through which the German peoples would achieve the status of a world power with an empire to match.

Yet, on 21 June 1919, the day that the Versailles Treaty was due to be signed, he gave the order to scuttle those units of the fleet anchored at Scapa Flow. This was a form of ritual suicide for the defeated Navy and one means of retaining some semblance of honour. The logic was simple enough, as he did not want to see the pride of the *Kaiserliche Marine* scrapped or, even worse, passing into the fleets of the victors. He probably did not foresee some ships being used for bombing practice by an American airman, William 'Billy' Mitchell. In defeat and without the best of his ships, Trotha saw his role as sowing the seeds of a new fleet, 'so that when the time comes a useful tree will grow from it.'

The seeds afforded him were poor material indeed. The Versailles Treaty banned Germany from manufacturing or operating aircraft or airships, while submarines were also banned. The restrictions applied to both services, with the Army limited to 100,000 men. Another condition was that the Rhineland was demilitarised. The Navy was allowed six elderly coastal battleships, often referred to as *Panzerschiffe*, armoured ships, with their eventual replacements limited to 10,000 tons displacement, as well as six cruisers, twelve destroyers and twelve torpedo-boats. This was not the navy of a maritime power, but of a continental power, a brown water navy restricted to the Baltic and the coasts of the North Sea. Yet, it was not the full disbandment that the German armed forces faced in

1945, and it meant that within a little more than eight months after the Armistice, the German armed forces were still operational. The Treaty terms also limited the Navy to 1,500 officers, so that Trotha immediately set about selecting the very best and most loyal as the core for his 'new' Navy.

One of those handpicked and offered the opportunity to serve in the new post-war German Navy, the Reichsmarine, was Dönitz, although the young lieutenant hesitated at first because of his monarchist sympathies from enlisting in a republican force. Nevertheless, he did so on 14 August 1919. He was later to claim that another officer had promised him that, despite the Versailles Treaty, they would have U-boats again within two years. That didn't happen, but there is no doubt that senior officers were again planning a submarine force within that timescale. In the meantime, the armed services supported the government-backed *Freikorps* in suppressing Bolshevik groups who attempted a number of localised insurrections across Germany.

It is difficult to give an exact idea of the state of Germany at this time, shorn of its gains from the Franco-Prussian War and divided against itself. Increasingly, the monarchist groups became a bigger problem than the insurrectionists. The crisis worsened when, in February 1920, the victorious Allies finally issued a list of some 900 'war criminals' and demanded that they be handed over to stand trial. The list included the Kaiser and several chancellors, the generals Hindenburg and Ludendorff, and many naval officers, including Tirpitz, Trotha and Scheer, as well as individual U-boat commanding officers. This did at least have the effect of unifying much of the nation as a humiliation too far, but it unified it against the government. Wolfgang Kapp, a Prussian official, led a naval *Freikorps* that marched on Berlin shortly before midnight of 12 March, and without Army support, the government fled the city. The so-called Kapp *putsch* then added to the confusion, and while order was maintained at Kiel, at Wilhelmshaven officers were arrested by petty officers and men in a rerun of the 1918 mutinies. Even at Kiel, the local commander, Admiral von Levetzow, was unable to prevent workers from joining a general strike called by the deposed government from its temporary headquarters in Stuttgart. The situation was defused on 17 March, when Kapp stood down, having no plans for the future of the country other than protest. Nevertheless, the unrest and mutinies continued, while Dönitz, given temporary command of a torpedo-boat and ordered with the others to help maintain order, suffered sabotage aboard his craft when salt water was induced into the fresh-water feeding the boilers. The unrest and indiscipline in the Reichsmarine was by this time so great that many felt that the service must be disbanded.

This grave situation continued until the end of May, when a *Reichstag* committee investigating the Kapp *putsch* reported, and its recommendations were quickly implemented, with almost 200 officers, including Trotha, discharged or retired, as well as the entire list of deck officers, who had joined the men in the mutinies. Those officers who had taken no part in the actual *putsch* were reinstated. This display of strength in fact showed a major weakness of the new republic, for the officer corps had shown that, as a whole, it had no sympathy with the government, which nevertheless needed them to suppress the uprisings that were continuing to afflict Germany. The officer corps in both armed services for their part realised that they could not take over the country without the support of the majority of the population, and this was not forthcoming. The lesson was learned for the future, that they were to remain away from and above politics.

WAR CRIMINALS

In the end, out of the original list of around 900 war criminals, just a dozen were brought to trial. This was no Nuremberg war trial. Instead, the accused went before the German Supreme Court. Two of the dozen had been watch officers aboard *U-86*, accused of sinking the hospital ship *Llandovery Castle*, itself contrary to the Geneva Convention and a breach of international law. The crime was compounded by the fact that they then gunned the survivors in the five lifeboats that had got away after it was discovered that the ship had not been carrying ammunition and combat troops, the excuse used for the attack. The commanding officer, *Oberleutnant zur See* Helmut Patzig could not be brought to trial as he had disappeared, although he later reappeared in the *Abwehr*, the Counter Intelligence Organisation.

The two hapless watch officers maintained that they had not fired the U-boats weapons and were simply obeying orders. Nevertheless, in a precursor of the eventual Nuremberg's judgements, the court decided that:

Patzig's order does not free the accused from guilt . . . the subordinate obeying an order is liable to punishment if it was known to him, that the order of the superior involved the infringement of civil or military law. This applies in the case of the accused . . . it was perfectly clear to the accused that killing defenceless people in the lifeboats could be nothing else but a breach of the law.[1]

Despite this, the two men received sentences of just four years for their involvement in the mass murder of the ship's company and wounded men, and even these lenient sentences provoked widespread public outrage. Neither man served the full term with one 'escaping' after four months and the other after just six months. No attempt was made to find them once on the run. This was par for the course, as another man found guilty and imprisoned at the time found himself better off in prison than when he had been free: that man was Adolf Hitler.

PLANNING FOR WAR

Unable to command U-boats, many of those who had been wartime U-boat commanders or second-in-command of a U-boat, were assigned to the torpedo-boats. Some maintain that many of them started to use their craft to practice U-boat surface attacks. Meanwhile, within the Torpedo and Mines Inspectorate at Kiel, a clandestine U-boat department was created, planning, ready for the day when the Reichsmarine could once again operate the forbidden craft. The German aircraft industry had not expired but in effect had gone into exile, with designers working in the Soviet Union, the Netherlands and elsewhere, so that there was no danger of a generation of progress in aircraft and aero-engine design being lost to Germany. Initially, submarine design was more difficult to send into exile in this way, but the means did exist. German plans for a new generation of U-boats, designers, engineers and construction experts went to Japan to help that country establish a strong submarine fleet, including a force of cruiser submarines. Other countries also welcomed the experience of the Germans.

In 1922, three German shipbuilders, AG Vulcan, Germaniawerft and AG Weser, finally grasped the nettle and established a company in the Netherlands, *Ingenieurskantoor voor Scheepsbouw, IvS*, (the engineering office for shipbuilding) based at Rotterdam, to enable German submarine experts to continue their construction work in exile. The three companies that owned the Rotterdam business actually carried out the design work at their own facilities in Germany. The company operated for eleven years, but was wound-up after the Nazi Party assumed complete power in Germany in 1933.

Operations for Germany's small Navy were seriously inhibited during the winter months by most of the Baltic freezing. While their ships were refitted and the crews drilled, many of the officers were given *Winterarbeiten*, 'winter work', conducting studies into naval theory. This almost amounted to providing staff college training for the small and exclusive cadre of officers, and in the winter of 1921–1922, no less than three of these exercises dealt with submarine warfare. Marschall, a former wartime U-boat commander, wrote one of these, covering surface attack by U-boats. This was timely as the late adoption of the convoy system by the Royal Navy during the First World War had forced the U-boats to adapt their tactics. Marschall allowed no doubts about a resumption of hostilities, writing that: 'The coming war may or may not involve war against merchant shipping.' He continued writing that U-boat commanders must be able to attack convoys since a warship squadron was also in effect a convoy. This was slightly doubtful reasoning as surface warships would be faster and more manoeuvrable than a merchant convoy. The paper advocated night surface attack, listing its many advantages, for these were the days before radar.

Admiral von Rosenberg, commanding the Baltic Fleet, read the report and noted at the end that the arguments in favour of night surface attack were valuable and of interest to torpedo-boat officers as well as those serving in U-boats. This was true, for a surfaced U-boat was in effect a torpedo-boat, albeit much slower.

These exercises and the planning they resulted in were the preparation of war plans for the U-boats and E-boats during the Second World War. The tactics were that the target should be identified and followed out of sight during the daylight hours, with U-boats and E-boats then attacking under cover of darkness. The implication was that both types of vessel would operate in a flotilla or 'pack'. This period seems almost certain to have been the time when the concept of the U-boat pack emerged and that Dönitz adopted the strategy early on rather than, as many suggest, inventing it. This was reinforced by a paper prepared in July 1922 for the *Wehrabteilung*, or Naval High Command in Berlin, by *Kapitanleutnant* (lieutenant-commander) Wassner, who recalled that as a U-boat commander he had found surface attacks to be the most successful, but that solo U-boat attacks on convoys were relatively ineffectual so that 'in future it will be essential for convoys to be hunted by sizeable numbers of U-boats acting together.'[2]

Step by step, the Versailles Treaty was being circumvented.

In planning for the future, the identity of a the potential enemy had to be established. The Germans were not alone in this, and it was not until the early years of the twentieth century that the Royal Navy had stopped using France as a potential enemy in its planning and its exercises. While the Germans wanted to return to war with the British, and specifically to see battle with the Royal Navy, that was some way in the future. In the meantime, the 'enemy' was Poland, which under the terms of Versailles had been given a link to the Baltic port of Danzig, known as the 'Polish Corridor' although it was not in fact the shape of a corridor. The Polish Corridor isolated East Prussia from the rest of Germany and so the threat existed of Polish annexation of the territory. The strategic thinking also considered that in the event of hostilities with Poland, France would intervene on the side of Poland, and U-boats would be necessary to stop French battleships and battlecruisers forcing their way through the Skaggerak and Kattegat into the Baltic.

Helping in the preparation of these war plans was *Kapitan-leutnant* Dönitz, posted to the U-boat department within the Torpedo, Mine and Intelligence Inspectorate at Kiel in spring 1923, as a *Referent*, an expert or adviser. While Dönitz maintains in his memoirs that he was not happy with this posting, to his superiors he was ideal, with his U-boat and torpedo-boat experience.

Earlier that year, in a show of strength and to enforce collection of arrears in war reparations, a joint force of Belgian and French troops had invaded the Ruhr. The German government's response was to call a general strike in the region, and to finance this it made the grave mistake of printing money, so that the value of the currency started its dramatic fall and the period of hyperinflation began that impacted most on the middle and professional classes, but also led to a vast army of industrial workers becoming un-employed.

During a period of such economic turmoil, the government never-theless managed to give the German armed forces 100 million marks in gold, effectively inflation-proofed, so that it could commence a rearmament programme over and above what was permitted by the Versailles Treaty. While most of the money went into the German Army, the Navy received a share and this was allocated between two secret rearmament funds, one in the Naval Transport Department under *Kapitan zur See* Lohrmann and the other into the Weapons Department under *Kapitan zur See* Hansen. The latter worked closely with the Torpedo, Mine and Intelligence Inspectorate at Kiel.

Meanwhile, the German industrial giants played the economy, expanding their tangible assets by discounting huge bills of exchange at the Reichsbank, buying them back as the currency devalued further, and using the resulting funds to expand through the acquisition of struggling small and medium-sized concerns. This consolidation of German heavy industry was eventually to be of considerable use to the Nazi Party, making it easier to control the economy and direct industry.

Under the terms of the Versailles Treaty, the German Navy, the Reichsmarine, was allowed to replace its ships as and when necessary. The first warship to be ordered post-Versailles was the light cruiser *Emden*, 5,400 tons, completed in 1925. Initially, she burned coal, the one fuel that was abundant in Germany, but in 1934 she was converted to burn oil. Another three cruisers were completed in 1929, *Karlsruhe*, *Koln* and *Konigsberg*, all of 6,000 tons, and then in 1931, these were joined by the *Leipzig*, also of 6,000 tons. These four ships were diesel-powered, giving much longer range, with the implication that their future use as surface raiders was already in mind.

DÖNITZ MOVES UP

In autumn, 1924, Dönitz was posted to an even more senior staff appointment at the *Marineleitung*, part of the *Wehrabteilung* or Naval High Command, in Berlin. Before moving he went on a short formal staff course run by Rear Admiral Raeder, who had been on Tirpitz's staff during the war and post-war had been an aide of Trotha. After the Kapp *putsch*, Raeder had been moved sideways into a low profile position. Raeder, the future commander of the wartime German Navy, was impressed by Dönitz, and recommended strongly that he should not be retained in technical positions, but given the opportunity to broaden his experience. In particular, his leadership skills made him suitable for the development of younger officers.

In fact, the staff course may also have been a screening exercise to see whether or not Dönitz would fit the future German Navy. It was clear that he and Raeder saw eye to eye at this stage.

Dönitz was moving ever closer to the centre of power and of rearmament plans for the Reichsmarine. His memoirs indicate that his main preoccupation was with service regulations and a new military code, which involved him in liaison with the Army to ensure that the conditions were coordinated, as well as being adjusted to reflect the specific conditions in the Navy, while the whole had to be approved by the Reichstag. Clearly, in view of the Supreme Court judgement on war crimes, his work was highly sensitive.

These continued to be difficult times for the new German republic. There continued to be constant activity against the republic and the armed services by the Communists. Again, it was the role of Dönitz's department to combat propaganda, which at times took on bizarre forms. An organisation known as the *Rote Marine*, Red Navy, staged as a propaganda exercise the 'proletarian theatre' production commemorating the 1918 naval mutinies and proclaiming the cruelty of the officers and ending with the execution of the leaders of the mutinies.

The *Marineleitung* continued the clandestine planning for rearmament that had started immediately after the Armistice. Dönitz's immediate superior was *Kapitan zur See* Werth, who worked closely with Wilhelm Canaris, the future wartime head of the *Abwehr*, as well as Arno Spindler and von Loewenfeld, and all of them reported to Rear Admiral Adolph Pfeiffer. As pressure for the reestablishment of the U-boat arm increased, responsibility for planning was transferred from the Torpedo, Mines and Intelligence Inspectorate in Kiel to Berlin and Spindler was put in charge, under the guise of U-boat counter-measures. Meanwhile, in a bid to continue U-boat development outside Germany, Canaris became the link between the *Marineleitung* and Spain, which it was hoped would develop a submarine arm under German tutelage.

Spindler wasted no time in planning the specification for U-boats that would be needed for the foreseen war with Poland and France, by this time known in German military planning circles as Case A, starting in January 1926. He studied the wartime logs of the U-boats and interviewed most of the surviving commanders. Canaris became involved as he wished to have firm proposals to offer the Spanish. Spindler settled on three types. The first of these was a small 270-ton U-boat for operations in the Baltic. The other two were both of 500-tons and intended for operations in the North Sea, or the Mediterranean, with one fitted for torpedoes and the other for laying mines. The intention was that the larger craft would be used to defeat any attempt to enforce a blockade against Germany, as well as protecting the Baltic from entry by enemy warships.

The actual design of these craft was by the parent companies of the IvS organisation in Rotterdam, which took the specifications and up-dated them in line with current developments in warship building. Just as the Soviet Union was being used by the aircraft manufacturers, the Reichsmarine then encouraged the USSR to become involved in U-boat production. In July 1926, no less than three naval missions visited the USSR, with which secret trade treaties were fostering the development and production of aircraft, armaments and ammunition, and armoured vehicles, in the hope that contracts would be placed for the new U-boats. Development was furthered by an international commission having recommended a loan of 800 million gold marks to support the Reichsbank and stabilise the German economy. Far from being used for its intended purpose, this money was for the most part used by the major German industrial concerns to develop weapons and also enhance the production systems, as well as continuing the clandestine re-armament by the two armed services.

In helping to foster Soviet armaments industry for her own ends, Germany was playing a dangerous game for senior officers at this time made no secret of the fact that Bolshevism and the so-called 'Slavic wave' were the main threats not just to Germany, but to Europe as a whole. Poland and her ally France were seen as more immediate threats because Russia was still backward and under-industrialised, as were the other Slav nations in post-Versailles Europe. Nevertheless, the USSR was advancing industrially and therefore militarily, with German help.

Just as the pre-war German government had accelerated the development of its armed forces while placating foreign governments, the foreign minister, Stresseman, was assuring the Allies that Germany was doing her best to fulfil the conditions of the Treaty of Versailles. In January 1927, the Allied Control Commission withdrew, despite its final report which maintained that Germany had failed to disarm and was unlikely to do so, but instead was actively seeking to re-arm, and had done everything possible to make inspection by the Commission difficult. The situation would not have been made any easier by the death of the first president of the republic in 1925, for his successor was none other than Field Marshal von Hindenburg, not only a popular choice amongst the armed forces and their officer corps, but also a reassuring symbol of the 'old' pre-war Germany.

Meanwhile, a retired senior officer, Rear Admiral von Loewenfeld was publicly expressing views that were almost identical to those of Adolf Hitler. Even before the Fuhrer took power, unofficial links were established between the Reichsmarine and the Nazi Party, and Admiral Levetzow, who had commanded the naval base at Kiel at the time of the Kapp putsch, later became Hitler's adviser on naval matters.

The Reichsmarine continued its policies and that included the annual *Winterarbeiten*. It was a sign that the secret preparations were leaking down into the officer corps that no less than eight of the ten produced during 1926–1927 dealt with submarine matters. Werth and Spindler started to prepare a course on U-boats for midshipmen as part of their torpedo course. In April, the first of a batch of submarines for Turkey was completed at Rotterdam, and the sea trials were conducted by Werner Furbringer, a former wartime U-boat commander, with the aid of a former U-boat engineer, so that a full report could be prepared for the *Marineleitung*.

REARMAMENT EXPOSED

Hitler's rearmament and rebuilding of the armed forces shocked Western sensibilities in the mid-1930s, especially when the Luftwaffe or Air Force was unveiled, but rearmament had been the plan from the Armistice onwards. The first revelations about re-armament were the reservations expressed by the Allied Control Commission in January 1927, but a second and public revelation followed in August of that year. The financial editor of the *Berliner Tageblatt* newspaper decided to investigate the financial affairs of a film company, Phoebus, which produced propaganda, and in his researches discovered the network of companies funded by the *Seetransport* office at the *Wehrabteilung*. When published, it awakened the concerns of the pacifists in the Social Democrat party and also alerted the anti-militarist Communists. Dönitz had to prepare the Reichsmarine's case for the *Reichstag*, and also help the Army as well, which in his liaison with them had discovered that the seafarers were far better at handling political matters, and had set up a department that was the mirror-image of his own.

Anxious to appease opinion both within and without Germany, the government hastily distanced itself from the Reichsmarine. A number of senior naval officers were sacrificed in the cause, including the head of the *Seetransport* officer, Lohrmann, while others, such as von Loewenfeld and Werth, were sent back to sea. Some were retired, others discharged and the more fortunate moved to less sensitive posts. The Defence Minister was another victim, as was the commander of the Reichsmarine, Zenker, who was succeeded by none other than Dönitz's former tutor on staff matters, Raeder. Dönitz and Canaris were both sent to sea, and out of the way. The former became navigating officer aboard the cruiser *Nymphe* in the Baltic, flagship of the Commander-in-Chief, Baltic, who was none other than Rear Admiral von Loewenfeld!

International concerns over rearmament have to be placed in the context of the day. While the Treaty of Versailles had broken the Austro-Hungarian Empire and deprived Germany of Alsace-Lorraine and its few overseas colonies, such as South-West Africa, and limited the armed forces, other treaties had affected the victors. The Washington Naval Treaty of 1922 had been a serious effort to limit the size of the world's navies and prevent a further naval race. No longer were the British allowed to work towards a 'Two Power Standard', but instead had to accept parity with the United States. The French and the Japanese had to make do with less than this. The Treaty imposed restrictions on total tonnage for each of the signatories, but also gave specific tonnage totals for each type of warship for each navy and a maximum tonnage for each type. It also intervened in the calibre of armament. Here were the victors accepting restrictions while the defeated were contemplating breaching the rules imposed upon them.

The Paris Air Agreement of 1926 opened the way for resumption of civil aircraft manufacture and civil aviation within Germany. With official blessing, gliding became a national hobby, and within this supposedly innocent activity, a large number of Germans became pilots, a good grounding for later conversion to fixed-wing flying and ultimately preparing the way for the birth of the Luftwaffe.

By this time, the sea trials for the Rotterdam-built submarines for Turkey had also taken on the role of training a nucleus of submarine crews. Furbringer not only conducted the trials of the second submarine for Turkey, but delivered the submarines to Turkey and remained there with his chief engineer to train Turkish submariners. In Germany, from 1930, Rear Admiral Walter Gladisch, signed himself as BdU, or Commander of U-Boats, although no one was listed officially as having this role. U-boat training also began in 1930, using a craft designed by IvS at Rotterdam, but built in Finland by German engineering workers. German naval personnel went to Finland as civilian tourists, and conducted trials with the U-boat from July to September.

Hitler had still to come to power when important decisions were taken about the future of the Reichsmarine. In 1929, the first of a new class of armoured warship, *panzerschiff* to the Germans, but described by the British media as 'pocket battleships', was ordered. These were certainly larger than most cruisers and more heavily armed, but to describe them as battleships was misleading as they had 11-in guns compared to the 15-in more commonly specified for this type of warship. The case for building these ships was that they were to replace the coastal battleships allowed by the Versailles Treaty and which were obsolete, and indeed Germany insisted on the right to build a total of six, but in the end just three were completed, *Deutschland*, *Admiral Graf Spee* and *Admiral Scheer*. Shortly after the outbreak of the Second World War, *Deutschland* had a name change to *Lutzow*, as Hitler suddenly considered the impact on national morale if *Deutschland* was sunk! That such ships could be built indicated that Germany was indeed rearming, since with their powerful, but economical, diesel engines these ships had a very long range. They were in fact surface raiders and certainly not intended to remain in the Baltic, or even the North Sea for that matter. In designing these ships, the maxim was that they should be 'stronger than faster enemies', in other words cruisers, and 'faster than stronger enemies', meaning battleships.

Whether or not the revelations about rearmament played any part, elections in 1928 saw a marked swing to the left, while the recession sweeping the industrialised countries left debt-ridden Germany in a vulnerable economic position. Just as fears of revolution had helped to harden attitudes during the years immediately before the outbreak of the First World War, these fresh fears forced many otherwise moderate people to view Hitler and the Nazis as their best hope for salvation. Many of these were doubtless people who thought that Hitler could be used and dropped when necessary; simply to overcome what they hoped would be a temporary difficulty. They were to be proved wrong.

Notes
1   Cameron, J., (ed), *The Peleus Trial*, Hodge, London, 1948
2   Rossler, E., *The U-boat*, Arms & Armour Press, London, 1981

CHAPTER FOUR

The Nazis Plan a War Machine

In September 1930, Hitler saw his party become the second largest in the *Reichstag*, with 107 seats. The new Chancellor, the Roman Catholic nationalist Heinrich Bruening, was confronted by an economy once again in crisis and had imposed a regime of strict austerity. While not a Fascist, his policies were acceptable to the majority of the Nazis. He denounced reparations, proposed a customs union between Austria and Germany, and an increasingly proactive policy in Central and South-Eastern Europe, with exclusive bilateral trade agreements with Hungary and Romania, and, despite the desperate financial situation, ordered two new battle-cruisers for the Reichsmarine. He had earlier rejected a French proposal for closer economic relations with Germany, and in 1931 Bruening rejected an offer that the French capital markets be opened to long-term German borrowing.

Germany needed borrowing to fulfil the requirements of the Young Plan, an American attempt to stabilise the Germany economy. German reparations to France and the United Kingdom were to be offset by a linkage to their wartime debts to the United States, but while the German government would be in control of reparations and released from foreign oversight, the scope for delay in making reparations was also reduced. Nevertheless, in June 1931, the wartime Allies were forced to consider a moratorium on reparations, and a year later at a conference held in Lausanne the reparations scheme was formally cancelled. In the intervening period, French delay in approving the moratorium led to the collapse of a major German bank, the state losing vast sums in an attempt to prop up its ailing currency, and then a general closure of the German financial system and Germany being forced off the gold standard. In mid-July, a new and draconian system of exchange controls was introduced, while private holdings of foreign currency were confiscated by the state.

The Lausanne Conference was designed to resolve issues surrounding international debt, but there was also another conference, at Geneva, as a further step towards the ever elusive goal of disarmament. This was to be far less successful. The Geneva Conference resulted from an American fear that the cancellation of British and French war debt would release funds for rearmament. In one sense, there was logic to the American aims, as it followed on from earlier attempts to impose limitations on armaments, such as the Washington Naval Treaty of 1922. The American action was not unwelcome to the British, who throughout most of the 1930s, until war became inevitable, tried to lower the maximum individual tonnages for the major warship types.

It was not until January 1933 that Hitler assumed power, marking the end of the Weimar Republic. He was carried to power by an alliance with the DNVP, but a further general election had to be called on 5 March, and this proved to be a disappointment, the Nazi's support having peaked the previous year. Considerable pressure was applied to the Catholic Centre Party to give Hitler a working majority in the *Reichstag*. The majority was used for the Enabling Law of 23 March 1933, which finally freed Hitler to rule by decree. Democracy in Germany was dead.

HITLER'S GERMANY

It was not just the Nazis and the nationalists who saw the outcome of the First World War as one of constant injustice. The feeling was widely felt throughout all classes of German society. In addition to the burden of reparations, the country had also lost its few colonies. Hitler was not alone in seeing colonial possessions as providing a captive market, and also space or *Lebensraum* into which expanding populations could move. Indeed, not only Germany but also both Italy and Japan were inspired by the need to establish empires, having missed their share of the colonial expansion of the nineteenth century, largely because Italy itself had been fragmented and because Japan had been isolationist.

Another factor that all three countries had in common was a paucity of natural resources, with Germany having massive reserves of coal, but nothing else, while Italy and Japan didn't even have this to any appreciable extent.

One difference between the Kaiser and Hitler was that *Weltpolitik* was less important than securing adequate natural resources, once again Germany was looking east, but within

Europe, but at first such intentions were kept from the world at large and simply mentioned within the National Socialist Party and the core of the future German armed forces.

Seldom has anyone been projected into such high office in a major country with so little experience of political life and of government as was Adolf Hitler. His party had been one of protest, in some ways a little more than a brutal pressure group. Inter-war Germany had had its fleeting taste of democracy, and the new national diet was to be dictatorship rather than monarchy.

Having first come to power on 30 January, two days later, on 1 February, Hitler made the first radio broadcast of his life. At the time, only a small minority of the German population had radios in their homes. Nevertheless, his first broadcast had to deliver a decisive policy address that would set the tone of his government. With a further general election looming, he had to gain the support of the vast majority of Germans at a time when popular support for his political party had passed its peak, and also encourage his own followers. While Germany was still militarily and financially weak, he also had to avoid alarming the democracies. Radio was important as his address would be taken seriously by listeners both within, and without, Germany at the time. Perhaps it was as well that television wasn't available, for Hitler has been described as sweating profusely with anticipation and, no doubt, nerves.

Hitler's speech concentrated on domestic issues. The recurring theme of his speech was the need for national unity. He harked back to Germany's surrender in November 1918, and to the Communist revolutionaries that had come to the fore in the period immediately following the armistice. In the speech, and in the years that followed, the trauma of German surrender in 1918 became a recurring theme, an obsession with defeat.

Relieving both unemployment amongst industrial workers and ending the poverty of the German peasant farmers were two specific objectives promised by Hitler, as well as reforming the relationship between the Reich, and the provinces or states, known as the *Lander*, and local government. Given the traumatic impact of hyperinflation on the population during the 1920s, his promise to promote efficiency and economy in public services, but to maintain health care and pensions must have reassured many sceptics, as well as promising to protect the German currency. All of this was innocuous, very much a case of 'motherhood and apple pie', and for domestic consumption.

On foreign policy, in many respects it was what Hitler did not say that mattered more than his actual words. Doubtless aware that his words would be considered carefully by the former wartime allies, Hitler gave conditional support to the Geneva disarmament negotiations. He even went as far as to stress that he would even accept the abolition of the German army, if every other country also disarmed completely. Yet, he laid equal stress on the fact that the state's primary duty was to protection of society and 'the restoration of the freedom of our *Volk*'. Few would argue that the first duty of government is the defence of the people, but as the German people were at this time still free, the stress on restoring freedom implied a hidden meaning. Many believe that by 'freedom', Hitler meant the freedom for Germany to do much as it pleased, placing her own national self-interest above all other considerations. The German *Volk* that he wanted to set free were those living outside Germany as minorities elsewhere in Europe.

What Hitler dared not say in public at this time was contained in his message for the armed forces. On 3 February, the new Defence Minister, General Blomberg, invited Hitler to address the country's senior military officers. The message was much clearer to this select and loyal audience. At home, Hitler's new administration would destroy Marxism and reconstruct the economy, while preparations would be made for a rearmament programme. Rearmament was essential because Hitler was anxious lest the former wartime allies might re-intervene whenever they felt like it, while he also saw Germany as vulnerable to attack from Poland and France, the German Case A again. The fact that Poland lacked the financial, industrial and military strength to do very much, and attacking Germany was far beyond its capacity, was conveniently overlooked.

The real meat of Hitler's address to the high command lay in his foreign policy ambitions. The concept of *Lebensraum*, 'living space', was to the forefront of his ambitions. He also called for new 'export opportunities', which was Hitler-speak for new colonies. By colonies, Hitler did not mean looking for tracts of Africa or Asia, at least not initially, but by expansion to the east, followed by a ruthless and single-minded Germanisation of the occupied territories that could be incorporated into the Reich and thus provide the *Lebensraum* that was so necessary. This was colonisation with a continental twist.

An even clearer indication of the way in which the new regime was to evolve followed on 9 February, when Hitler chaired a cabinet committee on job creation. The sole theme of the work creation programme was to be rearmament, whatever the country's representatives might say at Geneva. 'The future of Germany depends exclusively and only on the reconstruction of the Wehrmacht,' demanded Hitler. All other tasks must cede precedence to the task of rearmament . . . the interests of the Wehrmacht must in every case have priority.'[1]

After the general election on 5 March 1933, the nature of the new Germany was soon apparent. A good example was that, doubtless noting the promises to relieve unemployment and rural poverty, the socialist trade unions convinced themselves that they could work with the new government. For the first time in Germany, 1 May 1933, became a public holiday, with Hitler, Goebbels and the trade union leaders joining in a celebration of national labour. The day after, the trade union leaders faced reality. On 2 May 1933, large squads of brownshirt militia stormed the trade union offices and closed them, while trade union funds and property were confiscated. At works level, there were also Nazi activists on the shop floor, but their activities were getting out of hand and becoming an embarrassment for the party, so the National Socialist Party launched a German Labour Front, which acted as a controlling organization for a regional network of 'trustees' of labour.

Meanwhile, members of the other political parties, including the Communists and Social Democrats, were subjected to violent attacks, as well as members of the Jewish minority, whose homes and businesses were attacked.

Gradually, Hitler's ambitions started to become apparent to a wider audience. In June 1933, Hitler told the Hungarian prime minister, Julius Goemboes, in private, that he intended to crush France. Before that, the German government had imposed a moratorium on all of Germany's foreign debts, to take effect from 30 June, and at the same time a massive programme of rearmament was initiated that would account for up to 10 per cent of the gross national product for the future. The initial debt moratorium was to be short-lived due to the volume of protests from the wartime allies, and payments at the rate of half the interest and capital due soon restarted, but in December these sums were reduced to 30 per cent.

Meanwhile, in response to a British initiative calling for a further round of reductions in national armed forces, and British rejection of German plans for limited rearmament, Hitler withdrew from both the Geneva disarmament talks and membership of the League of Nations on the grounds that he could not accept Germany's second class status. It seems that if not Hitler himself, then several of his close associates, expected intervention at that time, especially from France and Poland. Both countries could have acted together and probably succeeded, but France suffered from internal civil unrest at the time aroused by its own Fascists, and Poland was placated in early 1934 by a combination of economic concessions and a treaty of friendship.

HITLER AND THE ARMED FORCES

From the start, Adolf Hitler was popular with the armed forces and enjoyed their support. The small size of the Army and the Navy had meant that it had been possible to screen new recruits and only those who were safe and without Socialist connections were accepted. This was especially true of the officer class. The support was more open and more widely felt in the Navy, with many Army officers, especially those of the 'old school' regarding the Fascists and the Communists as simply being different sides of the same coin, both being revolutionaries and both ruling by dictatorship. Hitler's background would not have endeared himself to the old Prussian elite. What both armed services had in common was support for the Nazi promise to free Germany from 'the shackles of Versailles.' When the President, von Hindenburg, appointed Hitler Chancellor, Dönitz recalled that: 'We soldiers also hoped that through this change in the leadership the Communist danger would be removed.' In fact, the Navy also saw the Nazis as resurrecting Germany's idea of a world role as a maritime power.

The Navy also needed to embrace Hitler and in effect gain his favour. It had failed during the First World War, suffered mutinies and desertions in 1918, and again there had been unrest in 1923. The Army had regarded the Navy as being better able to handle political matters and publicity, and it was to need this edge with the new regime.

The naval bases at Kiel and Wilhelmshaven were filled with many Nazi sympathisers, so much so that when Goebbels visited in spring 1932, he reported that 'everyone, officers and crews, are entirely for us.'

The initial plans for reconstruction of the armed forces had included plans for a secret air force. Initially, German manufacturers had continued their work abroad while gliding schools in Germany ensured that young pilots were being nurtured. In 1932, the air force was planned to have 200 aircraft, but in September 1933, this was raised to 2,000 combat aircraft, due to be operational by 1935. For the army, there were two four year plans, at the end of the first, in 1937, it was to have 300,000 men in twenty-one divisions, with adequate reserves to expand to sixty-three divisions on the outbreak of hostilities. This required conscription, forbidden by the Treaty of Versailles. Plans were laid to reoccupy the Rhineland by 1937. The Navy was not neglected, with an initial five year plan to begin rebuilding and modernising the fleet.

'No people have more right to the idea of world mastery than the German people,' declared Hitler at a speech at Mannheim on 5 November 1930. 'No other nation has had such a right to claim world mastery on the grounds of ability and numbers. We have come in short to this first world partition and stand at the beginning of a new world revolution . . .'

By April 1934, with a German military budget that forced the French to withdraw from discussing military issues with Germany, it was clear that the country was embarked on a course of military expansion of a degree that had not been seen for some years. Until 1934, most foreign observers could remain blissfully unaware of German intentions, but that time onwards, the course was set. Individual projects could be hidden or their full extent disguised, as when one new battlecruiser was laid down officially, but two, *Scharnhorst* and *Gneisenau*, were actually built. Airliners were developed that had a concealed military role, with the Junkers Ju52 trimotor originally being intended to double up as a transport and as a bomber, although it was obsolescent by the time the opportunity came. Until the mid-1930s, this means of aircraft development was none too difficult to sustain or conceal, as it was not until the late 1930s that the basic designs of bomber and transport aircraft began to diverge significantly, and many air forces, including the Royal Air Force, had operated bomber-transports. As the bombers became slimmer and leaner, some of the Dornier airliners produced during the 1930s must have been extremely uncomfortable for the passengers of Deutsche Luft Hansa (now Lufthansa), the national airline, so cramped and slender were their 'bomber' fuselages.

Hitler planned a two stage development of Germany's ambitions. The first stage would be continental hegemony, with the emphasis on the colonisation of Eastern Europe by Germans. This could only be achieved while maintaining good relations with the United Kingdom, which would protect his western flank. It would not only provide the *Lebensraum* that Germany craved, it would also provide the oil and other resources needed to give Germany security of supplies and also end the ever returning balance of payments problems that afflicted the country between the two world wars. The second stage was to be a struggle with the English-speaking world, essentially the United Kingdom and the United States, for world domination.

It is clear that at this time Hitler accepted the rationale that war on two fronts would be beyond even rearmed Germany's abilities. The trick would be to keep the British and the Americans quiet while Germany moved east. This was not completely unrealistic. The Munro Doctrine meant that the United States would be reluctant to intervene in Europe, although they had done so in 1917 and a long time before this in 1816, when they joined the British and Dutch in finally disposing of the Barbary pirates. All that would be expected would be that Germany would not interfere with the Americas. It could even be that the United States would welcome the opportunity to extend her influence over British, French and Dutch Caribbean and South American territories, and perhaps incorporate the Canadian provinces as states of the Union. US support for Britain would not be automatic, he reasoned.

The same reasoning continued to argue that the British would be reluctant to become involved in yet another European war. This was still the time when a country such as Czechoslovakia could be described by a British statesman as a 'far off country of which we know little.' Nor was there any love lost between the British, or at least the British establishment, and the Soviet Union. There was a shared fear of Bolshevism in both Britain and Germany. Initially, the proposal would be that the United Kingdom could have a free hand in the wider world in return for Germany having a free hand in Europe. The fact that by this time the warning signs that the British Empire's days were numbered, and meant that many even in the United Kingdom would not necessary favour their country having a free hand, escaped the Germans. Already, Canada and South Africa, and to a lesser extent Australia, were showing signs of increasing independence, while many in India were actively agitating for independence.

Many senior officers in the German armed forces maintained after the Second World War that they could not have foreseen where Hitler's ambitions would have led. This is nonsense. Not only did they have his speeches and briefings to senior officers passed on to them, but there were many in Germany, such as a member of Field Marshal von Moltke's family, Helmuth, who even before Hitler came to power maintained that 'whoever votes for Hitler votes for war.'

THE NAVY BACKS HITLER

Despite the way in which Dönitz's department had dealt with the *Reichstag* over matters such as the new military penal code, most senior naval officers had little time for democratic institutions, even less understanding, and for the most part contempt for those in the mainstream political parties. As early as May 1933, an important figure in the Reichsmarine, none other than the leader of the staff officer training scheme established by Raeder, addressed a joint meeting of members of the SS, SA, *Stahlhelm* and Nazi Party.

> Now the forces which in the last fourteen years were splintered through struggles in Parliament, are free to overcome . . . all the infamous sabotage attempts of Social Democrats, doctrinaires and pacifists . . . Now we must again awake and strengthen the understanding, the love of the sea and the will of the nation and never again allow the life veins to be cut, which for a free, great people lie on the free oceans.[1]

The old pre-war concept of *Weltpolitik* was clearly alive and well in the Reichsmarine.

The wider ambitions of the German people were aided to a minor extent by a scheme initiated by von Hindenburg, under which a travel grant was awarded annually to an outstanding officer in one of the two armed services to enable him to travel abroad and broaden his knowledge. In 1933, Dönitz was the lucky recipient, and chose to visit the British and Dutch colonies in the Far East. Leaving Germany in February 1933, he was away when the Nazis began their brutal campaign against their enemies and began to extinguish democracy.

Hitler's actions were those of a mad man who would brook no opposition, but Dönitz was also viewed by some as being unbalanced. One of those who viewed him in this way was Canaris, under whom he served during the early 1930s. A single officer's report can sometimes be discounted, especially since Canaris himself was something of an enigma, but the US Consul General in Berlin during the early 1930s swore an affidavit which was read out at the Nuremberg International Military Tribunal, saying that he 'was not always well balanced mentally.' Yet, even his own writings suggest that he was also something of a fantasist.

Some of the fantasies can be discounted as exaggerated tales of wartime to enliven the dinner table conversation. He admitted to talking about his experience as a U-boat commander during the First World War when a lady at the same table aboard the ship taking him to the east demanded to hear about the war as it really happened. He then related a completely fabricated story about a time when he was on watch aboard *U-39*. According to his account, they chased a small British merchantman through a smoke screen and when they reached the other side, found her drifting with her flaps open and four guns trained on them. *U-39* escaped because she was too close for the guns to be trained on her, and Dönitz ordered a crash dive, saving his boat.

Another story concerned when he had his own command, *UC-25*, in the Mediterranean, and had attempted a submerged night attack on a convoy off Cape Bon on the coast of Tunisia. Finding himself too far from the convoy for a torpedo attack, he surfaced and headed at top speed in bright moonlight towards the convoy, but as *UC-25* closed on the ships, the escorting destroyers opened fire and he was forced to dive. Once he was submerged, the destroyers steamed overhead making a depth charge attack.

He also related a story about his time as a prisoner of war in Malta, maintaining that when he refused to tell his interrogator, an admiral, the identity of his own vessel, a British staff officer immediately handed the correct information to the admiral.

There is absolutely no record of any of these events having occurred. In any event, it would have been unlikely for a U-boat commander to be interviewed by such a senior officer. In any case, he had survived the sinking of *UB-68*, yet related that the staff officer described him as the commander of *UC-25*, one of his earlier craft. In this last tale, he also maintained that he had sunk a large British merchantman in a Sicilian harbour, when in fact he had simply sent a coaling hulk to the bottom. His language in describing these events was also fantasist, describing his moonlight attack on the convoy as 'charging like a blind madman . . .' It was not surprising that Canaris found him not only unbalanced but immature.

One story that he did not recount was the loss of the submarine *UB-68*, sunk in the Mediterranean on 4 October 1918. He was amongst the survivors, with the engineer staying on board and three others being drowned. On his homeward voyage, he had the steamer stop at the point where the boat had gone down and saluted the dead from the stern rail.

Amongst the places visited were Ceylon, now Sri Lanka, India, Netherlands East Indies, including Java and Bali, and Singapore.

Dönitz returned home to find that not only was the internal security situation much calmer, with the Communists and others in detention camps, but that Hitler had launched a five year programme for the Navy. In October, he was promoted to *Fregattenkapitan*, a rank that does not exist in the Royal Navy but equates to a captain, second class or junior, and the following year returned to sea as commanding officer of a light cruiser.

The German five year shipbuilding plan was limited in two ways. The first was that the country could not afford to expand the Army and develop an air force at the same time as engaging in a major expansion of the Navy. It was also important not to antagonise the United Kingdom until Hitler's eastern ambitions had been realised, so the fleet was deliberately planned not to be of a size that would alarm the British. By offering the British a treaty that would confirm German naval inferiority, it would break the shackles of Versailles and separate the British from the French, while leaving Germany free to start on rebuilding the fleet. The Japanese had already attempted to overcome the limitations of the Washington Naval Treaty at the London Naval Conference in 1930.

Hitler meanwhile had realised that the SA had become an embarrassment, and was attempting to infiltrate the officer corps. He reached an agreement with Blomberg, head of the Army, that the SA and its leaders would be liquidated under the pretext that they were planning a *coup d'etat*, in return for Army support for Hitler as successor to President Hindenburg, by this time in poor health. Hindenburg died and the office of President and Chancellor were combined on 1 August 1934, while the next day, the commanders of both services reaffirmed their oath as 'unconditional obedience to Adolph Hitler, Fuhrer of the Reich and of the German people, Supreme Commander of the armed forces . . .' and every member of the Army and the Navy followed in a series of local ceremonies. The next step was to incorporate Nazi Party insignia into the uniforms.

Meanwhile, the expatriate engineers and designers who had been working outside Germany on the banned aircraft, armoured vehicles and U-boats, had returned home. The USSR was increasingly being presented as the enemy, while Polish fears about German intentions were allayed by a non-aggression pact. French fears over German rearmament meant that they realigned their foreign policy to seek an accommodation with the Soviet Union.

THE LONDON NAVAL AGREEMENT, AND BEYOND

The planning for the London Naval Agreement started in 1934. Anxious to expand the fleet without setting alarm bells ringing in the London, Raeder's staff worked out that Germany should seek displacement tonnage amounting to a third of that of the Royal Navy for the three largest types of warship, battleships, aircraft carriers and cruisers. Such a ratio would mean that a rerun of the Battle of Jutland would not be possible and the British would not feel threatened. For smaller ships, such as torpedo-boats and U-boats, the ratio sought was almost 100 per cent, justified on the grounds that as these were short-range vessels, they would not be perceived as a threat, but in case of sustained British objections, for U-boats ratios of 50 per cent, 35 per cent and 33.3 per cent were also considered as a negotiating ploy. The expansion of the fleet thus proposed also marked a considerable increase on the Navy's five year programme.

Such a fleet would be large enough to defend the Baltic and the North Sea. But it was to be no more than the first step in the expansion needed to confront the British Empire. Nevertheless, some of the vessels envisaged were far larger than anything that needed to be used against the French or the Russians, and in any event, war with these two countries would revolve around invasion and ground battles supported by overwhelming air power.

The year of the London Naval Conference, 1935, was the one during which the German Navy changed its name from Reichsmarine, 'State Navy', to Kriegsmarine, 'War Navy', suggesting a more aggressive role. The resulting Anglo-German Naval Treaty laid the foundation for the reconstruction of the German fleet, with a surface fleet of up to 35 per cent of that of the Royal Navy, based once again on tonnage rather than warship numbers, and given the impact of the German U-boat fleet on the United Kingdom during the First World War, what was surprising was that the negotiators allowed the Kriegsmarine to have parity in submarines with the Royal Navy if the extra submarine tonnage was subtracted from the tonnage allowed for surface vessels. While hindsight is generally credited with perfect 20:20 vision, in this case it seems that the negotiators were blind to the potential of the submarine and ignored the lessons of what was at the time the still recent history of the First World War.

It was strange that the British Admiralty, which was already worried about a German-Italian-Japanese alliance, should have allowed the negotiators to be so relaxed. The British Foreign Secretary, Sir John Simon, believed that nothing could stop German rearmament, while others thought that giving Germany what she asked for limited the European end of arms expansion. There was also the feeling that if they agreed to Germany's proposals, she would abide by them, but if they denied Germany her rights, she would go ahead and exceed the limits. No one discussed the agreement with any of the other wartime Allies, although by this time the United States was not interested and Italy was already being seen as a role model by Hitler.

Hitler could hardly believe that the London Naval Treaty was so generous, telling Raeder that it was the happiest day of his life. He felt that the British position at the negotiations came as a clear indication that Germany and the United Kingdom would not be at war, and that any future conflict would be with France or the Soviet Union. It was not until 1938 that war between Britain and Germany became inevitable in the eyes of the Fuhrer.

The problem that faced the commanders of the German armed forces is that Hitler would not allow effective coordination between them. He feared that a committee comprised of his chiefs of staff would in effect become a pressure group with its own policies. Instead, they had to report directly to him. This has become widely known as the 'Fuhrer System'. It left Hitler vulnerable since his own knowledge was completely inadequate and he had no conception of military command. It also meant that the individual service chiefs had to time their conversations with the Fuhrer so that none of the others, who had to be regarded as rivals, would be present.

During one of these conversations in June 1934, Raeder raised the question of the planned battlecruisers, which eventually entered service as *Scharnhorst* and *Gneisenau*, and was told by Hitler that they must be described as improved 10,000-ton ships with a speed of 26 knots rather than the planned 25,000-tons and speed of 30 knots. This was ridiculous, as the first ship, *Scharnhorst*, had already been announced and declared as a counter to the French Dunkerque-class. Her sister, *Gneisenau*, was laid down in secret. In one sense, both ships were less than expected, for while their

55

displacement was 31,800 tons, their armament was just 11-in calibre, using gun turrets ordered for the second batch of three *panzerschiff*, which were never built. The intention was that these would be replaced later by 15-in guns, but this never happened. The British classed them as battlecruisers, but the Germans always listed them as battleships.

During this meeting with Hitler, Raeder took the opportunity of asking whether all future heavy ships should have 35-cm (14-in) guns, to match the latest British ships, to which the Fuhrer gave his agreement. This meant that the next class of battleships, *Bismarck* and *Tirpitz*, were more heavily armed, although in the end they had guns that equated to 15-in rather than 14-in. The official German record preserved in the archives noted:

> Commander-in-Chief of the Navy stated his opinion that the fleet would have to be developed later against England, that therefore from 1936 the great ships would have to be armed with 35-cm guns (as King George-class).

Raeder continued with his meeting with the Fuhrer, moving on to U-boats. Orders had been placed for the first fifteen, although construction had still to start, which would be mainly of a smaller type, and the first batch of executive officers and engineers as well as some seventy ratings had completed the first *U-Schule* long course, which had run from October 1933. Hitler's orders were that the entire U-boat scheme was to remain secret until after a referendum in the Saarland, which was under League of Nations Control, whose inhabitants were to decide whether or not they wished to be part of the Reich.

There were other pressures that were hampering the arms build up. The German economy was still relatively weak, and the rearmament programme was already feeling the strain. When Dönitz was introduced to Hitler for the first time as commanding officer of the light cruiser *Emden*, about to depart on a foreign cruise, Raeder was present and once again sought the Fuhrer's ear. He complained that the funds available to the armed forces for 1935 were inadequate for the new plans and would affect the Navy's schedule. Hitler's reaction was that he did not believe that the funds would be reduced by too much. If problems did arise, Hitler would order funds to be diverted from the works programme because of the need to rebuild the Navy as quickly as possible. Without a strong Navy, ore supplies shipped from Sweden through Norwegian ports, could not be guaranteed. Swedish ore had to be transport by rail to Norway rather than direct from Swedish ports because the Gulf of Bothnia froze in winter. At the same meeting, Hitler also agreed with Raeder that he could go ahead and have the first six U-boats completed for the first quarter of 1935.

The ultimate objective of German naval planning was to have a fleet that was the equivalent of the Royal Navy or the United States Navy. The head of the Navy, Grand Admiral Raeder, believed that a substantial surface fleet, pre-positioned in foreign waters, would be able to deal with the Royal Navy. The weakness in this argument was that suitable foreign bases would be a problem for Germany which had lost its small number of colonies in the defeat of 1918, and the ships would be heavily reliant on a good fleet train for re-supply, which would be vulnerable.

HITLER'S DOUBLE SURPRISE

March 1935 was the month in which Hitler began to make his intentions clear to a wider world. It was an abrupt breaking of the shackles of Versailles. On Saturday 9 March, the Air Minister, Hermann Goering, revealed the existence of the Luftwaffe, the most fundamental breach of the terms of the Versailles Treaty. Exactly a week later, the second Saturday surprise was Hitler's announcement on 16 March that conscription was to be introduced and that the *Wehrmacht* was to have a peacetime strength of twelve army corps and thirty-six divisions.

Hitler had already ordered the construction of the first U-boats on 1 February, maintaining secrecy by having them assembled in large sheds that had been specially constructed.

Those who had wanted to know, as opposed to those who buried their heads in the sand, had been aware that Germany had started to rearm, despite the attempts to maintain secrecy. Nevertheless, the blatant rejection of the terms of Versailles after just sixteen years set the alarm bells ringing in capital cities across Europe. The Nazis liked to maintain that other nations had never disarmed, but the normal reduction in the size of armed forces once peace had returned had also been increased by the economic pressures of the inter-war years and by the presence of a strong pacifist movement in many of the democracies. These moves were aided by many who believed that the First World War had been so terrible that never again would nations go to war. These were also people who ignored Japan's aggression in China, and who had a rude awakening when Italy's actions in Abyssinia, present day Ethiopia, became widely known.

There were those, especially in Great Britain, who agreed that the terms at Versailles had been too strict and that it was only to be expected that Germany would want to rearm. Others saw the main threat to Europe as Communism, and wanted Germany as a bulwark against the westward march of this brutal and oppressive ideology.

Unknown to himself, Karl Dönitz had been selected as head of the U-boat service. While this was not known generally when the Naval High Command held a conference in March, it was agreed that the chief of the pending U-boat 1st Flotilla would report to the admiral in command at Kiel, at this time Admiral Foerster. When the idea was put to Foerster, he responded on 8 April, agreeing but also proposing that a *Fuhrer der U-boote*, FdU, be appointed early in 1936. The name of Karl Dönitz was put as commander of the 1st U-boat Flotilla when the autumn appointments were announced on 6 June. It is not known who proposed Dönitz for the post, and it seems that it was done verbally.

When Raeder told Dönitz about his new post, actually visiting the *Emden* on her return to Wilhelmshaven, Dönitz recorded his reaction as being unenthusiastic. He had been looking forward to taking his ship to the Far East, and by comparison, felt that U-boats were unimportant in the plans being prepared for an enlarged German Navy and that, in effect, he was being pushed into a siding. In fact, as in the Royal Navy and the Imperial Japanese Navy at this time, the *Marineleitung* was dominated by 'big gun, big ship' men who saw the battleship and battlecruiser as the naval weapon of the future.

There were U-boat enthusiasts at the *Marineleitung*, however, and at senior level, there was considerable disagreement over the future shape of the German Navy. Raeder was a big ship man, and his logic was that the increasingly widespread use of Asdic, as sonar was known at the time, meant that submarines were obsolete and vulnerable, and that surface raiders would be more important. The U-boat advocates were fervent supporters of the submarine, and believed that unrestricted submarine warfare against British merchant shipping would bring the United Kingdom to starvation and its armed forces would be unable to fight for want of fuel and munitions. Uncertainty over Asdic meant that some advocated firing torpedoes at long ranges, around 3,000 yards, while others believed that the detection system was underrated and had severe limitations.

As for Dönitz, his return home, followed by leave with his family, sailing with his two sons in the Baltic, was interrupted when he was sent to Turkey to see the U-boat school established by Furbringer, and which had retained the link with the Kriegsmarine through the presence of another wartime U-boat ace.

On 21 September 1935, the Reichsmarine ensign was replaced by the Kriegsmarine swastika ensign, amidst celebration amongst the officer corps of the German Navy.

COMMUNISTS AGAINST FASCISTS IN SPAIN

The Kriegsmarine was less involved in the Spanish Civil War, which broke out in July 1936 and lasted until April 1939, than the other two armed services. The Condor Legion was raised to enable the German armed forces to participate in supporting the Nationalists against the anti-monarchist and pro-Communist Republicans. The air element fielded by the Luftwaffe was especially successful in using the conflict to develop its tactics and create a battle-hardened core of airmen. Italy also supported the Nationalists, while the Soviet Union and, to a lesser degree, France supported the Republicans.

It was not uncommon for warships to be sent to areas of such great danger even by neutral nations to protect their own nationals, and it still happens today.

The German presence offshore was the *Panzerschiff Deutschland*, and she soon received a timely reminder of the danger that air power posed to surface vessels. On 29 May 1937, she was attacked by Republican aircraft while in Ibiza Roads, with at least two bombs hitting the ship and exploding, killing more than thirty members of her ship's company.

Admiral Scheer was also present off Spain, and in retaliation for the attack on her sister ship, she bombarded the coastal town of Almeria.

The attack on *Deutschland* undoubtedly helped influence the decision to rename her *Lutzow* in November 1939, and it also reflected pessimism on the part of senior naval officers.

Notes
1   Bird, K., *Weimar, the German Naval Officer Corps and the Rise of National Socialism*, Amsterdam, 1977.

CHAPTER FIVE

Plan Z Emerges

Dönitz may not have been enthused when he first heard that he was to become commander of a U-boat flotilla, but he must have quickly realised the advantages of being in a new arm of the Fleet at the beginning, and perhaps also recognised that the U-boat was once again to demonstrate great potential. Either way, even before he took up his post, he sent a paper to the *Marineleitung* giving his views about the organisation of the German submarine service. He prefaced it with an introduction on the role of the U-boat in wartime.

> The U-boat is essentially an attack weapon. Its great action radius makes it suitable for operations in distant enemy sea areas. In consequence of its low submerged and surface speed its tactical ability against fast forces is fundamentally excluded. Its employment will therefore in essence be only stationary.
>
> The operational mission of U-boats in war will be dependent on the war tasks of the Navy. In a war against an enemy whom is not dependent on overseas supplies as a vital necessity, the task of our U-boats, in contrast to the World War, will not be the trade war, for which the U-boat in consequence of its low speed is little suited. The U-boat will be placed in a stationary position as close as possible before the enemy harbours at the focal point of enemy traffic. Attack target, the enemy warships and troop transports.[1]

From this, it is clear that Dönitz was considering a future war against the Soviet Union and her ally France that had replaced Poland as a potential foe. He was also considering attacking French forces in the Mediterranean, correctly guessing that there would be substantial numbers of troop transports carrying reinforcements from North Africa to France. He was not thinking about war against the British Empire. There is little in his paper about U-boat strategy

60

as it was practised during the Second World War. Indeed, his paper advocates night surface attack, suggesting that his thinking had not moved on from the First World War and from his experience with the torpedo-boat exercises post-war.

Dönitz advocated the creation of an attacking spirit amongst the crews. Like the British admiral, 'Jacky' Fisher, so many years earlier who believed that 'Our drill ground should be our battle ground,' he pressed for considerable sea time and training in the planned operational areas. He also advocated using the surface fleet for exercises. The flotilla should not be tied to a home port, but instead should have a depot ship capable of supporting up to twelve submarines. A note of realism about the hardships of life aboard a submarine was that he also specified that the depot ship should have 'numerous baths'.

Foerster, the admiral in command at Kiel, was delighted with the paper, and allowed Dönitz complete freedom with training and exercising his flotilla. In September, all but one of the first twelve U-boats, all small 250-ton craft, had been commissioned. Out of necessity, many had been allocated to the *U-Schule*, and when he took up his appointment on 28 September, he had just three U-boats. His flotilla was named 'Weddigen' after the First World War ace. On 1 November, he became *Kapitan zur See*, or captain. Dönitz was not a desk officer at this time, for he joined his men in training and exercises in their submarines, despite his rank.

DEVELOPING U-BOAT TACTICS

Initially, U-boat tactics were based on those evolved for torpedo-boats, but these evolved until the tactics became more suitable for the submarine. Dönitz and his flotilla practised many different means of attack and in different numbers. It was not until November 1937 that he produced a long paper and for the first time argued in favour of group tactics, the wolf pack. He was later to claim that he started in the U-boats with the plan for group tactics already in mind, but there is nothing to prove this. One feature introduced during these exercises was that of centralised control and co-ordination, for which he used a command ship.

By this time, Dönitz was finally *Fuhrer der U-Boote*, FdU, although still in the rank of captain, having been given the title on 1 October 1936. A second flotilla was already forming, using the large Type VII which displaced 625 tons, by far the most numerous U-boat class built.

He took up his command at a difficult time for Germany. The unrealistic goals of the rearmament programme meant that the country was consuming iron ore, oil, rubber and other vital but always imported materials faster than it could pay for them. The demands of the armaments industries were such that it was difficult to spare capacity for exports that could have helped redress the balance of payments deficit. The Fuhrer system meant that each of the three armed forces had its own programme, which it pursued regardless of the impact on the economy or of the other armed forces. It is usual for each service in any country to be in some form of rivalry with the others, especially for public funds, but this was taken to extreme lengths by Hitler who, as already mentioned, had rejected any form of committee for the service chiefs. When faced with demands by his own economic adviser, Schacht, in 1936 for an easing of the rearmament programme to cut imports and increase exports, Hitler formulated a new 'four-year plan', this time to make Germany self-sufficient in those raw materials essential for armaments. Vast sums were ploughed into research and development of artificial oil and rubber, but these proved to be several times the cost of the real thing, with oil between four and five times as expensive, while the rubber proved extremely difficult to produce in quantity.

As for the Kriegsmarine, despite Hitler's desire for a strong navy, it was suffering from a limited steel quota. Eight battleships were now planned and in 1937, Raeder considered adding a ninth ship to the programme, with an armament heavier than that for the British *King George V*, but already the programme was suffering delays for want of steel.

Frustrated, Raeder started to appeal for larger quotas of steel and other metals during 1936. On 25 October 1937, he lost patience and issued an ultimatum, award the Kriegsmarine higher quotas or face having shipbuilding back drastically so that he could complete a few modern warships 'in a conceivable time'. This prompted one of the few occasions on which Hitler brought together all of the chiefs of his armed forces, as well as the Foreign Minister. He began the meeting by reiterating the question of finding *Lebensraum* for the German people, but went on to remind them that France and Great Britain were both 'hate-enemies'. He mentioned the weaknesses in British and French positions and looked back at the policies of Frederick the Great and Bismarck. His audience was told that he intended to resolve the question of *Lebensraum* by 1943–1945 at the latest, but might possibly bring this date forward should an opportunity present itself should France be weakened by war with another country or by an internal political crisis.

Hitler by this time clearly recognised that the British were unlikely to be fooled for long by his self-imposed limits on warship construction, and might intervene in any continental war.

For the first time, the Kriegsmarine started to consider the possibility that in any future war with France, the British might side with their First World War ally. This was a nightmare scenario that everyone had tried not to consider earlier. The prospect was given formal recognition when the Operations Division produced a study entitled 'The Tasks of Naval Warfare 1937/8'. Meanwhile, Krupp was ordered to expand their steel mills so that Germany could fulfil the Fuhrer's promise to Raeder that his annual steel quota would be increased from 40,000 to 75,000 tons. Raeder then began to worry that war might break out before his plans were completed, but the Fuhrer reassured him.

It was at this time that Dönitz started to change his ideas for naval warfare. The changes in strategy were highlighted in his report, 'The Employment of U-boats in the Framework of the Fleet', dated 23 November 1937, which called for the use of U-boats to threaten enemy commerce. This took a realistic view of a state that lacked a good strategic position and lacked colonial bases, as well as having a limited surface fleet. It argued that the U-boat might be the only means to threaten enemy sea communications. In this report, Dönitz was clearly thinking of war with the United Kingdom, and that would only happen if the country sided with France, something on which Hitler was taking a gamble.

The report also considered the possibility of the U-boats operating with surface vessels. The U-boats could provide reconnaissance, patrolling off enemy ports and reporting movements, and as attacking groups in the path of the enemy. Good communications were to be an essential part of this, with a good communications centre ashore to collect and coordinate information from the U-boats and issue orders, all of which recognised the poor visibility from an individual U-boat, although it tended to ignore the risk to the U-boats from enemy direction finding or code-breaking.

A feature of the report was that it also took aircraft into account. Aerial maritime-reconnaissance had featured in the First World War, with Royal Navy semi-rigid airships for convoy protection and flying-boats for active maritime-reconnaissance. The presence of aircraft would undoubtedly hamper U-boat operations and force the craft to remain submerged, but he did not envisage constant air patrols, so decided that aircraft would only restrict operations for a short time.

Finally, he proposed research and development of faster U-boats so that tests could be conducted on their potential.

FEARS OF WAR

It is tempting to compare Hitler's position in 1937 with that of the Kaiser in 1912. There were essential differences. In 1912, it was the Army that received the lion's share of the available resources, leaving Tirpitz opposing von Moltke's demands for war. In 1937, it was Blomberg and Fritsche, the Army chiefs, who feared war. They simply could not believe that Great Britain and France would allow Germany even to begin its continental expansion, the incorporation of Austria and the German-speaking areas of Czechoslovakia into the Reich, let alone the other more ambitious plans involving Poland and, ultimately, the Soviet Union. Raeder on the other hand fully accepted Hitler's assurances that there would be no war with the UK before 1943.

Not brooking any disagreement or independence of opinion, or taking advice from experienced and well-trained professionals, Hitler soon moved to replace the Army chiefs. A homosexual scandal was arranged to force Fritsche to resign, while Blomberg followed after he disgraced himself by marrying a former prostitute. Hitler then appointed himself Commander-in-Chief of the Armed Forces before replacing the Foreign Minister von Neurath, a professional diplomat, with von Ribbentrop, doubtless as a reward for his *coup* with the London Naval Treaty, and finally sacking Schacht, his economic adviser, with the economically-illiterate Funk. Just Goering and Raeder survived the October, or 'Hossbach', meeting. Only Raeder was a true professional, for despite having been a First World War fighter ace, Goering was simply another party hack with no experience of high command or staff work.

Hitler then proceeded with the first stage of his plans. In mid-March 1938, the *Anschluss* was declared after 100,000 German troops marched into Austria, and the Austrian government decided not to oppose these overwhelming forces. The *Anschluss*, meaning coming together, was at first very popular with the majority of Austrians. In contrast to other later occupations, the Germans were anxious to make the whole affair seem as un-military as possible, but the troops initially stationed in Austria were under strict orders to suppress any opposition.

Austria not only provided Germany with additional territory and manpower, with a population of some 6.7 million, it also brought additional industrial capacity, energy and raw materials for the increasingly hungry German industrialisation. Austria's gold and foreign exchange reserves were a welcome windfall. The *Anchluss* with Austria added around 7.5 per cent to Germany's industrial output, although it gave only an extra 4 per cent in steel production, and half of this was destined for export. Nevertheless, there was one invaluable asset, the Erzberg, a mine of the highest grade iron ore, much of which was exported to neighbouring countries. This was not of itself sufficient to meet German demand, but it certainly cut the balance of payments strain of importing all of Germany's iron ore.

Germany had had earlier designs on Austria, which had lost much of its territory to neighbouring Czechoslovakia, Hungary, Italy and Yugoslavia, including areas such as the South Tyrol, ceded to Italy, which were German-speaking. Immediately after the First World War, the name chosen for the country at first was *Deutsch-Österreich*, and union with the new post-war German republic was planned, but banned by the Treaty of Versailles, anxious to avoid creating a new power group.

Incorporating Austria in the Reich had other benefits over and above the industrial resources gained. It increased Germany's influence over the nations of central and southern Europe. Hungary suddenly found that instead of Germany taking 26 per cent of the nation's exports, it now accounted for 44 per cent, while Yugoslavia found that Germany took 43 per cent of its exports instead of 32 per cent. These were market shares that would be impossible to replace within any reasonable time, so both nations were drawn into the German orbit.

The annexation of Austria was a boost to German confidence. They had seen that the rest of the world seemed to lack the will to intervene. Now was the time for Hitler to demonstrate what he meant when he described the German people as *ein Volk*, one people. He had his eyes on those Germans living beyond the country's borders, of whom the most obvious were the Sudeten Germans, living in the west of Czechoslovakia. The Sudetenland had been ceded to Czechoslovakia, a new state created from the ruins of the Austro-Hungarian Empire, by the Treaty of Versailles.

The German population of 3 million was a substantial minority of the 14 million people living in Czechoslovakia.

Hitler's demands for the Sudetenland to be incorporated into Germany became increasingly strident, and Europe appeared to be on the verge of all out war. Nevertheless, the British and French were anxious to avoid another war if at all possible, and in the Munich Agreement of 30 September 1938, signed by the United Kingdom, France, Germany and Italy, Czechoslovakia was effectively compelled to cede the territory to Germany.

Often criticised, usually with the benefit of hindsight, the Munich Agreement bought the democracies time in which to continue their rearmament, but unfortunately it also reassured Hitler that an aggressive tone could win the day. With Czechoslovakia reeling from the loss of so much of its territory and almost a quarter of its population, and the democracies standing by, Slovakia, by far the poorer end of the country, began to come under the sway of the Germans, while Hungary annexed part of its territory. In the north, the Poles seized their chance and annexed the main area occupied by the 60,000 people of Polish descent living in Czechoslovakia. Despite the original German demands having been met, in March 1939, Germany occupied most of what remained of Czechoslovakia.

Earlier, on 28 May 1938, Raeder once again met Hitler, who had wired him with proposals for a massive acceleration in naval construction. By this time, it was clear that Hitler did not expect the United Kingdom to stand idly aside in the future as she was also rearming. To avoid war, the Fuhrer needed to have such a strong Navy, and in particular such a massive submarine force, that the British would hesitate to intervene in the planned continental expansion and war for fear of being blockaded and cut-off by U-boats.

If further evidence was required that Italy and Germany were embarked on a course that could only ultimately lead to war, it came on 7 April 1939, Good Friday, when Italy invaded Albania, a poor, mountainous country on the other side of the Adriatic. Once again, the United Kingdom and France did nothing, with the UK recognising the annexation in an attempt to discourage Italy from allying itself with Germany in the future conflict that was increasingly being seen as inevitable.

Once again, appeasement had been the preferred option.

PLANNING FOR WAR WITH BRITAIN

Even before the Munich crisis of 1938, Raeder considered that there was a danger of war with both France and the United Kingdom, but this was still not discussed officially. While it is possible to draw parallels with the situation before the First World War and before the Second World War, there were differences, not least in the attitude towards war of the Army and the Navy. Another big difference was that Raeder and his staff envisaged a war against shipping rather than the major confrontation between the opposing fleets that had so concerned Tirpitz.

The naval staff appreciated that Britain enjoyed a commanding strategic position that barred Germany's access to the open seas, but that her weakness was her dependence on overseas trade and supplies. Nor was there any question of Germany rivalling the strong British battle fleet. On the other hand, if Germany could seize Denmark, Norway and the Netherlands, the situation could be improved, but it would need the occupation of the entire northern coastline of France as far as Brest to have complete access to the oceans of the world. This would not only benefit the Kriegsmarine, it would also give the Luftwaffe the bases it needed to attack British shipping in the Channel and the Bay of Biscay, and British ports.

Much of this was outlined in a paper, *Seekriegsfuhrung gegen England*, 'Sea Warfare Against England', prepared on 25 October 1938, by Admiral Heye.[2] Nevertheless, it gave little idea of the way in which the war would be conducted at sea. It was very dismissive of U-boats.

> There are grounds for assuming that the English countermeasures against U-boats, in the first line detection, have reached a high standard. U-boats' attacks on English forces will therefore not be too successful. So long as no unrestricted U-boat war can be allowed, 'cruiser war' against merchant ships – if it is only conducted by U-boats – will have a limited effect. It comes down to the fact that the single U-boat by its nature does not come into question for 'cruiser war' on the high seas, but must be employed in a more or less stationery role.

The conclusion drawn from this was that Germany should build large 'cruiser U-boats' armed with four 12.7-cm (5-in) guns and a surface speed of 25 knots. Even so, once forced to dive, the low speed of submarines would mean that it would be at the mercy of

Asdic. This was an interesting concept, although not quite so heavily armed as the French concept of the *Corsair* submarine, such as *Surcouf*, or the British M-class, by this time withdrawn. The medium-sized U-boats proposed by Dönitz were simply classed as 'Other U-boats' and would be positioned outside enemy harbours and in the main shipping lanes, but it was anticipated that they would be playing a sacrificial role as strong counter-measures could be expected at such locations.

The strategy proposed was one of commerce-raiding by fast armoured cruisers, in effect the *Panzerschiff* or 'pocket battleship' (reclassified as heavy cruisers by the Germans during the war), escorted by light cruisers, while a squadron of powerful battleships would be needed to assist these vessels in their breakout into the open seas. It was also envisaged that the Kriegsmarine should have its own aircraft, indeed, it was vital.

The document was circulated for comment. The commander of the fleet, Admiral Carls, was enthusiastic, and advocated planning for war. Raeder moved him to head a staff committee that would implement the recommendations in Heye's paper. A succession of plans had in fact been drawn up by the naval staff, starting with Plan X, which was in turn superseded by Plan Y, and then ultimately came Plan Z.

Plan Z was Raeder's dream. This was the plan for the big battle-ships and aircraft carriers, armoured cruisers and other vessels, including 249 U-boats. Formulated in late 1938, it received Hitler's approval in January 1939, and was due to be completed by 1947, although the bulk of it would be completed by 1945. The initial plan included four aircraft carriers, six large battleships known as the H-class and three battlecruisers, the O-class, no less than twelve Kreuzer P-class *Panzerschiff*, two Hipper-class heavy cruisers, which would be *Seyditz* and *Lutzow*, two improved M-class light cruisers, and six Spahkeuzer-class large destroyers, as well as 249 U-boats.

In fact, as the table shows, the Plan ultimately envisaged that by 1947, in addition to the above there would be another four aircraft carriers, albeit of a smaller type than the *Graf Zeppelin*, up to twelve battlecruisers and eight heavy cruisers, twenty-four light cruisers, thirty-six scout cruisers, seventy destroyers and seventy-eight torpedo-boats. There would be 162 Atlantic-type U-boats, sixty coastal U-boats and twenty-seven special purpose U-boats, almost certainly either minelayers or supply boats.

Kriegsmarine Plan Z Projections 1939–1947

Number of ships to be completed by:

Ship Type:	1939	1940	1941	1942	1943	1944	1945	1946	1947
Battleship (Type H)	–	–	–	–	2	6	6	6	6
Battleship	–	–	1	2	2	2	2	2	2
Battlecruiser (*Scharnhorst*)	2	2	2	2	2	2	2	2	2
Type P	–	–	–	–	3	3	8	8	10*
Panzerschiff (Deutschland-class)	3	3	3	3	3	3	3	3	3
Aircraft carriers	–	1	2	2	2	2	2	3	4*
Heavy cruisers	2	5	5	5	5	5	5	5	5
Light cruisers	–	–	–	3	3	4	5	8	12*
Scout cruisers	–	–	–	2	6	9	12	15	20*
Destroyers	22	25	36	41	44	47	50	53	58*
Torpedo boats	8	18	27	35	44	54	64	74	78
U-boats									
Atlantic	34	52	73	88	112	133	157	161	162
Coastal	32	32	32	32	33	39	45	52	60
Special	–	–	6	10	16	22	27	27	27

Source: Bekker, C, *Hitler's Naval War*, London, 1974

The problem was that Germany did not have the shipbuilding capacity for this work, let alone the necessary materials. There had been no sustained new construction of major warships for many years and so the slipways were simply not available. Worse still, the fuel needed exceeded the total fuel consumption of Germany in 1938.

Construction had already started on the first German aircraft carrier, the *Graf Zeppelin*, in 1936, and after she was launched in 1938, plans were laid to begin work on a second ship, the *Peter Strasser*. During 1939, orders were placed for carrier versions of the Messerschmitt Bf109 fighter and the Junkers Ju87 Stuka dive-bomber, designated as the Bf109T and Ju87C. In mid-1939, the two battleships *Bismarck* and *Tirpitz* were both launched, and then the keels were laid for the first three of the giant H-class battleships.

* A number of vessel types were intended to increase in numbers after 1947, with the Type P battlecruisers eventually rising to 12 ships, aircraft carriers to 8, light cruisers to 24, and scout cruisers to 36.

Nevertheless, the Luftwaffe, or to be precise the Minister for Air, Hermann Goering, would not relinquish control of any aspect of military aviation. This was at a time when the British had realised their mistake in combining all service aviation in the Royal Air Force and were returning naval aviation, the Fleet Air Arm, to the Royal Navy. The lack of any earlier German interest in aircraft carriers also meant that the *Graf Zeppelin*'s design was obsolete even before she was launched. The best comparison was with the British Courageous-class and the French *Bearn*.

Even so, Dönitz started to lobby for a stronger U-boat arm, creating tension between himself and his superior, Raeder, but eventually Plan Z was amended to allow 300 U-boats. Given the state of the German economy, already on a war footing and heavily in debt, Dönitz's ideas were in fact far more realistic than those of Raeder. Even though the latter had no immediate ambitions for a major fleet battle with the Royal Navy, at least not until 1947 or 1948, he was still a 'big gun, big ship' man. His subordinate *Fuhrer der U-Boote*, argued that only U-boats could deliver the necessary attack on British shipping while Germany waited for its armies to reach the Atlantic coast of France. He was also on firm ground when he argued that U-boats were quicker to build, used fewer raw materials, and were far cheaper than the large ships Raeder favoured. There was also the question of manpower, and even today, one advantage of the submarine is its low manpower requirement.

Early in 1939, Dönitz had a book published, called simply *Die U-Bootswaffe*, 'The U-boat Arm'. The book avoided mention of such matters as the wolf pack or group tactics, but it left the reader in no doubt that the U-boat was to be a major offensive weapon in the Kriegsmarine and that merchant shipping would not be spared. He also held firm to his belief in night torpedo attacks, for which he argued that the U-boat was ideal because of its low silhouette. 'The destruction of the enemy trade,' wrote Dönitz. 'The attack on the enemy sea communications is the proper purpose of sea warfare . . .'

In short, anyone reading the book had been warned, but British Naval Intelligence did not obtain a copy until 1942.

RED v BLUE

While the long term fleet planning was due to reach its full potential in 1947, Dönitz instead worked on a naval engagement based on what he saw as the conditions that would prevail in 1943. This was the earliest date for a war with Great Britain. The war game covered 'Atlantic war operations with U-boats, including combined operations between surface commerce raiders and aircraft with U-boats; employment of artillery – and fleet U-boats.'

The Naval High Command saw the enemy or 'Red' side as bringing together substantial numbers of warships from the Home and Mediterranean fleets, and the American and African stations, to give a total of five aircraft carriers, twelve battleships and heavy cruisers, twenty-seven light cruisers and a hundred destroyers to protect five convoys. The convoys would include two from Cape Town and one each from the River Plate, the West Indies and Canada. The rules of the war game also allowed that the Royal Air Force would be providing cover for the convoys when within reach of its bases in the United Kingdom and Africa, and possibly France as well.

Ranged against these convoys were the German or 'Blue' side, with fifteen torpedo U-boats of Type VII and the larger 1,000-ton displacement Type IX, two large fleet U-boats, two large artillery U-boats, a minelaying U-boat and an armoured cruiser commerce raider with attendant supply ship. This was a small force to set against five target convoys that were extremely well-protected.

The Blue commander deployed his torpedo U-boats in five groups each of three, with the most northerly accompanied by the armoured cruiser positioned on the shipping lanes between Canada and the Western Approaches. Another three were positioned around the Azores and the Canaries to intercept the convoys coming from Cape Town and the River Plate. All were kept well away from the British coastline to avoid being detected by maritime-reconnaissance aircraft. The result was inevitable. The U-boats were spread far too thinly and so three convoys were not even sighted. One of the Cape Town convoys met the River Plate convoy west of Cape Verde, and the combined convoy was intercepted by a U-boat, which kept radio silence initially to avoid giving away her position, then belatedly radioed the other two boats in her group, which were promptly detected and destroyed by the convoy escorts.

Dönitz concluded that the small numbers of the boats and the vast expanses of the ocean combined to ensure failure. Nevertheless, he could see a solution to this problem. While wireless telegraphy between U-boats had been possible in the Mediterranean and the English Channel as early as 1918, what had not been possible had been shore-based communication that would assimilate the overall picture and direct the U-boat wolf packs accordingly. This was the strategy of 'concentration against concentration'. He advocated having three boats form a group deployed over a breadth of around 50 miles and a depth of 100–200 miles, with additional groups positioned at some 200–300 miles away along the shipping lane. All would be directed by BdU in Germany. Once a convoy was reported by the boats in a group, they should attack independently, while BdU would decide whether to order the other groups to the attack. The Luftwaffe and surface vessels would provide reconnaissance, otherwise fast fleet U-boats would have to be used.

Essentially, he wanted ninety boats at sea, which meant that BdU would have to have 300 U-boats available allowing for time spent on the passage to and from operational zones and time in port refitting the U-boats and resting the crews. The problem was that this was a paper calculation, and no one really knew just how many U-boats would be needed at sea, or the concentration required.

Dönitz went on to suggest that the large artillery or 'cruiser' U-boats be used for distant operations, with three each in the South Atlantic and the Indian Ocean, suggesting that a total of eighteen would be required, while he wanted three large mine-laying U-boats and ten fast fleet U-boats which would displace 2,000 tons, known as Type XII, and which would operate with surface vessels and reconnoitre harbours in the United States, then track convoys from the US and direct the waiting wolf packs in mid-Atlantic to them.

The gist of Dönitz's paper signed in April 1939, was that war was likely to break out before 1943 and in any case well before Plan Z was completed. Therefore, it was important that the U-boat arm be built up as quickly as possible.

That spring saw Dönitz take the U-boat fleet for a spring cruise in which he decided to test his group tactics. Starting early on 12 May and ending during the evening of 14 May, the exercise was conducted in the Bay of Biscay and off the Portuguese coast. Dönitz commanded the exercise from aboard the *Erwin Wassner*, his command ship, which represented a surface raider for the exercise, while his former command ship, the *Saar*, represented her escort. Fifteen U-boats of types VII and IX represented the rest of the 'Blue' force, while the target was a convoy, 'Gold', represented by a tanker and a cargo vessel. The convoy could steam at a maximum of 13-knots, and the commander could vary its course as he wished on the condition that his overall point-to-point convoy speed must not drop below 11-knots.

The convoy was set to steam from a point 130 miles west of Lisbon towards Ushant, and the Blue U-boats were deployed in four groups at intervals of 200–300 miles along the convoy's intended path. The *Erwin Wassner* made long searching sweeps. In visibility of less than five miles, it took just four hours for the convoy to be sighted by the most southerly of the U-boats, *U-46*, at 12.05, which signalled the position, course and speed of the convoy before attacking, but she was driven off and later lost contact. The other three U-boats in *U-46*'s group responded to her signals and found the convoy at dusk, but the continued poor visibility and rising seas with spray ensured that they too lost the convoy.

The second group was ordered by the flotilla leader to patrol in the latitude of Finisterre, and shortly after dawn on 13 May, *U-37* established contact and attacked. Once again, in poor visibility and worsening sea conditions, the convoy managed to escape. The flotilla leader then deployed the third group across the course of the convoy in the Bay of Biscay, while the seven boats of the two southern groups made the best speed possible on the surface chasing the convoy in heavy seas. The *Erwin Wassner* sighted the convoy at 15.00, and two of the third group's boats, *U-32* and *U-34*, joined the 'surface raider', but the *Saar* drove the convoy off to the west and contact was lost again. Nevertheless, the third boat of the group, *U-35* made contact with the convoy at 19.00 and maintained contact until darkness, before attacking, and then maintaining contact until the *Erwin Wassner* caught up and attacked the convoy at 03.00 on the final day of the exercise. The *Saar* then followed with the remaining southerly submarines, before the *Erwin Wassner* changed sides to become a convoy escort. She was repeatedly attacked, although she did force the U-boats to dive.

By dawn, seven U-boats were in the vicinity of the convoy. At 07.45, *U-47* attacked from 500 yards, and then attacked from 300 yards ten minutes later. There were further attacks during the day, some from a range of up to 3,300 yards, and at the close of the exercise, at 20.00, the convoy was surrounded by thirteen U-boats.

Not surprisingly, Dönitz concluded that for effectiveness, a 'great number' of U-boats was essential, and that this depended on the U-boat in contact with the convoy calling up others. This would overwhelm the convoy and stretch its escorts. He accepted that in the vast reaches of the Atlantic with the course of the convoy open to doubt, even larger numbers of U-boats would have to be deployed, and believed that this justified his proposal for larger and faster reconnaissance U-boats. Command would be divided between BdU in Germany which would deploy the U-boats along the expected course of the convoy and a flotilla leader or *Fuhrer* aboard a U-boat who would exercise tactical control. This, of course, indicated a heavy wireless traffic, and the risk of direction finding discovering the location of the U-boat groups, but Dönitz believed that accuracy would be difficult and that there would not be time for reinforcements to get into position to save the convoy.

While he ignored developments such as radar, although he was to become involved with a trial scheme to fit basic radar aboard two U-boats, Dönitz anticipated correctly that a convoy would send its escorts on a dusk sweep astern of the convoy to detect tracking U-boats, although these ships would be vulnerable to torpedo attack, and he believed that the convoy would change course after dark.

He also argued that there should be a small number of repair U-boats taking into account the more distant operations conducted away from U-boat bases.

Nevertheless, Dönitz had his ideas challenged even by senior officers with U-boat experience. *Konteradmiral* (Rear Admiral) Furbringer argued that the Royal Navy was stronger so that surprise was essential for success, and that until U-boats could be made immune to Asdic, attacking against this defensive aid would be suicidal. Furbringer saw attacks on the escorts as essential, but dangerous, and that U-boat operations would have to be closely linked with those of a naval air arm.

Dönitz was dogmatic about the importance of the U-boat, however, and even questioned the value of naval aviation in mid-Atlantic. There was no question that he was pleased with himself, completely confident that the May exercise had been a great success.

CASE WHITE

Meanwhile, events had been hurtling towards war. On 11 April, the directive for 'Case White', the long-planned attack on Poland after 1 September, had been issued by Hitler. He saw internal difficulties in France as pre-occupying her, and that this would mean that Great Britain would have to consider attacking on her own, an unlikely prospect. He argued convincingly, certainly as far as Raeder was concerned, that despite British and French guarantees to Poland, the conflict could be contained. Raeder was later to concede that many naval officers did not share this view, including Dönitz. Even so,

Raeder followed an inspection of the U-boat flotillas on 22 July with a speech to the officers in which he told them that he had Hitler's personal assurance that war with Great Britain would not occur in the near future.

'Do not believe that the Fuhrer would bring us into such a desperate position,' he assured his audience. 'For war with England would mean *Finis Germania*!'

In some of his official reports and other papers, Dönitz wrote as if he accepted the official line. Meanwhile, the U-boat specialists at the *Marineleitung* started to accept Dönitz's arguments. This was despite one paper by the first staff officer in the U-boat department, worrying over the impact that carrier-borne aircraft would have on the U-boats, forcing them to keep submerged and therefore unable to track a convoy on the surface. On the other hand, the same paper also anticipated the Kriegsmarine being able to field adequate battleships and surface raiders to force the Royal Navy to deploy its own battleships as convoy escorts, and because of the limited numbers of such ships, having to concentrate all convoys onto one route, from the United States. This could only mean that he expected Plan Z to be implemented, at least for the most part if not in its entirety, which meant that war was not expected in autumn 1939.

One interesting fact that emerges from this paper, is that he fully expected the United States to remain neutral, but nevertheless to continue to provide substantial support for the United Kingdom. Supplies from throughout the world would be concentrated in the US and convoys sent from East Coast ports across the Atlantic.

In fact, the paper, written by a humble *Kapitanleutnant* (lieutenant-commander) glossed over a number of problems. It was remarkably prescient in seeing the threat posed by carrier-borne aircraft, but for some reason failed to consider the implications for the large, fast reconnaissance U-boats. It accepted Dönitz's proposal for 300 U-boats, but then increased the numbers of other U-boats, with a figure of twenty for Fuhrer U-boats, so that sixty would be needed, and for reconnaissance suggested fifteen, making a total of forty-five. In addition, the author also proposed smaller boats for operations in the Baltic and the North Sea, as well as tanker U-boats to extend the patrol times, so that, in total, he was proposing a force of around 500 U-boats! This was a massive increase on even the final version of Plan Z – already extended at Dönitz's request, and could only be realised by cutting the surface fleet element.

Case White required all U-boats not required in the Baltic for the campaign against Poland to be deployed around the British Isles to attack merchant shipping should the United Kingdom honour its pledges to Poland. Senior officers in the Kriegsmarine were well aware of the secret treaty signed between Germany and the Soviet Union. In August 1939, just thirty-five boats were actually available for extended operations, and these left Wilhelmshaven in late August. Additional U-boats, the small Type IIs, were deployed to the North Sea while fourteen were left in the Baltic. Despite the relatively small number of submarines at this stage, and the frantic planning of the years from 1933, and even before, one problem encountered was a shortage of torpedoes. Of course, with virtually all of the 56 U-boats at sea, there would be nothing to replace them when they returned to base. Dönitz took the *Erwin Wassner* to Swindemunde, indicating that he was expecting action in the east, but it had been decided earlier that should war with the United Kingdom and France break out, he would take his command ship to Wilhelmshaven. Then came the news that both the UK and Poland were mobilising.

The Kriegsmarine was now feeling the lack of ships of all kinds, not just U-boats. The two *Panzerschiffe Graf Spee* and *Deutschland* (not to be renamed *Lutzow* until November), with their supply ships, were being sent to their Atlantic patrol areas.

As the Kriegsmarine prepared for war, Dönitz was disappointed when he was ordered to send his U-boats to their Atlantic stations taking a northerly course around the Faeroe Islands, using extra fuel and reducing their time on station to mid-September at the latest.

Hitler was also suffering a major disappointment at this time. As war loomed, like the Kaiser before him, he attempted diplomacy. He even promised the British ambassador to Germany that he would guarantee the continued existence of the British Empire, even placing German forces at the disposal of the British government. One major setback to his plans was that he had learned, virtually at the last moment that he could not count on his ally, Mussolini. Italy would not declare war.

The news that Germany was at war with the United Kingdom reached both Dönitz and Raeder within minutes of the uncoded signal being sent to all units of the Royal Navy, 'Total Germany', on 3 September 1939. Those around Dönitz saw his shock, and he left the room briefly to prepare a message of encouragement to his staff. Raeder was also surrounded by his staff when the news reached him, at his daily conference, and he too left the room. He detailed the fleet he would have had available under Plan Z had the war been postponed until 1944 or 1945, when with the cooperation of Japan and Italy, they could even have had a chance of defeating the Royal Navy.

'Today the war breaks out against England-France,' he noted in a memorandum, 'which, according to the Fuhrer, we need not have reckoned with before about 1944 and which until the last moment the Fuhrer believed he should prevent . . . (the Kriegsmarine) could only show that it understood how to die with honour in order to create the foundations for later reconstruction.'

Notes
1 *Organisation der U-Boote Waffe*, 21 September 1935.
2 Salewski, M., *Die Seekriegsleitung, 1939–1945*, Bernard & Graefe, Munich, 1970–1975 (five vols)

CHAPTER SIX

The German War Economy

With the absorption of Austria and, thanks to the Munich
Agreement of 1938, the Czech Sudetenland into the Third Reich,
Hitler had created a *Grossdeutschland*, making Germany the pre-
eminent continental power in a way that the Kaiser had never
achieved. Pre-First World War Germany had been a continental
power without doubt, but pre-Second World War Germany was
something else. Of course, Hitler wasn't finished. There were those
areas of Poland that had originally been part of Prussia, and these
were still outside *Grossdeutschland*. The former Austrian territory
of South Tyrol, German-speaking and as a result of Versailles, part
of Italy was safe, at least for as long as the alliance between Germany
and Italy lasted, which was effectively the same as saying as long as
Hitler and Mussolini survived. There do not seem to have been plans
to absorb the German-speaking part of Switzerland, but although
the country was officially neutral, German aircraft did intrude into
Swiss airspace during the war, and were intercepted by Swiss
fighters.

Nevertheless, in this moment of triumph, having faced down the
British and the French and gained the territory he so desired, Hitler
was faced with some practical and increasingly pressing problems.
The massive demands of rearmament, which not only placed a great
strain on the economy but also precluded industry having sufficient
capacity for exports to earn much needed foreign currency, were
increasingly being met by the Reichsbank printing money. In the
wake of Munich it was forced to admit that there was no longer
'complete stability of the German currency', and indeed that
although it was 'not yet fully apparent', 'an inflation of the
Reichsmark had begun.' Inflation, the debilitating evil that had
swung so many Germans behind Hitler and helped him to gain
power, was on the march once again.

PRESSURE FOR A PEACETIME ECONOMY

The bankers and economists wanted to see a transition from a war economy to a peacetime economy so that printing of money to meet the demands on the exchequer could end. There had been no alternative to this policy throughout 1938, with the Reich unable to raise long-term loans on the international markets, the gold and foreign currency reserves wiped out, and the arms effort demanding the import of fuel, rubber, ore and non-ferrous metals. The Reichsbank noted that the nation's leadership had managed to 'avoid a war that would have jeopardised its earlier successes' and warned that it had now to face the challenge of 'avoiding . . . inflation whose consequences could be almost as dangerous.'

The problem was that the financial world had taken Hitler at his word when he pronounced himself satisfied with the Munich Agreement, yet Hitler wanted the rest of Czechoslovakia and he wanted the territory lost to Poland as a result of Versailles. Hitler and most of the senior members of the armed forces now realised that they would have to fight the Western powers before they could make any significant advances in the East. Yet, Germany had to advance eastwards if it was to gain not just the much desired *Lebensraum*, but also the food, raw materials and most of all the oil reserves that Germany needed.

Even before Munich, the military-economic office of the Oberkommando Wehrmacht was advised that it was to prepare for war against England in 1942. Already, the Fuhrer's promise of no war with England until after 1943 was broken. It took just another two weeks for Goering to make his famous speech to senior Luftwaffe officers and prominent industrialists about needing a 'gigantic programme compared to which previous achievements are insignificant.' The Kriegsmarine's role in this was to start a six year build up, Plan Z, which, of course, took it to 1944, two years after the date just given to the Oberkommando Wehrmacht for the outbreak of war.

The problem was quite simple. Germany could not afford the level of armaments production experienced in 1938, let alone the further increases outlined by Goering in October, which effectively meant tripling production. As the year drew to a close, the Reich faced a massive cash flow crisis and an equally difficult foreign exchange situation. In the aftermath of Munich, with not just the ordinary German but also financial institutions buoyed up by optimism and the seeming assurance that peace lay ahead, the

79

Reichsbank had been able to raise loans internally, issuing government bonds to the tune of 1.5 billion Reichsmarks, and then even managing to add another 350 million on top at short notice. Nevertheless, the Reich's appetite for money was endless, and in late November, another attempt to raise 1.5 billion Reichsmarks in this way failed, with a third of the bonds left unsold.

Hitler was left with the stark choice of imposing massive cuts in public spending or ordering the Reichsbank to print money, meaning accelerating inflation. Goering had already extended price controls beyond armaments contracts, but price controls were, and remain, an ineffectual and crude weapon favoured only by the economically illiterate.

In short, the planned armaments programme meant that 30 per cent of Germany's gross domestic product would have to be spent on the Wehrmacht alone. This ignored the demands of the other projects also needed to make the country ready for war, including development of communications and manufacturing industry, and, of course, the synthetic fuel and rubber production processes in which so much hope was being placed.

It is clear that during the winter of 1938–1939, the Reichsbank used economic arguments in an attempt to dissuade Hitler from following his rearmament plans. It was not that the president of the Reichsbank, Horace Schacht was opposed to German rearmament. He was a Nazi and a follower of Hitler, but he believed that rearmament should be within limits. In other words, that it should only proceed at a pace that the country could afford. It mattered not at all with Hitler that this was well-intentioned advice from a supporter with a sound grasp of economics. Within two weeks of receiving the advice, Schacht was dismissed, along with his deputy, Friedrich Dreyse and the Director, Ernst Huelse. Two other signatories to the report resigned to show solidarity with the dismissed men, and to emphasise the importance of the advice. Perhaps appropriately enough, Schacht was replaced by a man called Funk! Walther Funk has been described as compliant. He was helped by a change to the Reichsbank's constitution in June 1939, which abolished any formal limits to expansion of the money supply. Although the Reichsbank's value remained at parity with the gold standard, in reality the country had abandoned the gold standard. This had been a long term Nazi aim, to free the Reich from the constraints that adherence to the gold standard implied.

The truth was that, increasingly, Germany was becoming an

artificial and closed economy, with growing restrictions on who could do what. In some ways, this was not unlike the hated Communist system which the National Socialists despised so much. There were differences, however. It is not for nothing that some say that Communists nationalise property, while Fascists nationalise people. Hitler had become an absolute dictator, and could determine the money supply as he wished. So often, the Fuhrer's refusal to take advice is associated with his disagreements with his generals later in the war as the tide swung decisively against Germany, but this is wrong. In 1938 and 1939, he was already over ruling the advice of those with the training and experience that made them well qualified to pronounce on issues, whether they be of economics or of strategy.

Inevitably, contradictory messages were being issued by the regime. In early 1938, the foreign exchange situation was dire, but temporary relief was given by the *Anschluss*, which brought Germany not only the territory and people of Austria, but that country's foreign reserves. By August, exports were down 20 per cent compared with the same month in 1937. In mid-October, Goering was calling for a renewed export drive, and in November, the Wehrmacht was informed that exports would have priority over everything else! That was the same month that the Wehrmacht received the shocking news that its steel allocation for 1939 was to be cut from 530,000 tons to just 300,000 tons.

Nevertheless, even Hitler could not conjure up everything that the Wehrmacht wanted. The country was at peace but the economy and industry were both on a war footing. Hitler could play with the Reichsmark and print as many as he liked, but he could not generate additional industrial capacity at whim, and nor could he magic additional foreign reserves with which to increase the supply of essential materials for the war effort. The overall level of military spending experienced in 1938 continued, which was far less than the Wehrmacht wanted, but it was already at a ruinous level. A sign of the state of the country was that the national budget was a state secret. For 1939, the Wehrmacht budget was set at 20.86 million Reichsmarks, of which 11.6 billion was for recurring expenditure and the remainder for expansion. There was considerable disparity between the armed forces. The Kriegsmarine thought it was doing well with a budget of 2.744 billion Reichsmarks, as did the Luftwaffe with 7.018 billion Reichsmarks, but the Army had to manage on 10.449 billion Reichsmarks, less than in 1938. The reduced steel allocation for 1939 also impacted heavily on the Army as the Navy was given priority.

SHORTAGE OF RESOURCES

This was an inevitable consequence of the shortage of resources, including skilled industrial manpower. It was impossible to ensure the high level of spending and expansion for all three services equally. If the Kriegsmarine was given priority, then another service had to suffer relative neglect, and in this case it was the Army. That the Navy was inadequate for the tasks expected of it in the coming conflict was clear enough, but the Army was hardly fully equipped either for the task ahead, and nor was the Luftwaffe.

As we know, the Kriegsmarine lacked aircraft carriers and sufficient big ships, and indeed, it entered the war with far fewer U-boats than it needed, and throughout the war there was a shortage of destroyers. The Luftwaffe lacked heavy bombers capable of carrying out a strategic air war, while its transport aircraft were obsolescent and there were no dedicated transport squadrons, so that major airborne assaults relied on instructors from the bomber schools switching roles, interrupting training, often to a devastating degree if losses were heavy. The Army appeared impressive and capable of overwhelming force, but it achieved this by switching units around so that there was always sufficient armour to spearhead an assault, but the front had to be narrower than it needed to be. Worst of all, the German supply line was weak, with not only supplies but also artillery pulled by horses. Horses were slower and weaker than motor vehicles, and while the latter required fuel, it was less bulky for the power it produced than the feed for the horses, which also needed water. For their 'tractive effort', horses also required more manpower to control and look after them than motor vehicles. One can forget the image of a fast, modern, motorised army.

There was another problem. Before starting any major campaign, an army needed large stockpiles of munitions and other supplies. This at the current rate of production and expenditure, the Army could not do. It had sufficient stockpiled for a short campaign, not for a major war.

So, we have Goering demanding a massive rearmament programme in October 1938, and that same month insisting on an export drive. Even Hitler took up this theme in January 1939, telling people that Germany must 'export, or die', having been given the Reichsbank's monthly report that stated simply, and

Plan Z was drafted under Grand Admiral Erich Raeder, but he was one of many German naval officers who regarded the U-boats as being at risk from improved Allied counter measures, especially Asdic.
(IWM No A 14906)

Donitz was an enthusiastic proponent of the U-boat, and increased the numbers allowed under Z – here he is congratulating the crew of a returned U-boat. *(IWM No HU 40217)*

German ideas on carrier design were dated, and were not too dissimilar from that of the British sisters, HMS *Glorious*, seen here, and *Courageous*.

Except briefly at the height of the war, the Germans also ignored the potential of the escort carrier, such as *Avenger*, seen here, which could at least have provided reconnaissance and fighter cover for their surface ships. *(IWM No FL12*

only aircraft carrier laid down by Germany was the *Graf Zeppelin*, seen here on the slipway.
(US Naval Historical Records Centre)

concept of the corsair or cruiser submarine, armed with larger calibre guns, was also considered,
never built. The best example of this type of submarine during the war was the French *Surcouf*,
ch was seized by the Royal Navy at Portsmouth in 1940.   *(IWM No A410)*

Instead the Germans placed great faith in their *Panzerschiffe*, daubed 'pocket battleships' by the British media, such as *Deutschland*, seen here, but reality had them change her name to *Lutzow* after the start of hostilities. *(US Naval Historical Records Centre)*

Scharnhorst showed just how unprepared for war the Kriegsmarine really w – the intention had been t replace her 11-in guns wit 15-in, the usual armamen for a battlecruiser, but this never happened. Here she is under construction. *(US Naval Historical Reco: Cent*

roup of U-boats at an anchorage, with the larger one in the right foreground clearly meant to vide anti-aircraft cover.

(US Naval Historical Records Centre)

iore familiar base for U-boats after the fall of France was in heavy protected pens, which were iervious to Allied bombing until the advent of the heavy earthquake bombs, the RAF's 12,000-lbs lboy' and 22,000-lbs 'Grand Slam', which undermined the sides of the pens.

(US Naval Historical Records Centre)

The mighty *Tirpitz* safe in a Norwegian fjord, with *Scharnhorst* bottom left, almost hidden. Torpedo nets are deployed.   (*IWM No C 56*

Bismarck, the only other German battleship to be completed, at the start of her first, and last, cruise, 'Operation Rhine Exercise'.   (*IWM No HU 3*

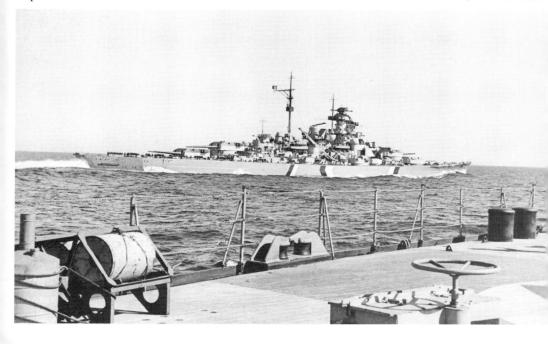

cerned over the safety of his major warships, Hitler ordered them home and took the daring
sion to bring them on the most direct route through the English Channel. Here are Scharnhorst
Gneisenau during the famous 'Channel Dash' with Prinz Eugen. *(IWM No MH 4981)*

le the Germans made extensive use of captured French artillery and railway rolling stock, the real
e could have been the French fleet, although these ships at Alexandria were safely out of way. In
foreground is the cruiser *Tourville* with the destroyer *Forebin* alongside. *(IWM No A9937)*

When the Germans belatedly tried to seize those ships in French waters in late 1942, they were scuttled or blown up, here is the battlecruiser *Strasbourg* with a scuttled cruiser lying alongside at Toulon. The Germans simply gained a small number of French submarines. (IWM No A256

The biggest wasted Axis asset was the Italian fleet, with three of the six battleships put out of action by the Fleet Air Arm at Taranto on the night of 11/12 November 1940. Here is the battleship *Littorio* down by the bows after the attack. (IWM No HU 523

starkly, that its gold and foreign exchange reserves no longer existed.

If the Reichsmark was starting the process of being reduced to Monopoly money, there were other measures that the state could take meantime. On 20 March 1939, the *Neuer Finanzplan*, or New Finance Plan, enforced the payment of services and goods by the Reich using tax credits for a minimum of 40 per cent of the contract value rather than paying in cash. Industry was able to offset its future tax liabilities using these credits and they also provided some worthwhile tax exemptions, but no interest was paid. This meant that having exhausted the willingness of the public and financial institutions to buy government bonds, the Reich was now insisting that its suppliers provided it with interest free loans.

Such measures were needed to ease the desperate cash flow situation of Hitler's government. They were inadequate at the time, and could only afford temporary relief. After all, logic dictates that future tax receipts would be much reduced by the use of tax credits by industry. There was another problem. The tax credit scheme also imposed a desperate shortage of liquidity on government contractors at a time when they were supposed to be investing heavily in expansion and accumulating stocks of raw materials against the inevitable interruption that would come with the outbreak of hostilities. The impact of receiving at least 40 per cent of the money due in tax credits rather than cash can be best guessed at by the fact that it is very rare for any business to make a profit margin of more than 20 per cent, and often profit margins will be less than 10 per cent, especially given the price controls already in force. In short, German industry was subsidising its main customer to an incredible degree.

FOREIGN POLICY FAILURES

Hitler was counting on diplomacy to restrain the democracies from engaging in war with Germany until his rearmament plans were completed. He must have realised that his scope for manoeuvre was becoming increasingly limited as his pledge that war would break out after 1943 had already been trimmed back to 1942. His Foreign Minister von Ribbentrop believed that he could enable Hitler to absorb the remains of Czechoslovakia at the same time as he concluded an alliance with Poland, but Poland rejected the German offer and instead moved closer to the Soviet Union. This was a difficult and dangerous course of action as the Soviet leadership also

83

viewed much of Poland as its territory, the country having achieved its independence from Tsarist Russia during the Russian Civil War.

Ribbentrop also wanted to conclude an alliance with Italy against Britain and France, but Italy was pre-occupied with Africa and the Balkans, its own form of colonial expansion. An alliance with Japan against both the British Empire and the Soviet Union was also hoped for, but Japan's priority was its expansion on the mainland of China, its own quest for *Lebensraum*.

Given the short interval between the Munich Agreement and the occupation of the remains of Czechoslovakia in 15 March 1939, no one should have been surprised at the diplomatic uproar that followed. Poland's border defences were outflanked, but the country rejected the German offer of an alliance. By the end of March, the United Kingdom issued a public guarantee that it would protect Poland's territorial integrity. Unfortunately, this ensured that Anglo-French efforts to conclude an alliance with the Soviet Union against Germany were fruitless.

Germany was counting on strict American neutrality, but the one success of Britain and France was to open the door to deliveries of US armaments, hitherto banned because of US neutrality. The French in particular were having massive difficulties with aircraft production, with their aircraft industry in chaos following national-isation, but President Franklin Roosevelt ensured that a French purchasing mission was shown the very best that American industry could offer. The Germans began to believe that an Anglo-American Trade Agreement, signed on 2 November 1938, included secret clauses on military aid, although this was untrue. Nevertheless, the growing rapprochement between the United States and the two European allies was in stark contrast to Washington's attitude towards Berlin. The United States was fully aware of the plight of the German Jews and especially the horrors of *Kristallnacht*. The Munich Agreement brought some time for Germany, but the occu-pation of Czechoslovakia in March 1939 brought a 25 per cent punitive tariff on German exports to the United States, the world's biggest and richest market. The Germans regarded this as a declaration of economic war.

Despite the growing threat of action by the United Kingdom and France, and the increased willingness of the United States to support them, Hitler still hoped that his occupation of Poland would not result in a wider conflict. He still believed that it would be possible to repeat his success over the Sudetenland, especially after effectively

84

concluding his conquest of Czechoslovakia without any threat of military intervention. The Wehrmacht was instructed to prepare plans for the invasion of Poland, provided that the exercise could be isolated diplomatically. On 23 August, a secret pact was signed between Ribbentrop and the Soviet Foreign Minister, Molotov, covering the occupation of Poland and this must have increased Hitler's confidence, since it would deny the United Kingdom and France their much sought after third partner and prevent Germany from being squeezed between East and West as in the First World War. On the debit side, and at this stage there was always a drawback to any diplomatic advantage gained, Germany's agreement with the Soviet Union made it impossible for the Japanese to ally themselves with Hitler, struggling as they were to keep the Soviet Union out of Manchuria. When the Nazi-Soviet Pact was announced, the pro-German civilian government in Tokyo resigned and power passed to the Japanese Army.

Again, there were contradictions in policy and in announcements. The Soviet Union was effectively an ally with regard to Poland, but Hitler still believed that Germany, Hungary, Italy and Spain could provide an anti-Comintern alliance capable of defending Germany and allowing the plan for *Lebensraum* to be implemented. There were also hopes that Romania and Turkey would ally themselves with Germany. In fact, the Soviet leader, Joseph Stalin, was using Germany for his own ends. By concluding a pact with Germany, he bought time. If, as he expected, Germany ended up fighting the British and French, he expected all three countries to exhaust themselves. The beneficiaries of such a conflict would be the Soviet Union and the United States.

The one success of German diplomacy at this time was the signing of a German-Romanian Trade Treaty on 23 March 1939. This was achieved through bribery and coercion, including the threat of invasion by Hungary, but it secured oil and grain supplies for Germany. It seems that the Romanians had also been buying time and trying to stave off German pressure, for they soon managed to persuade the French to guarantee their security and the British had little option but to agree as well. Meanwhile, the French joined the British in the guarantee to Poland.

Turkey, meanwhile, was drifting away from Germany and towards the Allies, although initially this seemed to be because the country expected Britain and France to conclude an alliance with the Soviet Union, Turkey's difficult neighbour. A belief in an

Anglo-French-Soviet alliance also pushed Yugoslavia and Greece, and even Bulgaria, towards London and Paris. Romania also started to show that she was not prepared to give Germany everything she wanted, insisting that oil and grain deliveries be paid for by arms deliveries. In June 1939, Romania suspended oil supplies for Germany, forcing Germany to agree to divert Messerschmitt Bf109s from the Luftwaffe to Romania, but Hitler vetoed the deal, largely because he suspected that Romania could not be relied on if war did break out. Nevertheless, those directing the Four Year Plan suddenly realised that without Romanian oil, peacetime petrol rationing might be necessary. Goering intervened and Romania got its fighters delivered and oil supplies to Germany resumed. The solution was clear, but at the time unspoken, as the Wehrmacht had already estimated that Romania's oil production would only be sufficient for German needs if the country was occupied and its entire oil output sent to Germany.

To achieve a balance of power, Hitler needed to forge an alliance with both Germany and Italy, but this continued to elude Ribbentrop throughout most of 1939. A sharp dose of reality was provided for the Nazi regime on 24 May 1939 by Major-General Thomas of the military-economic office of the Wehrmacht. Thomas compared the defence expenditure planned by the United States, United Kingdom and France for 1939–1940 with that of Germany and Italy combined. After making adjustments for differences in spending power, he estimated that during the period being reviewed, the three democratic countries would outspend Germany and Italy by at least 2 billion Reichsmarks. The contrast was even worse if military expenditure as a proportion of national income was taken into account, for while Germany was planning to spend 23 per cent in 1939, France was planning to spend 17 per cent, the United Kingdom 12 per cent and the United States just 2 per cent.

There were two ways of looking at Thomas and his estimates. On the one hand, he may well have been quietly hoping that the sums would force Hitler to take a longer view and wait rather than rush into war. Certainly, it is known that he was opposed to premature war, knowing full well the weaknesses of the different German armed services. On the other, to Hitler and his henchmen, the figures also suggested that Germany could not win an arms race. Time was not on her side.

If we return to the naval context, and consider just the aircraft carriers included in Plan Z. The plan promised four aircraft carriers by 1944, but the Royal Navy would have six fast, armoured carriers by that time in addition to the latest ship, *Ark Royal*, while France would have at least two new carriers, possibly three or four. Germany had the first of a new class of battleships fitting out, as had France, while the first of a new class of British battleships was already building. As for aircraft, the Supermarine Spitfire was just entering RAF service, an aircraft that could engage the Messerschmitt Bf109 in combat, while heavy bombers were planned. Most significant of all, Britain and France could clearly count on American support. What would the outcome be if the United States decided to increase its defence expenditure, even if it just doubled or trebled it as a percentage of gross domestic product? Germany could not compete with American industry. Indeed, even Great Britain was matching the current reduced rate of aircraft production in Germany.

As time passed, and Hitler managed to occupy Czechoslovakia, his attention turned to the true state of his armed forces. In April 1939, he demanded to know the position in respect of ammunition in April and October 1940. The reply was anything but reassuring. If raw materials continued to be allocated as at July 1939, there would be less than 37 million rounds of infantry ammunition produced each month instead of the 375 million rounds considered necessary. Worse, 3.7-cm anti-tank round production would amount to 39,000 per month instead of 650,000; and there would be just over 56,000 light howitzer shells produced instead of the 450,000 needed.

The mad dreams of massive armaments production in the wake of the Munich Agreement were dissipating in the cold light of reality. It was not money as such that was lacking, but the lack of foreign exchange.

Meanwhile, the Germans enjoyed an advantage in the air and on the ground as a result of having been building up their armed forces since 1934. Even with British aircraft production matching that of Germany in 1939, the British were making up for lost time, leaving Germany ahead. The Germans had also tested their aircraft and refined their tactics during the Spanish Civil War. Even at sea, the comparison between the Kriegsmarine and the Royal Navy had to be set against the tremendous global demands on the British. This still left the Royal Navy stronger in home waters, but the difference was not that vast, especially if a continental war was envisaged.

Increasingly, the logic of Germany's position pointed to war sooner than later. If the British and French failed to support Poland, a gamble would have paid off handsomely. If they did support Poland and war resulted, the sooner and quicker it was over, the better.

WAR AT LAST

Major-General Thomas attempted to persuade his superiors to see reason in the last days of August 1939. His first approach on Saturday 26 August, was not well received. He tried again the following day, and earned a sharp rebuke from the Fuhrer himself. Thomas was not alone, and nowhere was pessimism about the outcome more marked than in the Kriegsmarine. Admiral Raeder, its commander-in-chief, noted that the Kriegsmarine was 'not at all adequately armed for the great struggle', concluding that the service 'can only demonstrate that it knows how to go down with dignity . . .'

Surprisingly to many, the Luftwaffe was also pessimistic. Its senior officers were chronically aware of the weakness inherent in scrapping the heavy bomber programme during the late 1930s. The RAF could reach Germany, and would no doubt suffer heavy losses in doing so, but the Luftwaffe would find it more difficult to reach Britain *unless* it could gain bases in Belgium and Northern France. Bases in Northern France would also help the Kriegsmarine, with surface raiders and U-boats spared the lengthy voyage around the north of Scotland, which consumed fuel and time as well as adding to the dangers of being caught by the Royal Navy or the Royal Air Force.

In short, everything depended on the Army. Yet, it had been the Army that had been worst affected by the cuts in the steel allocation in 1939. It was the Army that still used horsepower. Surprisingly, most of the generals engaged in planning operations in Poland did not share Thomas's pessimism.

The invasion of Poland enjoyed popular support. This was Germany reversing the injustices of Versailles and regaining her territory in the east. It was also yet another case, as with Austria and the Sudeten Germans, of reuniting the German people as a significant minority of those living in Poland were German speakers, and in future would become German nationals. *Ein Volk!* Much as hatred of Britain had been fostered by the German leadership, hatred of Poland was even stronger.

Poland was an easy victim. Her armed forces were ill-equipped.

She had a very small navy. Once fully mobilised, the Polish Army was strong on paper, but poorly equipped and lacked the ability to manoeuvre of the Germans. Even so, the German Army and the people were surprised at how easy victory was, with Warsaw occupied in just three weeks and the Polish armed forces destroyed. The mood of pessimism evaporated. There were even those who expected both the United Kingdom and France to be broken and suing for peace by the end of the year. Confidence was further boosted by *U-29* torpedoing and sinking the British aircraft carrier HMS *Courageous* on 17 September. The following month, on 14 October, there was a further boost from *U-47* penetrating the British Home Fleet's forward anchorage at Scapa Flow in Orkney, torpedoing and sinking the battleship HMS *Royal Oak*. This was something that the Germans had failed to do during the First World War when anti-submarine detecting devices were in their infancy.

The Kriegsmarine needed these early successes from its still small fleet of submarines. As soon as war broke out, Plan Z was scrapped and only those capital ships close to completion had work continue. This even extended to the first German aircraft carrier, the *Graf Zeppelin*. The Army and the Luftwaffe would from this time onwards have priority, save for the U-boat fleet, for which production of 25 boats a month was envisaged, later rising to 40. Dönitz's argument that the production of U-boats required far less resources and manpower than the surface fleet was clearly accepted, if only tacitly, but it took some time before production built up and it was not until autumn 1940 that significant numbers of U-boats were being launched.

Despite the onset of winter, Hitler was pressing for action in the west. With the two Allies now at war with Germany, and the United States passing legislation that would allow both countries to buy arms and ammunition from the United States, time was not on Germany's side. There was also the danger, Hitler argued in a memorandum on the conduct of war in the west, that if delayed too long, the United States could well intervene. Memories of US involvement in the First World War were still fresh. Only in the air had American involvement in the First World War been weak, but the arrival of US troops in France had boosted Allied morale, and the Americans had been quick to send warships to Ireland and had even attached a battle squadron to the Royal Navy's Grand Fleet, while also pressing for the introduction of a convoy system.

In theory, the legislation passed in the United States could have enabled Germany to also buy American equipment. Nevertheless, a factor in the passing of the legislation through Congress was the anger aroused by the invasion of Poland, and Germany was fast becoming a pariah. Before the days of 'Lend-Lease', the conditions attached to the sale were described as 'cash and carry', meaning that armaments had to be paid for in cash and transported in the customer's own ships. Germany lacked the foreign exchange and would have been unable to protect her ships on the voyage across the North Atlantic. The Wehrmacht estimated that the combined purchasing power of the United Kingdom and France amounted to US $7.37 billion (£1.9 billion at the prevailing rate of exchange), while Germany would have struggled to raise as much as US $700 million.

WEAKNESSES

Yet, despite the ease with which Polish resistance had been suppressed, all had not gone well in the Polish campaign. Serious weaknesses in the training of troops had been exposed, especially amongst mobilised reserve units, which at times had suffered incidents when troops under fire had panicked.

Hitler had also been disappointed that Italy was proving lukewarm about war, and he was still not certain whether Japan would join Germany, even though the advantages to that country were considerable, not least because she could gain the oil and rubber of the British Empire and the oil of the Dutch. He realised that his new ally, the Soviet Union, would be unreliable in a prolonged war. In fact the alliance was a temporary expedient, buying time for the Russians and enabling Germany to continue to receive supplies from the east, but in military terms, it was simply a case of dividing Polish territory.

Hitler's case for striking now, regardless of the winter weather, was in many ways impeccable. The longer he waited, the worse the German economic situation would become and the better equipped his enemies would be. There was just one major problem; indeed, it was an overwhelming problem, a chronic shortage of ammunition. This was the consequence of the reduced allocations of steel and copper experienced earlier in the year. The Luftwaffe alone had used most of its stock of bombs simply to support the invasion of Poland. During September, consumption of bombs had exceeded production sevenfold. Even while still assembling their forces in France, the British and French would still be a far more potent opponent than the Poles.

While the image of the Panzer armoured formations was one of modern tanks and efficiency, even if the numbers deployed were far less than the original re-armament programme would have wanted, the true story was that these too suffered weaknesses. In less than a month of fighting, a quarter of the tanks had either been knocked out or had simply broken down. Most of the tanks used were Mark I and Mark IIs, obsolescent and clearly unsuitable for a prolonged campaign in the west. The German Army feared the French Char B, at the time the world's best tank. It was also the case that the combined strength of the British, French, Dutch and Belgian armies was, at least theoretically, a match for the Germans in manpower and equipment. On the other hand, the Low Countries were placing their faith in neutrality, and even the British and French had not exercised together.

The hastily prepared German plans for attack in the west were simply an updated version of those used for the First World War. Given more modern equipment and Luftwaffe support, they envisaged a rapid advance to the Channel Coast to provide bases for the Luftwaffe and the Kriegsmarine, but failed to provide a means of destroying the French Army. It is interesting that the Germans envisaged a war similar to that of the First World War, for this was also the assumption of the British and the French.

General Werner von Brauchitsch, Commander-in-Chief of the Army, pleaded for more time. They needed to re-equip and retrain, rebuild ammunition stocks, and in addition move as many troops as they dared from Poland to the west. Given the poor state of the railways and the lack of mechanised transport within the Army, this last was no easy feat. They also needed another million troops. Even at this early stage of the war, Hitler ignored their advice. He insisted that the offensive against France and the Low Countries should begin in early November.

Brauchitsch had as chief-of-staff General Franz Halder. Halder had been appointed in 1938 after the resignation of his predecessor General Ludwig Beck, who resigned after failing to unite the Army's senior officers in a collective stand against Hitler's plans for Czechoslovakia. As with others opposed to the breakneck pace and the strains of the rearmament programme, Beck had not opposed Hitler's ultimate objectives, but had opposed the timing and felt that rearmament should proceed more slowly, placing less strain on the economy and not provoking an arms race with the United Kingdom and France. Now, in late 1939, Halder was also sounding out opinion over resistance to Hitler. He toured the commanders of the three army groups to sound out their opinions on an immediate attack in the west, and amongst those he could trust, he sought their opinions on a military-led *coup d'etat* to overthrow the Nazi regime.

Meanwhile, tension between Brauchitsch and Hitler rose steadily. On 5 November, the two men met. Brauchitsch, feted as a hero for his victory in Poland and ever the consummate professional, went armed with statistics prepared by the Quartermaster General, General Eduard Wagner, which detailed the poor state of the army's equipment and stockpiles of supplies. He reported the true state of the army to the Fuhrer, who listened impatiently, and when Brauchitsch has finished, he was subjected to a devastating tirade. For the rest of the day, Hitler fumed over the 'sabotage of the army command'. His commander-in-chief was sufficiently shaken by Hitler's outburst to have left the meeting shaking. He immediately put Halder in the picture, who feared that the Gestapo had discovered his plans. He destroyed the incriminating evidence immediately, and without his leadership and coordination, the *coup d'etat* was over. Just how close Hitler came to being assassinated is still difficult to assess, but Halder met Hitler almost daily and later confided to an associate that he attended those meeting with a loaded pistol in his pocket and firmly intended to shoot 'Emil down'. 'Emil' was the code-name for Hitler. Many believe that what saved Hitler during those crucial meetings in autumn 1939 was Halder's sense of duty making it difficult for him, a professional soldier, to kill the man to whom he had pledged an oath of loyalty.

The date set for the invasion of France and the Low Countries was 12 November 1939, but the onset of the winter weather intervened. The concept of *Blitzkrieg*, literally 'lightening war', demanded that the air force and army operated together concentrating overwhelming force, but the weather grounded the Luftwaffe, and without it, the invasion could not go ahead. Even Hitler had to accept this.

A growing body of historians now believe that the delay saved Hitler, at least for another five and a half years. There were chronic weaknesses in the army and the air force that would have made victory in the west anything but inevitable, for while the air force had technical superiority over the two Allies, with the Royal Air Force even operating Gloster Gladiator biplanes in France, the Luftwaffe was, as already mentioned, chronically short of bombs, while the army was short of shells and trained men. Worse, Hitler could still not count on the unswerving support of the German people, who would soon fall in behind the regime under the pressures of war, the early victories and Allied bombing. Had the German people any idea of what was to be expected of them in the years ahead shortly after the outbreak of war in 1939, there would have been a very real danger of a mass uprising. Had the army known about the horrors of the Eastern Front, and the disaster that followed the capitulation at Stalingrad, then the nightmare of the Soviet occupation and the rape of Berlin, mutiny would have been inevitable.

As it was, the situation in economic and industrial terms was worsening. There was almost no oil or copper being imported while ore shipments from Sweden, via the Norwegian port of Narvik, were cut off. Overall imports were cut by around 80 per cent. The ore had to come via Narvik rather than direct from Sweden because the Gulf of Bothnia froze in winter. Sweden provided 83 per cent of Germany's iron ore, paid for by shipments of coal. A similar arrangement worked, but for precision machine tools and Oerlikon anti-aircraft guns, with Switzerland, also dependent on German coal. The impact of economic sanctions and British blockading was not unexpected. Hitler knew that Germany could only survive a short war having neither the money nor the natural resources for a sustained war of attrition over many years. Protests from the Gauleiters, charged with being the link between the Fuhrer and the civilian population, forced Walther Funk, by this time Minister for Economic Affairs, to desist from a programme of draconian mobilisation. He then tried to present his changes as a plan for moderation in mobilisation, and by the end of the year found himself stripped of his responsibilities for organising the civilian economy.

There were those who thought that with careful management of the economy, Germany might last a three year war. Once again, comparisons were made with the First World War. The reason why no one expected Germany to survive as long as she had in the earlier conflict was not simply memories of the starvation of 1918, but a realisation that the German economy was in an even worse state in 1939 than it had been in 1914. In the earlier conflict, Germany had also access to the resources of the Austro-Hungarian Empire, but in 1939, much of this was cut off.

By 'careful management', what was planned was a defensive posture for the armed forces rather than all-out war. In fact, this was completely unrealistic. Great Britain and France could simply continue re-arming and wait for Germany to collapse. Only if peace could be gained through diplomacy could this strategy work, which would have meant the two Allies accepting Germany's seizure of Poland.

STRIKING WEST

Before invading France and the Low Countries, Germany had to secure her supplies of iron ore. Hitler feared a British Expeditionary Force landing in Norway to take control of the port of Narvik. He decided that both Denmark and Norway would be occupied, ensuring that supplies could continue and also giving him control over the Skagerrak and Kattegat, the straits that linked the North Sea and the Baltic. The invasion of Denmark was relatively easy, but the Norwegians had time to implement a defence plan and the British, and then the French, had time to land an expeditionary force, with fighting beginning on 9 April and lasting for three months, before the Germans achieved their objectives, by which time the British and French had decided, too late, to withdraw their forces to reinforce those engaged in the Battle of France.

The invasion of Norway saw the Kriegsmarine suffer heavy losses amongst its small force of destroyers and also the light cruiser *Konigsberg* suffered the unwanted distinction of being the first major operational warship to be sunk by aerial attack. The attack was by the Royal Navy's Fleet Air Arm, although the aircraft were shore-based rather than carrier-borne. No doubt the loss of the British aircraft carrier, HMS *Glorious*, with most of those aboard, to the battlecruisers *Scharnhorst* and *Gneisenau*, during the withdrawal from Norway, more than compensated for the loss of a light cruiser and ten destroyers. On the other hand, earlier, the British battlecruiser *Renown* had inflicted serious damage on *Gneisenau* on 9 April, with her main armament put out of action, and had a German aircraft carrier been available, it might conceivably have turned the tables. The *Panzerschiff Lutzow* was torpedoed by the British submarine *Spearfish* on 11 April, and although she wasn't sunk, doubtless there was a sigh of relief in the upper echelons of the Kriegsmarine that her name had already been changed from *Deutschland*. Nevertheless, the Germans gave a good account of themselves during the Norwegian campaign, sinking one British aircraft carrier, two cruisers, six destroyers, a sloop and four submarines.

Meanwhile, Hitler had acted to safeguard the Reich's oil supplies.

In March 1940, he offered King Carol of Romania protection against the Soviet Union. At this time, the USSR was, at least on paper, Germany's main ally. Despite the needs of the armed forces, oil was more important, so the Romanians were offered arms for oil, but most of the arms were those taken from the Poles while the oil was to be sold at preferential prices. An interim agreement was intended to pave the way for a longer term deal, which happened to be negotiated just as France was on the verge of surrender. In fact, this proved to be a master stroke, with Germany granted a monopoly of Romanian oil supplies, while the United Kingdom, which had previously taken 40 per cent of Romanian production, lost these supplies virtually overnight.

Whatever the stresses and strains to which the German economy was being subjected, no matter how thin the margin of ammunition and fuel stocks for the German armed forces, the country had once again established itself as the supreme continental power, and the weaker states of Southern Europe hastened to get on the right side of the continent's proven strong man, Hitler. Mussolini, whose hesitation in entering the war had perplexed and frustrated Hitler, at one time an admirer, declared war on Great Britain and France on 10 June 1940. Hitler may have been pleased by this, but his military men were cynical, dubbing the Italians the 'harvest hands'. In a hint of things to come, Mussolini invaded the South of France, and demanded support from the Luftwaffe despite having a powerful air force of his own.

Still suffering from the ravages of the Civil War, Spain was in no state to declare war, but Franco shifted his stance from strict neutrality to one of a non-combatant state.

Neutral Switzerland had a significant number who argued for a reassessment of neutrality, and while the country did not join the Axis camp, it provided still more generous trade credits to Berlin and restricted strategic exports to the United Kingdom. Switzerland still depended on German coal, having few natural resources of its own, and also managed to buy German aircraft for its air force. The Germans in return received high quality precision machine tools and instruments as well as Oerlikon anti-aircraft guns.

The massive advance in the West had given the Germans not just territory, but bases in France for the Kriegsmarine and for the Luftwaffe. Commerce raiding by U-boats and surface vessels from French ports was now a practicality, while the United Kingdom, even as far west as Belfast, was within range of German bombers.

No less important were the strategic industries gained in the Netherlands, Belgium and, most of all, northern France, added to those of Czechoslovakia. Not only did Germany gain Swedish iron ore shipped through Norway, it also gained Norwegian and French aluminium production.

Had production in all of the industries in this new German empire or *Grossraum* been producing at pre-war levels, the combined output would have been greater than that of either the British Empire or the United States, while the land area was almost as great as that of the USA and the population, at 292 million people, even larger.

There were other gains as well. The German railways had been neglected in the rush to rearm, even though they were of vital strategic importance in war as in peace. In 1939, it had fewer goods vehicles than in 1922. The best rolling stock from the Low Countries and France was quickly transferred to Germany. The German Army hastened to seize French artillery and motor vehicles. All in all, no less than 5,017 French artillery pieces were seized, with 3.9 million shells and 2,170 tanks, while there were also 314,878 rifles. Even as late as March 1944, no less than 47 per cent of the German Army's artillery was of captured foreign origin, mainly French.

And of course, with Plan Z in abeyance, there was the Marine Nationale, the French Navy. It was a mixed bag, but there were also some excellent vessels, including new battlecruisers and the large, fast *contre-torpilleur* destroyers, while there was also an elderly aircraft carrier and even an aircraft-carrying submarine.

CHAPTER SEVEN

Comparing the Navies in 1939

'Finally, let it be remembered that when the present naval re-armament is completed in about 1940 our figures will be 21 capital ships as against 68 in 1914, 69 cruisers as against 103 and 190 torpedo craft as against 319.

'With the exception of Germany, every other leading navy will be substantially stronger than before the last war.'

So wrote Lt-Cdr E. C. Talbot-Booth, editor of the magazine *Merchant Ships*, on the eve of war in 1939.

For comparison, in September 1939, the Kriegsmarine had:

2 elderly battleships plus 2 building

2 battlecruisers

3 armoured cruisers

3 heavy cruisers

6 light cruisers

22 destroyers

20 torpedo boats and small destroyers

59 submarines

Talbot-Booth made a good point, but to some extent he was not comparing like with like. Many of the capital ships in 1914 had been obsolescent pre-Dreadnoughts, while the 1914 cruiser was a ship whose size could vary enormously, for although there were substantial armoured cruisers, light cruisers could be smaller than a twenty-first century destroyer. Many of the pre-First World War torpedo craft were supposed to be torpedo-boat destroyers, and often less than a thousand tons. Nevertheless, he was right inasmuch as the period between the two world wars had not been good for any of Britain's armed services, and it certainly had not been good for the Royal Navy. The First World War had marked a turning point. The nation that had prided itself on maintaining a fleet that was the equivalent of any other two foreign navies, the so-called 'Two Power Standard', had nearly been brought to its knees by a combination of the German U-boat menace and the reluctance of the Admiralty to institute a convoy system. The Battle of Jutland in 1916 had proved to be anything but decisive. On paper, the Royal Navy had lost, suffering heavier casualties in men and ships than the German Navy, although a strategic victory could be claimed as the German High Seas Fleet put back into port. The introduction of convoys and a sea blockade of Germany eventually meant that it was the Germans who were brought to the point of starvation.

Comparing the two navies, the most obvious deficiency with the Kriegsmarine compared to the Royal Navy was its lack of aircraft carriers and the small number of destroyers. Its surface force was also vastly inferior in numbers and it had nothing like the successful British Town-class cruisers. On the other hand, the Royal Navy lacked any equivalent to the E-boats, and had to struggle to get motor torpedo-boats and gunboats into service after the fall of France meant that E-boats were within hit and run range of British ports and coastal shipping. Neither navy had the means of mounting successful amphibious operations, but the deficiency was the more critical for the Kriegsmarine given Hitler's ambitious plans to invade England, and showed in the defeat of his surface forces during the invasion of Crete.

VERSAILLES AND WASHINGTON

While the Treaty of Versailles in 1919 had determined that the then *Reichsmarine* would be small and primarily designed to provide coastal protection, what followed was the Washington Naval Treaty of 1922 whose terms meant that the best the Royal Navy could aspire to was the 'One Power Standard'. This simply meant that it would be limited to the size of the navy of one other nation. The Washington Treaty was very specific, for its provisions allocating maximum tonnages to each navy of the signatories meant that other navy was to be the United States Navy. In addition to the Treaty stipulating not only a maximum tonnage of ships for the main navies, it also imposed restrictions on the total tonnage for each type of warship, and imposed maximum tonnages for individual vessels as well, with cruisers limited to 10,000 tons, for example, and capital ships to 35,000 tons, while aircraft carriers were limited to 27,000 tons, although both the British and

Americans were allowed two carriers of up to 33,000 tons each.

Both the Royal Navy and the United States Navy were limited to a total warship tonnage of 525,000 tons, while Japan, a First World War ally, was limited to 315,000 tons, and France and Italy were both limited to 175,000 tons each. These limitations had some unexpected results, with all three of the largest 'treaty navies' having battlecruisers in excess of their permitted tonnage, and all three took the option of converting two of these ships to aircraft carriers.

It was also the case that there were practical differences that meant that the state of the Royal Navy was worse than it might have been. The first of these was the determination of successive British inter-war governments to tighten the Washington restrictions, and drive down the tonnage of warships to much less than that allowed, aiming at a figure of around 8,500 tons for a heavy cruiser and 23,000 tons for an aircraft carrier. Not surprisingly, the future Axis powers took an opposing view, and consistently under-stated their tonnages. At the London Naval Conference of 1930, the Japanese attempted to obtain parity with both the UK and the USA. Four years later, the Japanese formally notified the other Washington Naval Treaty signatories that she no longer considered herself bound by its restrictions. German desire for rearmament became increasingly clear after Hitler assumed absolute power in 1933, but even the Weimar Republic had aspired to rebuild its naval forces and had conducted clandestine developments in U-boats, while the Paris Air Agreement of 1926 had already removed the restrictions on German commercial aviation and aircraft manufacture. The London Naval Treaty of 1935 paved the way for the reconstruction of the German Navy, granting Germany a total tonnage equivalent to 35 per cent of that of the Royal Navy, although within this figure, what can only be regarded as an oversight or collective memory loss allowed Germany parity with the Royal Navy in terms of submarines! The Germans even managed to build extra ships once new tonnage was permitted, ordering the battlecruiser *Gneisenau* secretly.

The second problem was that the Royal Navy had lost its aviation element, the Royal Naval Air Service, with the creation of the Royal Air Force on 1 April 1918. So it happened that between the wars, the navy that had invented the aircraft carrier and had come to know more about the operation of aircraft from ships than any other navy, found itself providing aircraft carriers for an air force to use. Many have drawn attention to the poor state of British naval aircraft at the outbreak of war, and some have blamed this on the Air Ministry, even though it too suffered from severe financial constraints until the late 1930s. The real problem, however, was the loss of experienced naval aviation personnel to the RAF in 1918. While the Fleet Air Arm of the Royal Air Force had included a number of naval airmen, especially for the catapult fights aboard battleships and cruisers, most naval officers knew little about aviation and cared even less. It was the Admiralty that believed that high performance aircraft could not be operated off aircraft carriers. By contrast, in the United States Navy, with control of its own air power and even including the shore-based long-range maritime-reconnaissance aircraft, there were senior officers such as Read and Towers with a real understanding of naval aviation.

In fact, the Royal Navy between the two world wars had quickly forgotten the teaching of Lord Fisher that the future of naval warfare would be in the air and under the sea. It still clung to the belief that future warfare would see major fleet actions dominated by the battleship, and officers were taught the 'lessons' of Jutland.

This was, and remains, the difficulty with international treaties that were intended to restrict the actions of dictatorships. The democracies played fair and abided by their treaty limitations, often hampered by tightly drawn public purse strings and by a zealous and unwarranted desire to reduce ship sizes on the part of the body politic, then had to face dictatorships that consistently ignored their treaty obligations and whose expansion plans were never limited by money, but by shipbuilding capacity and the availability of raw materials.

The impact of all this on the individual serviceman should not be underestimated. Certainly the Royal Navy had not had to face the mutinies and Communist uprisings suffered by the *Reichsmarine*, but in 1931, across the board pay cuts during the financial crisis resulted in mutiny amongst ratings aboard the ships of the Atlantic Fleet at Invergordon on the east coast of Scotland. Throughout the inter-war period until 1938, officers without a ship or a posting ashore awaiting them, all too frequently saw their careers interrupted by a spell on half pay, and this was a danger of service life for officers as senior as rear admiral!

The outbreak of war did not come as a surprise to the Royal Navy, which had expected war from October 1935 onwards, after Italy had invaded Abyssinia, present day Ethiopia, and indeed many in the Mediterranean Fleet at the time were surprised and disappointed that the League of Nations did not sanction war with Italy. The successive crises over Czechoslovakia and Italy's seize of Albania had also increased tensions.

AN IMPERIAL NAVY

The world's navies are generally divided into those that are 'blue water', or ocean-going, or 'brown water', which means that they are limited to coastal duties or perhaps a largely land-bound sea, such as the Baltic or the Black Sea. The Royal Navy was always the consummate blue water navy, with the worldwide British Empire to support. In contrast to the United States Navy, it also retained the tasks that also fell upon a brown water navy, such as fisheries protection and in times of war keeping ports open through minesweeping. The USN was largely able to overlook many of these tasks, except minesweeping, because of the existence of the United States Coast Guard, in many ways a brown water navy, which belonged to the US Department of Transportation (sic) during peacetime, but came under naval control in wartime.

Between the two world wars, the Royal Navy went through a number of reorganisations. The Grand Fleet of the First World War became first the Atlantic Fleet and, later, the Home Fleet. The Inskip Award of 1937 saw naval aviation handed back to the Admiralty, which formally took control of the Fleet Air Arm in May 1939.

In 1939, the distribution of the Royal Navy included both the Home Fleet, which was the largest single administrative formation, as well as the Mediterranean Fleet, with its bases at Malta, Gibraltar and Alexandria, plus the China Station, essentially meaning Hong Kong; the East Indies Station, mainly centred on Singapore; the American Station, meaning Bermuda; the African Station, based on Simonstown, near Cape Town in South Africa, and the West Indies Station.

On the outbreak of war in 1939, the Home Fleet was the strongest element within the Royal Navy and in many respects more than the equal of the entire Kriegsmarine. The commander-in-chief was Admiral Sir Charles Forbes, who had 5 battleships, 2 battlecruisers, 2 aircraft carriers, 3 squadrons with a total of 15 cruisers, 2 flotillas each with eight or nine destroyers, and some 20 or so submarines. The main forward base for the Home Fleet was Scapa Flow in Orkney. Scapa had been neglected since the previous conflict, and it was only as late as April 1938 that the Admiralty had decided that Rosyth would not be adequate for the coming conflict. All too soon,

Scapa itself was to prove insecure, but in any case this was more of an anchorage than a base, lacking the heavy repair facilities available at Rosyth. On the other hand, Rosyth, on the north or Fife banks of the Firth of Forth, was too far south, about twelve hours' steaming from Scapa.

Also in home waters and in addition to the Home Fleet, another two battleships and two aircraft carriers were based in the English Channel, with three cruisers and a destroyer flotilla, while another two cruisers and a further destroyer flotilla were based on the Humber. Further escort vessels were based on Plymouth and Portsmouth.

Under wartime pressures, new North Atlantic and South Atlantic Commands were created. There were also six home commands, Orkney and Shetland, Rosyth, Nore, Dover (created in October 1939), Portsmouth and Western Approaches. The last-named was initially at Plymouth, but soon moved to Liverpool. The China Station became the British Eastern Fleet on 2 December 1941, with its own commander-in-chief, and was augmented by ships that had previously been allocated to Force Z. After the fall of Singapore and the Japanese attacks on Ceylon, now Sri Lanka, the British Eastern Fleet moved its headquarters to Kilindini, or Mombasa, in British East Africa, now Kenya. Operations in the Indian Ocean were helped by a secret refuelling base at Addu Atoll, now known as Gan.

In addition, the Royal Navy had far closer links with the navies of the British Empire than would be the case today when these relationships have largely been overtaken by those with Britain's allies within the North Atlantic Treaty Organisation, NATO. There were differences, however, and the Canadians, for example, took a far more independent view than say the Australians or New Zealanders. Nevertheless, the four main Commonwealth navies were the Royal Australian Navy, the Royal Canadian Navy and the Royal Indian Navy, as well as the New Zealand Division, which later under wartime expansion became the Royal New Zealand Navy. None of the other colonies maintained a naval force, although locally recruited personnel were present in many cases. While officially Egypt was an independent kingdom, it was still at this time run virtually as a colony by the United Kingdom, and the Royal Egyptian Navy was commanded by a British admiral.

In 1939, no other navy had such a spread of responsibilities as the Royal Navy. The French came closest with the need to maintain ships in the Mediterranean and the Atlantic, as well as a small naval presence in their colonies, but as a far weaker force, much can be noted from the fact that instead of 'fleets', the Marine Nationale was divided into Atlantic and Mediterranean Squadrons, as well as a Far Eastern Station (in French Indo-China).

The Royal Navy and Royal Marines in June, 1939, totalled 129,000 men, of whom just under 10,000 were officers. To bring it up to maximum strength in wartime, it could depend on recalling recently retired officers and ratings, as well as two categories of reserves, which between them provided another 73,000 officers and men in 1939. Included in the 1939 total were 12,400 officers and men in the Royal Marines. By mid-1944, the RN had reached its peak strength of 863,500 personnel, including 73,500 of the Women's Royal Naval Service.

By contrast, the Kriegsmarine in 1939 had 122,000 personnel, rising to 190,000 the following year and peaking at 810,000 in 1944, as with the Royal Navy, after which the Kriegsmarine manpower figures plummeted as men were transferred to the Army to defend the Reich. In 1943, the year when war had originally been expected to break out, it had 780,000 men.

The Royal Navy's wartime casualties amounted to 50,758 killed with another 820 missing, presumed dead, and 14,663 wounded. The WRNS lost 102 killed and 22 wounded, mainly in air raids.

The Kriegsmarine lost 48,904 men due to enemy action, and 11,125 through other causes. Another 25,259 were wounded, while a staggering 100,256 were listed as missing.

The Royal Navy that went to war in September 1939 consisted of 12 battleships and battlecruisers, including HMS *Hood*, 'The Mighty Hood', that despite its battlecruiser designation had been the world's largest warship for many years, 7 aircraft carriers, of which 4 were either in reserve or earmarked for early retirement, 2 seaplane carriers, of little use in the carrier-age, 58 cruisers, 100 destroyers, 101 other escort vessels, 38 submarines and 232 aircraft. This compared badly with the 61 battleships, 120 cruisers and 443 destroyers, plus many sloops for convoy protection and two aircraft carriers of the previous global conflict, with which the Royal Navy had struggled to maintain control of the seas. Yet, by 1945, this fleet was to grow to 61 battleships and cruisers; 59 aircraft carriers; 846 destroyers, frigates and corvettes; 729 minesweepers; 131 submarines; 1,000 minor vessels and landing craft and 3,700 aircraft.

Much has been made by the contribution to Britain's armed forces of the dominions and colonies, but in terms of equipment, this was insignificant in 1939. In the case of a threat from Japan, Australia and New Zealand had been promised the support of the Royal Navy. No one seems to have considered the possibility of fighting three nations, a war on three fronts, while there was still time to do something about it.

By contrast, the Kriegsmarine, in 1939 had 2 old battleships, really the old coastal defence ships permitted under the Treaty of Versailles, 2 battlecruisers, 3 armoured cruisers, 3 heavy cruisers, 6 light cruisers, 22 destroyers, 20 torpedo boats and small destroyers, and 59 submarines. Still under construction at the outbreak of war were the two battleships, *Bismarck* and *Tirpitz*.

The Italian Navy was stronger still, and as Italy did not enter the war until June 1940, that has to be the relevant date for comparison. The Italians had 6 battleships and 7 heavy cruisers, 14 light cruisers and a coast defence ship, no less than 122 destroyers and torpedo boats and 119 submarines. Nevertheless, as the Second World War progressed, the Italian fleet, the Regia Navale, was to find its operations restricted by a growing fuel shortage.

On this basis, the Royal Navy was outnumbered and out-gunned by the opposition, even without the need to dilute its strength through maintaining a worldwide presence. The Imperial Japanese Navy was not to be an opponent until December 1941, by which time the United States was also in the war, but by that date, the Japanese could boast 10 battleships, with 2 still building, 8 aircraft carriers and 18 heavy cruisers, 20 light cruisers and 108 destroyers, as well as 65 submarines. The Imperial Japanese Navy was the only Axis navy to have aircraft carriers. An unusual feature in the Imperial Japanese Navy was the inclusion of aircraft-carrying submarines, something long abandoned by the Royal Navy after the loss of the experimental *M2*, and even more unusual was the fact that some of the Japanese submarines could carry two aircraft.

Looking at navies in terms of the numbers of ships and manpower is not enough. In 1939, the Royal Navy had radar, the Italians didn't. The Royal Navy also had Asdic, or sonar as it would now be called, which was far superior to the hydrophones used during the First World War. In fact, the Italian Navy did not expect to fight at night!

CHAPTER EIGHT

Seizing the French Fleet

War had come far earlier than the Kriegsmarine planners had allowed for. They had been led to believe that they would have had at least four more years before war broke out. Nevertheless, they were not caught quite by surprise. Many senior officers had doubted that Hitler could keep the British and French out of their war with Poland.

Poland itself had not presented a threat to Germany. The country was impoverished and amongst the most backward in Europe. It had gained independence from Russia during the Russian Civil War and had been awarded Germany territory, East Prussia, under the Versailles Treaty. It had been a virtual dictatorship since 1926, and even when Marshal Pilsudski died in 1935, his followers in the Sanacja ('cleansing) regime, continued his policies. The army had some 280,000 men, and although this could be increased by the mobilisation of some 3 million reservists, there was little modern equipment. The same could be said of the air force, with 400 aircraft, but few were modern and none were a match for the Luftwaffe or even for those of the Red Air Forces when the USSR invaded on 17 September. The navy was commanded by a rear-admiral and was little more than a coastal defence force, having just four modern destroyers, two of which had been built in Great Britain and the other two in France, and five modern submarines, as well as twenty-three aircraft. In addition to a small force of coastal gunboats and minesweepers, there were also river craft. There were just 3,500 personnel.

The Kriegsmarine was barely involved in the invasion, and as the invasion started, several Polish warships escaped to British ports, including three destroyers and two submarines, a supply ship and a training vessel, working to a plan agreed earlier with the Royal Navy. Thirty-eight merchant vessels also escaped, including three passenger liners.

Traditionally, navies have seized warships from their enemies and adapted them to their own use. Indeed, the most distinguished Royal Navy warship of all, the Second World War aircraft carrier HMS *Illustrious*, came from a line of warships to bear the name that had started with the captured French warship *L'Illustre*. There was little left by the Poles, or indeed by the Dutch and Belgians, with the former having its best ships in the East Indies, but the fall of France presented an opportunity.

Caught in a major war without sufficient warships of their own, the Germans must have considered seizing the French *Marine Nationale*, a substantial but even by the standards of the day, hardly well balanced fleet, with just one obsolescent aircraft carrier, the *Bearn*, and a marked absence of modern cruisers. Nevertheless, the French ships could have remedied the lack of progress on Plan Z. After all, the justification for building the battlecruiser *Scharnhorst* was to rival the French *Dunkerque*, an ominous warning of German intentions.

THE FRENCH FLEET IN 1940

Known officially as the 'Marine Nationale', in 1939, the French had the fourth largest navy in the world and once mobilised had 160,000 personnel. While the Marine Nationale had been limited to 175,000 tons of shipping by the Washington Naval Treaty, it had gone well beyond this by 1940, by which time it had a total tonnage well in excess of 600,000 tons, but many of the ships were old. It was strong in battleships and cruisers, and far stronger than Germany in 1939 and 1940 in terms of submarines and destroyers, but it was weak in aircraft carriers, with just one elderly ship, the converted battleship *Bearn*, 22,000 tons, and a seaplane tender, although two more aircraft carriers of modern design were under construction.

Between the two world wars, French defence planning had been based on the assumption that the country's most likely adversary would be Italy. The Italians viewed the French in the same light, and a naval race had developed between the two countries.

As war approached, the French had launched a programme of naval expansion, but in 1939, the fleet included:

1 elderly aircraft carrier
3 modernised battleships
4 old battleships

2 battlecruisers
7 heavy cruisers
12 light cruisers
32 large *contre-torpilleur* destroyers
38 other destroyers
1 seaplane tender
77 submarines

Of these ships, in 1940 the best were the two battlecruisers, *Dunkerque* and *Strasbourg*, rivals to the German *Scharnhorst* and *Gneisenau*, which had been built as Germany's answer to the French ships. These battlecruisers were in fact heavier than the older French battleships, at 26,500 tons displacement, and had their main armament forward in two quadruple turrets, but here the comparison ended, as the guns were of 330-mm calibre, 13-in, and so compatible with neither the older nor the new French battleships. Nevertheless, both ships outgunned the German battlecruisers, and would have made light work of the German *Panzerschiffe*.

It was not until 1936, when Germany became an increasing threat and war in Europe became increasingly likely, that a new warship building programme was agreed. The Marine Nationale's building programme included:

2 aircraft carriers
4 battleships
3 light cruisers
4 large *contre-torpilleur* destroyers
12 destroyers
40 submarines

Of these, the most interesting ships were the two 18,000 ton aircraft carriers, the *Joffre* and *Painleve*, which, while dated in outline with their hull not plated up to flight deck level, in plan view showed the flight deck and hangar offset to port to balance the large superstructure island. Some have suggested that this was an early version of the angled flight deck, but this was not so. Reputedly, a third ship was ordered on the eve of the German invasion.

Just as Plan Z was interrupted by the outbreak of war, so it was with the French. Just two of the four new battleships were completing in 1940. The first of these, *Richelieu*, was moved to Mers-el-Kebir as French surrender became inevitable. Her sister ship, *Jean Bart*, was not completed until the end of the war. These were ships worthy of their type, being much larger and faster than the three older ships, at 35,000 tons and capable of 30 knots. In some ways they were similar to the British battleships *Rodney* and *Nelson*, with their main armament all forward in 'A' and 'B' turrets, but unlike the three triple 16-in turrets of the British ships, for once the French chose a more conventional calibre, with two quadruple 15-in turrets. The secondary armament was also conventional, with 6-in guns in five triple turrets.

The French Navy in 1940 had twenty-two cruisers, but most of these were elderly vessels, and many had non-standard calibre guns, including some with 5-in which made their status as cruisers somewhat doubtful as the Washington Naval Treaty had stipulated 6-in guns for light cruisers and 8-in for heavy cruisers. Again, the more modern vessels did conform, with the *Algerie*, a heavy cruiser displacing 10,000 tons dating from 1933, having eight 8-in guns in four turrets arranged conventionally fore and aft. Six other cruisers, including the *Emile Bertin*, 5,886 tons, also dated from the later 1930s and had 6-in guns.

An unusual feature of the French Navy was the *contre-torpilleur* 'super' destroyers, developed in response to Italy's light cruisers. These varied between 2,000 and almost 3,000 tons in size, and had 5.5-in guns as opposed to the 6-in of a light cruiser. The newest and largest were almost 3,000 tons, with eight 5.5-in guns in four turrets, and capable of up to 43 knots in the calmer waters of the Mediterranean. Another six *contre-torpilleurs* had been completed in 1934 and 1936, and were slightly smaller, at 2,600 tons, and slightly slower as well. There were another twenty-four *contre-torpilleurs*, of 2,000 tons and 2,300 tons, as well as thirty-eight standard destroyers.

By 1940, the French submarine fleet had risen to 84 boats. A complete novelty in the French Fleet was the *Surcouf*, a corsair submarine similar to the British M-class, and at 2,880 tons, the world's largest submarine at the time. *Surcouf* was also referred to sometimes as a cruiser submarine, with two 8-in guns forward and a small aircraft hangar for a floatplane after of the conning tower. Given the tactics advocated by Dönitz for U-boat surface attack by night, this type of vessel would have been ideal for Germany's warfare against merchant vessels: U-boat commanders preferred to use their deck armament rather than their limited number of more expensive torpedoes.

Yet the official tonnage figures provide an exaggerated impression of the size of the Marine Nationale, or at least of its wartime fighting potential. Four old battleships were counted in the official figures, but these were of pre-First World War vintage; one of them, the *Courbet*, started the war as an anti-aircraft battery and later simply became a breakwater. Three other battleships that had been completed in the years immediately following the earlier conflict had been extensively modernized, given new boilers and their armament increased, with additional emphasis on anti-aircraft protection, but their 22,000 tons displacement was insufficient for a capital ship of the day, as was their speed, at 21 knots.

Many French ships displayed a highly individualistic set of gun calibres, such as 330-mm calibre guns, which equated to 13-in, as well as the cruisers with 5-in guns already mentioned.

Another unusual feature, which the French had in common with the Kriegsmarine, was a number of torpedo boats that were almost of destroyer standard at 1,000 tons. In contrast to the Royal Navy, the French had not neglected motor torpedo boats and small gunboats.

With this fleet, the Marine Nationale had to wield a worldwide presence, as had the Royal Navy, but being considerably smaller it operated large squadrons rather than fleets. The Atlantic Squadron equated to the British Atlantic, later Home, Fleet, and the same relationship could be applied to the French Mediterranean Squadron and the British Mediterranean Fleet. The main bases in France were at Brest on the Atlantic coast of France and Toulon on the Mediterranean coast, but there were other smaller bases and just as the British had Gibraltar and Malta, the French had Oran and Mers-el-Kebir in Algeria, Bizerta in Tunisia, Casablanca in French Morocco and Dakar in West Africa. Dakar had the only dry dock between Gibraltar and Cape Town.

There were also ships stationed in the Caribbean, in the Indian Ocean at Madagascar, and in French Indo-China, as well as at Beirut in the Lebanon.

THE FATE OF THE FRENCH FLEET

The big difference between France and the other nations invaded by the Germans up to June 1940 was that the country was not entirely overrun. This was never the German intention. They wanted the Channel ports of Northern France and the industry of the area around Paris as well as the coalfields of the north. Another difference was that, in common with Luxembourg, the Germans had high hopes that at least some of the population would join them, as Alsace and Lorraine had long been disputed territories with both France and Germany regarding these provinces as theirs. They had come under German control during the Franco-Prussian War of 1871, having become French territory during the late 17th and early 18th centuries, and returned to France after German defeat in the First World War. In May 1940, they were back in German hands, known to the Germans as Elsass-Lothringen, with the majority of the local population German-speaking. It must have been a provocation for the Germans when the French named one of their First World War battleships *Lorraine*.

An armistice between France and Germany was a difficult political question as the British and French had concluded a treaty that didn't simply commit themselves to an alliance, but went beyond forbidding either to conclude a separate negotiation with Germany or Italy. In complete contrast was the policy, advocated by Pierre Laval, another member of the government who had surrounded himself with a power base of senators and deputies. Laval wanted not simply surrender, but for France to change sides. His argument for the policy was that by allying herself with the victor and continuing the war against the United Kingdom, France would not only retain her sovereignty, but also all of her overseas possessions.

At the time, the Germans were looking for surrender, which with a substantial part of France unoccupied and with its own government, would make it much more difficult for France to continue in the war. In fact, Hitler's appreciation of the threat posed if the French chose to continue the war from North Africa, and perhaps the Lebanon and Syria as well, was astute. There were those who, realising that the Battle of France was lost, intended to continue the war from Africa and the French Empire using the French fleet. After all, none of the other countries overrun by the Germans had actually stopped fighting, but had continued to do so using those of their citizens who had managed to escape, first to France and then to the United Kingdom. The French had the advantage of strategically placed territories around the world that gave them the room and the manpower to continue fighting. Overall, the French forces in the Mediterranean theatre had been stronger than those of the British. The only weakness in the French fighting the war from their colonies was the lack of a manufacturing base, for which the British and the Americans, and perhaps the Canadians who were rapidly industrialising, would have to provide a substitute.

On 21 June, the terms of the armistice were presented to the French delegation. To emphasise that the French had been defeated in the field, there were no negotiations. As a result, the leader of the French delegation, General Huntziger, was simply handed the armistice agreement with its twenty-four articles, and told that they were non-negotiable. The Armistice with Germany was signed the following day.

With the Anglo-French alliance effectively in tatters, the condition that applied to the French Navy was Article 8, which read:

The French fleet (with the exception of that part which is left at the disposition of the French government for the protection of French interests in the colonial empire) will be concentrated in ports to be determined and will be demobilised and disarmed under the supervision of Germany or, respectively, Italy. The peace-time bases of these vessels will be used to designate these ports.

The German government solemnly declares to the French government that it has no intention of using during the war for its own purposes the French fleet stationed in ports under German supervision, other than the units necessary for coastal patrol and minesweeping. It further declares solemnly and formally that it has no intention of making claims in respect of the French fleet after the conclusion of peace.

With the exception of that element of the French fleet to be determined which will be allocated to the defence of French interest in the colonial empire, all warships at present outside French territorial waters should be recalled to France.

The lack of interest in taking French warships was interesting as it was completely contrary to what was happening elsewhere to the French armed forces. The defeated French Army had been a treasure trove for the Germans, who grabbed the artillery and stocks of ammunition for their own use. They also started to strip the French railways of their best rolling stock. It would have been tempting to have taken as many French warships as possible and convert them to the use of the Kriegsmarine. After all, U-boat construction during the first year of war had been slow. Yet, because the south of France was not occupied until November 1942, most of the active fleet remained outside the grasp of the Germans either at Toulon or in North and East Africa.

In fact, fourteen U-boats were pressed into service from the navies of the countries overrun by Germany. There was also *UA*, for *U-Ausland*, meaning U-Foreign, a large U-boat under construction for Turkey, and which was retained and commissioned into the Kriegsmarine on 21 September 1939, and later the British submarine, *Seal*, captured early in the war, seeing service as *UB*. Two Norwegian submarines were also pressed into service with the Kriegsmarine, as well as five Dutch submarines. Three French submarines were seized when their ports were occupied, and after Italian surrender, four Italian submarines stationed in the north of the country also saw service with the Germans. These U-boats were given special designations, with the Norwegian boats becoming *UC-1* and *UC-2*, the Dutch boats *UD-1* to *UD-5*, the French boats *UF-1* to *UF-3*, and the Italian boats becoming *UIT-22* to *UIT-25*.

Nevertheless, the bulk of the French fleet eluded the Germans with Admiral Darlan, at Bordeaux, by this time the seat of government, maintaining that the French fleet would never be surrendered to the Germans or the Italians, and also refusing to send the fleet to the UK while French troops were still fighting and declaring that the fleet had to remain in French waters while the fighting continued.

At the time of the armistice, Darlan went to great lengths to assure the United Kingdom that the French fleet would not fall into German hands. He ordered commanding officers to scuttle their ships should the Germans attempt to take them. Unfortunately, the British didn't trust Darlan, and seized or sank whatever ships they could, except at Alexandria.

Darlan harboured strong Anglophobe tendencies and attitudes. He also wanted a more equal relationship between France and Germany. In May 1941, Darlan offered Hitler the use of French bases in Syria, and after a visit to Berchtesdgaden he returned to France with plans for joint Franco-German operations in the Middle East. Petain refused to agree to these proposals, which were undoubtedly of great appeal to the Germans who had been unable to encourage their First World War ally, Turkey, to join them.

SUBSTITUTES FOR THE PLAN Z SHIPS?

Despite some incompatibility between the two fleets, many French warship types were available in far larger numbers than their German counterparts. In 1940, the French had more submarines than the Germans, with 84, of which 24 were lost between war breaking out and the French surrender. Manpower was one reason for the Germans not taking over the French ships, as German industry still needed skilled men and the army and air force had absorbed large numbers of men. Nevertheless, the Germans would have needed to seize Vichy France to be sure of seizing all of the ships actually in French home waters, with many of the large surface units at Toulon. At Toulon was the single largest element of the Marine Nationale, some eighty ships, more ships than most of the world's navies. In major surface units alone, the fleet at Toulon was close to matching the Kriegsmarine. Yet, had the Germans seized these ships, it might have persuaded the French authorities in North Africa, although officially under Vichy control, to send ships in their ports to the Royal Navy.

Of course, the real prize could only have come if the Italian invasion of the South of France starting on 10 June 1940 had been more aggressive and successful. Had the Italians swept along the Mediterranean coastline of France, the ships at Toulon would have been a prize worth having and just conceivably could have been taken before scuttling charges could have been set. Nevertheless, the most useful naval vessels would have been the French submarines, with a limited manpower requirement.

Even with the French surface fleet, the Kriegsmarine would still not have a balance with the Royal Navy. It would also have been a fleet 'in exile' and difficult to concentrate in one war zone, unless it could be sailed through the Straits of Gibraltar to Brest and have access to the open sea.

Had the French warships been seized and used by the Germans in 1940–1941, it could have made a difference and the availability of the battlecruisers as surface raiders during the Battle of the Atlantic would have made the position of the convoys even more difficult. Even problems with different calibre guns would not have been insurmountable as French production facilities could have been used.

In particular, the French submarines would have been a useful addition and allowed the Kriegsmarine to put a hundred-plus U-boats to sea in 1940. But this was not done, and it certainly was not done out of any sense of honour or of meeting the conditions of the Franco-German armistice.

There were three reasons for failing to make full use of the French maritime booty. The first was that increasingly the Germans saw a blockade of the British Isles using submarines as a way to force the United Kingdom into starvation and capitulation, and did not see a strategic plan in which naval forces would play a major role. This was due to the continental, land-centred, mentality. The second was that Hitler quickly became disillusioned with the German surface fleet's performance, whose one great success of the war was the sinking of the British battlecruiser *Hood*. When the Germans lost the *Bismarck*, the pride of the Kriegsmarine, shortly afterwards, it was the second in a growing list of major German warship losses, following on from the *Graf Spee*.

Perhaps most telling of all, there was a third reason for not making use of the French fleet, the German fuel situation. It was simply not possible to maintain the Panzer units and the Luftwaffe and also have a thirsty surface fleet. The situation was so bad that many minor warships, including minesweepers, were converted to coal-firing, as this was the one natural resource that Germany had in abundance. The manpower needs of burning coal in warships and the reduced range, as well as the time taken to re-coal, was a major drawback and indicative of the extent of the fuel crisis. Increasingly, the Germans found it difficult to spare sufficient fuel to keep the navy of their Italian ally, the Regia Navale, in the war.

Yet, in August 1940, *Reichsmarschall* Hermann Goering, the second highest member of the Nazi regime, demanded the complete exploitation of the occupied territories.

Meanwhile, from summer 1940 through to November 1942, the surviving units of the French Navy were allowed to protect Vichy convoys between France and her North African colonies, a reminder to the British that here was a great naval asset that could be used against them.

Eventually, after French forces in North Africa surrendered to the Allies following the invasion, on 27 November, the Germans tried to seize those French warships stationed at Toulon in the South of France.

At Toulon, the French commanders had been ordered by Darlan to move their ships to Dakar, out of reach of the Germans and for the time-being at least, difficult for the Allies as well. Toulon was home to the two powerful battlecruisers, *Strasbourg* and *Dunkerque*, although the latter had been badly damaged in her encounter with Force H at Mers-el-Kebir. There were three elderly heavy cruisers, two light cruisers, ten large 'super' destroyers of the *contre-torpilleur* type as well as three smaller destroyers. There was the battleship *Provence* and the seaplane tender *Almirante Teste*, two destroyers, four torpedo boats and ten submarines. In addition to these ships, fully or nearly fully-manned, there were another two cruisers, eight *contre-torpilleur* destroyers, six smaller destroyers and ten submarines decommissioned under the armistice terms and which simply had skeleton crews aboard. There were also minesweepers and other minor naval vessels and auxiliaries.

The major fleet units, including the destroyers but not the submarines, were steam-powered, which meant that steam had to be raised before they could leave port. Since it could take six hours to raise steam, once the Germans were at the gates of the dockyard, flight was not an option.

When the Germans were seen advancing on the port area at Toulon, all commanding officers were ordered to raise steam on their ships, and to be on their guard to prevent the Germans boarding any vessel. Then the order to scuttle was re-issued, and then repeated as the Germans attempted to enter the dockyard area, but encountered fierce resistance from Vichy forces, who had also been alerted by a despatch rider sent by a gendarmerie outpost. In the confusion, five submarines, *Venus*, *Casablanca*, *Marsouin*, *Iris* and *Glorieux* with their diesel engines providing power almost immediately, managed to slip away and out to sea. The ease with which they did this, their crews manning their deck armament, suggests that the whole procedure had already been rehearsed. They were bombed, strafed and depth charged by the Luftwaffe, leaving *Venus* so damaged that she had to be scuttled, while *Iris*, also damaged, was taken by her commanding officer and crew to Spain, where they spent the rest of the war in internment, but the other three boats reached North Africa.

When the Germans reached the piers alongside which the *Strasbourg* had been moored, they found that she was already drifting away after her crew had cast of all lines to the shore. A German tank fired an 88mm shell into 'B' turret, fatally wounding a gunnery officer. The crew responded, with machine guns and other light weapons. The officer in command of the German troops demanded that the ship be returned to the pier, but scuttling had already started and the ship was settling slowly in the water, accompanied by the first of a series of loud explosions that ripped through the ship, while the crew set about wrecking the ship's machinery with hand grenades and oxy-acetylene cutters. There wasn't enough depth of water for the ship to sink completely, but instead she settled on the bed of the port, leaving her distinctive superstructure sticking out of the water.

Nearby, the crew of the heavy cruiser *Algerie*, 13,900 tons, also had opened her sea cocks and her main armament had been destroyed by explosives. The ship continued to burn for the next two days during which occasional explosions could be heard as her ammunition blew up. This was far from a record, as the light cruiser *Marseillaise*, which had settled at an angle, took more than a week to burn herself out. Another cruiser, the *Colbert*, was boarded by a German party, but when they saw fuses being set and one of her officers setting fire to his floatplane, they left promptly, but only just in time before her magazine blew the ship apart. The German party that had set foot aboard another cruiser, the *Dupleix*, also had a narrow escape when she blew up.

Scuttling on its own often causes little damage, and ships scuttled in shallow port waters can be re-floated and salvaged, which was one reason why so much emphasis was given to setting off the magazines and ready use ammunition, not to mention the attacks by grenade and oxy-acetylene cutters. This point was brought home later when another cruiser, a sister ship of the *Marseillaise*, *La Galissonniere*, was scuttled, but then re-floated and taken by the Italian navy, but returned to the French in 1944.

In the confusion, the elderly battleship *Provence* was one ship that was nearly taken by the Germans, as her commanding officer hesitated when he was given the message that the Vichy premier, Pierre Laval, had ordered that there were to be no 'incidents'. Nevertheless, while he sent an officer to seek clarification, his crew, seeing the other ships sinking and blowing up, opened the sea cocks and the ship began to settle in the water even while the Germans argued with her CO on the bridge.

The battlecruiser *Dunkerque*, sister ship of the *Strasbourg* and pride of the pre-war French navy, was in dry dock and rather than being refitted and returned to service, she suffered the ignominy of being scrapped by a large gang of Italian workers imported for the purpose, so that she could be sent to Italy in pieces as part of a scrap metal drive intended to rebuild Italy's dwindling stocks of war materials.

The Italians also gained three out of the eight contre-torpilleur destroyers, *Lion*, *Tigre* and *Panthere* which were being refitted so their skeleton crews did not have enough time to sabotage them effectively, along with the smaller destroyer *Trombe*.

116

Four submarines that were left behind at Toulon were scuttled at their moorings.

German delay in seizing the ships had allowed the French to honour their pledge to scuttle their ships rather than surrender them, yet the way ships were handed over to Italy, shows that German intentions had been simply to honour the armistice only for as long as it suited them. Delay also meant something else, for the fuel situation from this time onwards became increasing critical and by 1943, the Italian fleet was largely confined to port.

CHAPTER NINE

Using the Italian Fleet

While Italy had pledged to be an ally of Germany before the war, the country's leadership did not declare war on Poland on 1 September 1939 and did not declare war on Great Britain and France on 3 September. It was not until the Battle of France had almost ended, on 10 June 1940, that Italy declared war. This late entry into the war, after most of the fighting had been done but just in time to share in the spoils, earned the scorn of many Germans, especially in the military.

Modern Italy was not a maritime nation, although it had a relatively short land frontier compared with its long coastline as the 'leg' of Italy stretched across and almost bisected the Mediterranean. After Mussolini's rise to power in 1925, and his successful conquest of Libya, he liked to feel that Italy controlled the Mediterranean, which he called *Mare* Nostrum, 'Our Sea'. This was nonsense as both the British and French navies maintained a substantial presence, with the former having strong bases at Gibraltar, Malta and Alexandria, and the latter in France and in Algeria.

Despite having been allies during the First World War, for most of the period between the two world wars, France and Italy viewed each other as the most likely enemy. This was due to the rhetoric and expansionist policies of Mussolini. Indeed, when Italy marched into Abyssinia in 1935 against League of Nations objections, war seemed imminent between Great Britain and Italy, but French reluctance meant that no action was taken, even though it would have been easy for the British and French to have stopped Italian shipping from using the Suez Canal. In 1939, Italy invaded Albania, and during the Second World War was to launch a disastrous invasion of Greece from which Hitler had to rescue her by committing German troops for the invasion of Yugoslavia and Greece.

A WASTED ASSET

When Italy finally entered the Second World War in June 1940, Hitler's expectation would be that his new ally would send her fleet and air force to bombard and then take the island fortress of Malta, which had been the British Mediterranean Fleet's main base. This would cut the Mediterranean in two and make it difficult for the British to resupply their forces in Egypt, defending the Suez Canal. While air raids on Malta started from the early hours of 11 June, the fleet remained in port, a wasted asset.

On entry into World War II, the Italian Navy had six battleships and seven heavy cruisers, as well as fourteen light cruisers. This was a powerful force for a nation with few maritime pretensions. Lighter forces included 122 destroyers and torpedo boats, and, something usually overlooked, there were 119 submarines, twice as many as the Germany Kriegsmarine possessed in 1939!

Mere numbers were not enough, however, and, while a modern fleet, the Regia Navale suffered from many shortcomings. Italian warship designers had placed more emphasis on style and speed than on effective armament and armour protection, but, more important still, they lacked radar. According to Britain's naval commander in the Mediterranean, Admiral Sir Andrew Cunningham, the Italians 'were no further advanced than we had been at Jutland twenty-five years before.' While an aircraft carrier was under construction, this was never finished.

The main bases for the Italian fleet were in the south at Taranto in Italy's 'instep', Genoa in the north-west, and La Spezzia, slightly further south, as well as Trieste at the northern end of the Adriatic, close to the border with Yugoslavia. Of these, only Taranto was well placed as a forward base as the war developed. It was close to Malta, and also provided the shortest mainland shipping route to North Africa, where Italian ground and air forces needed to be kept supplied. It was also close to Greece, and ships based on Taranto could effectively cut the entrance to the Adriatic. Indeed, an active fleet based on Taranto could have cut the Mediterranean in half.

A sheltered anchorage with both an outer harbour, the Mar Grande, and an inner harbour, the Mar Piccolo, Taranto offered everything a naval base could be expected to provide. The outer harbour provided moorings for the battleships, while the cruisers and destroyers could use both harbours. A large breakwater shielded the outer harbour from the full force of the elements, for even the Mediterranean can be unkind in winter. In the inner harbour, ships used what was known as 'Mediterranean mooring', that is instead of berthing alongside, they were berthed stern to the quayside, packed close together 'like sardines in a tin' as one British airman put it. This had the incidental advantage of making a torpedo attack on any one ship very difficult.

A seaplane station was also provided at Taranto, largely for the aircraft that would be used by the battleships and cruisers once they were at sea, literally the 'eyes of the fleet', and without radar the only eyes for Italian warships other than their own lookouts. The ship repair facilities were enhanced for wartime by the use of floating docks, while there was also a large oil storage depot.

Italy's geographical position, aided by air bases in Sicily, Sardinia and the Dodecanese, meant that the absence of an aircraft carrier in the Italian fleet was not so serious a drawback as it might seem. Italian aircraft could cover all of the Adriatic as well as a substantial proportion of the Mediterranean from shore bases, especially after the Greek islands started to be occupied, and, of course, after the fall of Greece and then of Crete.

THE REGIA NAVALE
On paper, major units of the Italian fleet sounded impressive enough. The Andrea Doria-class of battleships, which included the *Conte di Cavour* and the *Caio Duilo*, were vessels from the First World War, reconstructed between the wars, as indeed were a number of units in the British fleet. Nevertheless, their relatively low displacement of 22,964 tons and main armament of ten 12.6-inch guns, with a secondary armament of twelve 5.2-inch, ten 3.5-inch and nineteen 37-mm, the last being primarily for anti-aircraft protection, made them obsolescent, despite a reasonable speed of 27 knots,.

More modern and more impressive were the Impero-class, under construction just before the outbreak of war and intended to make full use of the maximum dimensions permitted by the Washington Treaty. The four ships included the *Littorio*. These were ships of 35,000 tons, capable of 30.5 knots. Their main armament consisted of nine 15-inch guns, with a secondary armament of twelve six-inch and four 4.7-inch, twelve 3.5-inch, twenty 37-mm and thirty-two 20-mm. For comparison, the British *Prince of Wales*, also weighed in at 35,000 tons, but was only capable of 28.5 knots. Her main armament was ten 14-inch guns, with a secondary armament of sixteen 5.25-inch, forty-eight 2-pounder pom-poms, a single 40-mm and twenty 20-mm.

Domination on paper was not the same as domination in reality. The Italian Navy had not been faced with a serious conflict since the Balkan Wars thirty years' earlier. They had not engaged the Austro-Hungarian Navy during the First World War, although the Italian Army had suffered a major defeat at the hands of their northern neighbours during the war.

Training was poor, and so too was the study of naval warfare by the officers.

On the other hand, it would be wrong to overlook the fact that the Italian Navy, and the other Italian armed forces, did excel in using small specialised forces, such as the two-man crews of the human torpedoes. These were a big success, known officially as the *Siluro a Lenta Corsa*, or 'slow running torpedo', but to their two-man crews as the *Maiale*, or 'pig'. These were ridden by their operators who sat on top, and once inside an enemy harbour and under the target ship, the warhead could be detached and fastened to the hull. The intrepid crew could then make their escape on the torpedo. Apart from the obvious dangers and difficulties of penetrating an enemy harbour at night, getting clear was important since the percussive effects of underwater blast meant that the crew were greatly at risk while close to the target. In fact, Italian and, later, British experience of human torpedoes was that their crews seldom managed to make a successful escape.

Skill, courage and imagination meant that such teams were a potent threat, but a wider *esprit de corps* was usually missing. Instances of Italian ships being well fought during the war in the Mediterranean were rare, although Cunningham's autobiography does mention one outstanding destroyer action.

While Italy had a major shipbuilding industry, the other problem faced by the Italian armed forces was the shortage of fuel. Britain had the fuel resources of the Middle East and, at times, North America, even after the loss of those in the Dutch East Indies and Burma. Italy depended on the Balkans, and on whatever Germany would offer her increasingly despised ally. Fuel was to be one of the objectives in Germany's ill-judged thrust eastwards into the Soviet Union, and later in the war, as this failed, so the Italian war machine also suffered and eventually faltered.

While the Italian Navy must have understood that war was likely, and that the United Kingdom would be the most likely opponent from the start of the Abyssinian adventure in the mid-1930s, no official indication was given to the armed forces until

April, 1940, that Italy would expect to fight alongside the Germans. Mussolini listened to and consulted the army, who dominated the Supreme Command, leaving the sailors and airmen to do as they were told.

The Chief of the Italian Naval Staff, Admiral Domenico Cavagnari, also held the political post of Under Secretary of State for the Navy, and should have had great influence. He wrote to Mussolini, effectively complaining that entering a war once it had already started, meant that any chance of surprise had gone. In the circumstances, Italy was in a weak position. He thought that Britain and France could block the Mediterranean at both ends and starve Italy of the fuel and raw materials needed to survive, let alone prosecute a war, or seek combat, in which case both sides could expect heavy losses. He stressed the difficulties inherent on being dependent on the cooperation and goodwill of the Regia Aeronautica.

Undoubtedly a pessimistic forecast, but very realistic, and certainly more so than that of the Italian Army. A convoy system had to be hastily instigated, but here the lack of Italian preparation was soon to be felt, as often one or two warships would guard a number of merchantmen, but not only were such convoy escorts insufficient in numbers, they were often the wrong kind of vessel, as when cruisers escorted convoys but were unable to provide protection against submarines.

COULD GERMANY HAVE TAKEN OVER?

It soon became clear that Italy was completely unprepared for war and that in all probability many members of the armed forces had little appetite for it. After the raid on Taranto put three Italian battleships out of action, half the battle fleet, for the loss of just two aircraft, Hitler was shocked. He might have accepted such losses, albeit reluctantly, from a major naval battle, but that this had happened while the ships had been safely moored in a well protected port was beyond belief. His reaction was that the offending British warship, the aircraft carrier HMS *Illustrious*, had to be destroyed. A crack Luftwaffe unit, *Fliegerkorps X*, with extensive experience of anti-shipping operations, was moved to Italy at New Year 1941. It was this force that surprised the carrier and other units of the Mediterranean Fleet on 10 January 1941, causing such serious damage to the carrier that she had to limp into Malta for repairs, where she prompted such heavy aerial bombardment compared to what had been experienced in the first seven months of war with Italy, that it became known as the 'Illustrious Blitz', with the worst day of raids on 16 January.

Again, that spring, German troops had to take over from the Italians in Greece and Yugoslavia, even though this meant delaying the planned invasion of the Soviet Union, Operation Barbarossa, that had been so important to Hitler's plans. This was not a simple matter of delaying an operation, it was a matter of starting so late that the chances of attaining its objectives before the onset of the Russian winter were lost. The Germans were completely unprepared for the severity of the Russian winter, and had outrun their supply lines, and so this became the decisive front in the Second World War in Europe.

Yet, could the Italian fleet, or at least its most modern units, have helped make up the shortfall in Plan Z? The four modern battle-ships would have made up for the lack of the Plan Z ships, or would they?

While the Germans effectively took over northern Italy after Italian surrender, to have done so before hand would have been difficult. After Italian surrender, many Italians continued to fight alongside the Germans, often for a variety of motives, some of which were undoubtedly political while others may have felt uncertain about their prospects under the Allies. While it is open to question whether they would have stood by while the Germans took over the Regia Navale, or at least the best parts of it, it was also the case that the situation in 1943 was not the situation in 1940 or even 1941. As it was, the Germans had to content themselves with just a handful of Italian submarines after Italian surrender.

Even if the Germans had been able to 'acquire' the Italian warships, what would have happened then? No doubt the four ships of the Impero-class, 35,000 tons displacement and capable of 30.5 knots, with their nine 15-inch guns, would have been a good replacement for the *Bismarck* after she was sunk in May 1941, and given the Kriegsmarine the heavy ships it needed. They could even have transferred the crews of the *Scharnhorst* and *Gneisenau*, since the Italian ships had a heavier armament, but, unfortunately, the Italian ships did not have radar. By 1942, the shortage of fuel was becoming a serious issue, but in 1941, getting the ships out of the Mediterranean would have been difficult with Force H in the way of any Axis ships trying to make a dash for the Atlantic. Only if most of the Italian battle fleet had made a bid for the open seas through the Straits of Gibraltar would there have been any chance of success.

Indeed, at one stage, Hitler had contemplated seizing the British outpost of Gibraltar, itself difficult to defend from a determined attack. There was even a code-name for this, Operation Felix. But to have done this, he needed the support of his ally, the Spanish dictator Franco. Franco was determined at all costs not to involve Spain in the Second World War. His country had been ravaged during the Civil War, and wartime shortages affected even neutral nations, making recovery difficult. The schisms in Spanish society were still deep and any external distraction could have opened the way for renewed internal unrest. Spain could not even have allowed German forces access across its territory without becoming involved. Spain would not have been an asset to the Axis at the time, with its armed forces in a poor state and fit for little more than internal security duties. Internal communications in Spain at the time were poor, with bad roads and a dilapidated railway system, using a broader gauge, at 5 ft 6 ins, than in most of Europe, including Germany and France. This would have meant that an invasion would, for the most part, have had to be by sea, with few good landing positions for paratroops on Gibraltar other than the race course, which was quickly converted into an airfield by the British.

Of course, a gung ho scenario could have had the Italian battle fleet in German hands and Malta bombarded and then invaded. This could have worked if the Italians had pressed ahead with the operation in summer 1940, but it was politically unlikely that the Germans would have been able to take Malta even in 1941. After the heavy losses amongst German paratroops and glider-landed troops during the invasion of Crete, Hitler banned further airborne operations, and such a means of assault would have been necessary to take Malta because of the few good landing places for an amphibious assault.

In essence, with Mussolini failing to keep in step with him, Hitler had to face the fact that his ally was almost as much a liability as an asset. Italy gave the Germans well-located bases, such as the airfields in Sicily used by *Fliegerkorps X*, but little else. After the Allies landed in Italy, even this asset was lost and it simply meant that Germany had yet another front on which to fight.

CHAPTER TEN

Could Plan Z have been Achieved?

Plan Z was intended to enable the German Navy, the Kriegsmarine, play its major part in winning a war with the United Kingdom. It would have given the Germans mastery of the seas in the sense that they would tie down the entire Royal Navy, and indeed the British would be neutralised at sea and unable to obtain the food, fuel, raw materials and war materiel that they needed to remain in the war. It was never intended to be a complete rerun of the plans entertained by Imperial Germany to become the dominant maritime power in Europe, and not just the dominant continental power.

On the other hand, had Plan Z achieved its objectives, had Germany gained the much wanted *Lebensraum* in the east, as well as the food, fuel and raw materials of the eastern territories, as well as unifying the German communities scattered throughout Europe and providing an enlarged pool of dedicated manpower, Germany would soon have been able to consider absolute maritime domination and if not world domination, at least domination of Europe, the Middle East and Africa.

If a sense of realism had dawned, Germany would have not only happily accepted Japanese domination of the Far East and even, perhaps, Siberia and India, but also American domination of the Americas. On the other hand, would a sense of reality have dawned? After all, the Germans had been heavily involved in South America between the two world wars.

The question arises, could Plan Z ever have been achieved? Could it have attained its goals?

KRIEGSMARINE V LUFTWAFFE V ARMY

Although it was not allowed to function fully effectively, the Wehrmacht was the overall high command of the armed forces, in effect a form of defence ministry. It suited Hitler to allow each of his service chiefs to function independently and for him to become

Supreme Commander-in-Chief of the Armed Forces. Even before the attempt on his life, he did not encourage, indeed he was deeply suspicious of, any attempt by the armed forces' chiefs to meet and plan for fear that they might become a unified opposition to his plans. This was the paranoia of a dictator.

Of the armed forces, the old school of army officers were the most suspicious of Hitler. The Heeres, or Army, had been the dominant service and had included members of the best Prussian families, all very much old school. The Kriegsmarine, or War Navy, as Hitler had renamed the old Reichsmarine, had been very much the second service and it had been the Kaiser elevating it to equal status with the Army before the First World War that had helped provide a basis for achieving the aims of *Weltpolitik*. Having suffered mutiny in 1918 and after the end of the First World War, senior naval officers were enthusiastic about Hitler. Nevertheless, they had also learnt an important lesson about keeping out of and above politics during the difficult days of 1919 and 1920.

The only service that was deeply politicised was the Air Force, the Luftwaffe, and then possibly only at the very top. The Luftwaffe had been kept a secret until1935, and alone amongst the armed services owed both its birth and its autonomy from the two traditional services to Hitler. More than that, the Air Minister, Hermann Goering, was a close political intimate of the Fuhrer and designated his successor until almost the very end of the Reich. This friendship probably accounted for the small naval air arm, reduced to flying reconnaissance aircraft off battleships and cruisers, being incorporated into the Luftwaffe once the Second World War started.

The result of what has become known as the 'Fuhrer System', the lack of coordination between the services and the constant attempts by the individual service chiefs to catch the Fuhrer's attention and curry favour with him, was that each considered only its own needs. It was a case of divide and rule. Inter-service rivalry is a fact of life in every country, and attempts to dispense with it in unified armed forces have only worked in countries either with small and insignificant armed services or where one service is dominant, as in land-locked Switzerland, for example. Nevertheless, properly managed and controlled, inter-service rivalry can be a force for good, a case of establishing an effective *esprit de corps*, but left to its own devices and without control and coordination, it is destructive.

Unbridled inter-service rivalry was the situation in Germany in 1938.

It was not that the Wehrmacht did not have the means of co-ordinating activity. Hitler had created a new level of command with the Wehrmacht, for which the full title was the *Oberkommando Wehrmacht*, *OKW*, and within its organisation was a military-economic office. On the day the Munich Agreement was signed in October 1938, its director, Major-General Georg Thomas, received a telephone call telling him that he was to initiate preparations for war against Great Britain, with a target date of 1942, a full year before the earliest date promised by Hitler to the Kriegsmarine. Time was running out.

Preparation for war does not consist of manpower and equipment alone. In modern warfare, the nation's infrastructure such as railways and airfields and roads all make a difference. The American Civil War was the first in which railways were used, while the start of the First World War has often been referred to as being dependent on the railway timetables. The absence of port handling facilities in Malta during the Second World War was a major drawback when the convoys, or what was left of them, arrived. Then, there is industry, which needs to be placed on a war footing. It is both a question of having the right capacity and enough of it for the war needs of the day, and of a system for directing raw materials, fuel and labour. If food supplies are likely to be uncertain or simply insufficient, or to become too expensive, thus causing industrial and social unrest, rationing is necessary.

On 14 October 1938, Goering gathered together the senior officers of the Luftwaffe and senior managers from the aircraft industry in the conference hall of his Air Ministry. He referred obliquely to the 'world situation', and then told his audience that the Fuhrer had ordered a gigantic programme against which 'previous achievements are insignificant'.

Hitler wanted nothing less than a fivefold increase in the size of the Luftwaffe and as quickly as possible. Meanwhile, the Kriegsmarine was to accelerate its own expansion and the Army was to procure offensive weapons in large quantities, with special emphasis on heavy artillery and armoured vehicles. Industry was to place top priority on production of fuel, rubber and explosives, while railways, canals and roads were to be improved. These targets nevertheless left each of the armed services with considerable freedom to decide what they would like to do.

The results were predictable. The senior officers went away and set the planners to work. The army already had a four year programme to complete, begun in 1936 and due to end in 1940. The soldiers did not take long. On 20 October, the Army declared that in 1939, it would need 4.5 million tons of steel, a quarter of total German output. This increase in demand from just one of the armed forces was so out of step with the capability of industry and so unthinking of the demands of other sectors of the economy, that in fact it was not achieved until 1942 when the Battle of Stalingrad was at its height, and when it was already too late. In late twentieth and early twenty-first century Europe, the perception of Germany is one of efficiency with everything working well. In the inter-war period, it was an impoverished country, bankrupted by the strains of 'the war to end all wars' and by post-war reparations, and then by the worldwide depression. While much attention has focussed on the autobahns, the railways were in a poor state, Indeed, one of the early benefits of the invasion of the Low Countries and France was that the Germans were able to lay their hands on much-needed railway rolling stock.

As for Goering's pride and joy, the Luftwaffe, its fivefold expansion meant that within four years it was intended to have 21,750 aircraft, making it the largest peacetime air force in the world. The decision had been taken to abandon four-engined heavy bomber development in production in favour of light and medium bombers, and especially the Junkers Ju88 of which a force of no less than 7,000 was envisaged. The reasons for this were partly that light and medium bombers were quicker and cheaper to build, and partly because these were the type of bombers most useful in the concept of *blitzkrieg*, 'lightening war', which meant fast-moving advances spearheaded by the Panzer tank divisions with overwhelming close air support. Now, the Luftwaffe also wanted 800 Heinkel He177 heavy bombers, which would be protected by a heavy concentration of long-range escort fighters in addition to the Messerschmitt Bf109 interceptors.

The Kriegsmarine, determined not to be outdone, wanted a warship construction programme that would enable it to compete with the Royal Navy within six years, that is by 1944. Nor would it stop in 1944. The plan would continue so that by 1948, the Kriegsmarine would have 797 vessels, costing 33 million Reichmarks. This fleet would include six battleships and eight cruisers, as well as the initial figure of 249 U-boats. This materialised as Plan Z, and was approved by Hitler on 27 January 1939.

Such a massive fleet was indeed a shock to the German industrial system. Shipyards needed to be expanded to provide the building capacity needed. Massive new dry docks were needed at Hamburg and Wilhelmshaven. The island of Reugen was selected as a naval base, for which it would need to be hollowed out. It was not just the demand for steel and other metals presented by the construction programme, the construction programme itself and then the facilities for maintaining such a huge fleet also added to the demand.

Put bluntly, the country simply could not afford these programmes. Industry simply could not deliver, even if it stopped exporting and made the deteriorating balance of payments situation even worse. The predicament that faced the German leadership at this time was stark. The country could not afford to expand military production to the scale required, or even maintain existing production, but could not risk going to war without the equipment included in the programmes.

Even in August 1938 before the revised plans were prepared, the Reichsbank stated that: 'the means of a peacetime economy are no longer sufficient, one must instead begin to reach for the tougher measures of the war economy.'[1] This meant that civilian demand had to be curtailed, that economic and industrial planning and control had to be imposed. Many of the measures needed were those which Stalin and the Communists would have understood, and were in complete contrast to the mobilisation of US industry after Pearl Harbour. To drive the new regime, Goering created a new *Reichsverteidigungsrat*, Reich defence council, while the planning came from Major-General Thomas in the OKW.

The first meeting of the Reich Defence Council was on 18 November 1938, a little more than a month after Goering had demanded a massive increase in armaments. Thomas and his colleagues drafted Goering's opening speech. Those present were left in no doubt about the appalling economic situation, with the conflicting demands of rearmament and exports, the undermining of the public finances and the growing danger of inflation. Foreign exchange reserves were 'non-existent'. Despite this terrible position, nothing short of a crisis, the Fuhrer had called for a trebling of armaments production, so armaments production had to be trebled! Industry had to be mobilised for war.

Most wartime economies rely to a greater or lesser extent on the direction of labour. This started in Germany even before war began. At the meeting on 18 November, Goering announced that the entire population was registered on a national card index administered by General Kurt Deluege, the chief of the SS police. Labour offices would direct every adult in the country to their most productive form of labour. Tax administration would be simplified to release labour, and so too would the legal system. Construction projects sanctioned by the Fuhrer would be completed, but everything else would shut down. Factories would be inspected to ensure that they were operating at maximum efficiency. Only those motor vehicles of interest to the military could be produced. There would be strict pricing guidelines for all public contracts, and not just those for the military.

Oddly, in the light of what came later after the war began, the Jewish community was expected to make its full contribution, partly through a new wealth tax, but it was also clear that they would be meant to work. Acts of violence and destruction such as *Kristallnacht* would have no place in the mobilised German economy. It was even suggested that the entire population would be expected to make a special sacrifice through a single surrender of wealth to the nation.

Once again, it was another example of the old saying 'Communists nationalise property, Fascists nationalise people', and this was the gist of it.

In December 1938, Goering appointed Fritz Todt to head the entire construction sector and ensure that rearmament was the absolute priority. By spring 1939, out of a total turnover in the construction industry of 12 billion Reichsmarks, no less than half was reserved for the Wehrmacht, 20 per cent for industry and 10 per cent for public construction projects, leaving just 20 per cent for housing, and even this was seized and allocated to accommodation for workers in the defence industries.

By the same token, the owners of privately-owned shipyards were told that the Kriegsmarine had the absolute power of veto over any other work.

Even if the massive effort had been directed to fulfilling the needs of just *one* of the three armed services, it would have been im-possible. The estimate for the fivefold increase in the size of the Luftwaffe amounted to 60 billion Reichsmarks, which meant that Luftwaffe expenditure alone between 1938 and 1942 would be 50 per cent more than that for the entire Wehrmacht between 1933 and 1938.[2] The Luftwaffe never got its 21,750 aircraft, and if it had, it wouldn't have been able to find trained personnel for them. The

Luftwaffe seldom had more than 5,000 aircraft at any stage in the Second World War. The United States Army Air Force, the most powerful air force engaged in the Second World War, peaked at 21,000 combat aircraft, and the Soviet Union only managed 17,000 in April 1945.

As for the Kriegsmarine's Plan Z, one of the problems was creating enough fuel storage capacity. To ensure that operations were not interrupted, it was estimated that the Kriegsmarine needed 9.6 million cubic metres of fuel capacity which would have to be protected from the effects of enemy action. In 1936, it was estimated that, given the expansion plans of the time, the Kriegsmarine would need 1.4 million tons of oil annually, and a further 400,000 tons of diesel oil. Under Plan Z, by 1948, it would need 6 million tons of fuel oil, and no less than 2 million tons of diesel fuel. Domestic production was estimated to produce no more than 2 million tons of oil and 1.34 million tons of diesel fuel by 1948. Not only would this not be sufficient for the Kriegsmarine, it did not take into account the needs of the Luftwaffe, the Army, the railways and electric power generation, or civilian transport! The Fuhrer envisaged exploiting the resources of the east, but Germany had to get there first.

THE MONEY RUNS OUT

Even as early as 1938, with the Sudeten crisis unfolding, the financial situation was grim. The government could not even raise money by a bond issue. Foreign investors kept away from a country that could be involved in a major war. The mood changed after the Munich Crisis and the resulting agreement. For the rest of October, the Reichsbank was able to borrow the money it needed from the German public, and almost 2 billion of Reichsmarks bonds were offered and snapped up. At the end of November, the mood changed. A further offering of 1.5 billion Reichsmarks in bonds failed, with only around two-thirds taken up. The problem was that the Reich had returned to the market requesting more loans too soon. It could also be that news of the impending armaments build up must have leaked out and the implications readily understood.

There was another problem. The markets had provided the money that the government needed in October, and struggled to do so the following month. Meanwhile, German industry, anxious to expand to meet the demands being placed upon it, found that the market had dried up, and could not raise the additional capital it needed.

131

If a government cannot borrow money when it needs it, it has to cut spending, or raise taxes, or a combination of both. The alternative is to print money, thus fuelling inflation.

Meanwhile, other problems emerged. As early as 24 November 1938, the virtual collapse of the export programme and the means of earning much needed foreign exchange, put pressure on the allocation of raw materials for the armaments plan. This was the day that the armed forces were told that their steel allocation for 1939 would have to be cut back from 530,000 tons to 300,000 tons. The Army was to be worst hit, with a steel allocation little better than that of 1937, and what was worse, the types of steel it needed most would be the most severely curtailed. To make matters worse, in January 1939, the Army and the Luftwaffe learnt that the Kriegsmarine was to have priority. By spring, orders for ammunition for the Army were being cancelled, less than six months before the planned invasion of Poland! Production of medium battle tanks was cut in half. The situation continued to worsen, with mortar shells no longer produced and ammunition production for infantry weapons almost drying up. During 1939–1940, 61,000 Model 34 light machine guns were due to be produced, but in the end, the Army received just 13,000. The Army had sufficient ammunition stockpiled for just fourteen days of heavy fighting.

By the end of 1939, the first winter of war, 300 infantry battalions lacked proper barracks or garages for their vehicles. Germany's Army was so large that a part of it could only spend the winter under canvas. Even without these problems, the planning still left the German Army in a poor state of mechanisation. The image of fast-moving Panzer divisions was not without foundation, but the bulk of the Army depended on railways being available, and away from the rail heads, transport was largely horse-drawn. Even artillery pieces depended on authentic horsepower rather than the mechanical variety.

In short, almost a third of Germany's 105 divisions were seriously under equipped. Some 90 per cent of training units were without weapons.

This was happening in a planned economy with everyone capable of work being forced into a job, but the net result was that more than 100,000 highly skilled armaments workers were being laid off.

The Luftwaffe was suffering similar problems. The total of 21,750 aircraft was kept simply by postponing deliveries and adjusting the plan so that increasingly, deliveries were moved to the later years. In December 1938, the Luftwaffe was due to receive 10,000 aircraft in the year ahead, but in January 1939 this figure was cut to 8,299 aircraft, with the air force's allocation of aluminium cut by a third. The copper allocation was cut by 50 per cent, and then finally, in July 1939, reduced to just 20 per cent of what had been promised. That month a further 20 per cent cut in aircraft production was imposed, with the sole exception being production of the Junkers Ju88, and to compensate for that, it was planned to phase out the older Ju87, the famous Stuka dive-bomber.

Freed from all of these cuts was the Kriegsmarine, protected by the Fuhrer's endorsement of Plan Z. The problem was that warships take longer than any other item of military equipment to produce, so there was little to see immediately for all the steel and copper that was being absorbed by the shipyards.

WAR BRINGS REALITY

The dream world of ever rising armaments production came to an end along with all hopes of being able to avoid war with Great Britain and France following the invasion of Poland. Late on 3 September 1939, Hitler, who had been so enthusiastic about Plan Z, abandoned it. Only those capital ships capable of being completed during 1940 were spared, all other work on major surface units was stopped immediately, including Germany's first aircraft carrier, the *Graf Zeppelin*. The major dockyards at Bremen, Kiel and Hamburg were ordered to switch production immediately to a standard design of U-boat, the Type VII. The new U-boat programme called for the production of no less than twenty-five vessels each month and for this, the Kriegsmarine was to receive priority in the allocation of materials, but in fact it took more than a year for production to build up. As it was, as Dönitz had predicted, the U-boats were cheaper and quicker to build, and also needed less materials, so that throughout the war, the Kriegsmarine received no more than 15 per cent of total armaments expenditure. The Luftwaffe and the Army received priority for the rest of the war. The Luftwaffe alone was to receive 40 per cent of armaments expenditure.

All hope of Germany emerging as a maritime power vanished with the onset of war, for it was continental power that now mattered.

Even the policy of concentrating on the U-boats was not set in concrete. As the war progressed, in March 1942, reality dawned,

133

when finally the Germans began to appreciate that, without naval air power, their remaining major surface units were at serious risk, especially from British aircraft carriers. Operation Barbarossa had not only failed to achieve its initial objectives and had left German army and air force units bogged down in the Soviet Union, but worse, the Allies had started to support the Soviet Union, sending convoys to Murmansk and Archangel, to Vladivostok, and to the Persian Gulf, with supplies moved by railway through present day Iran and into the southern Soviet republics. The convoys to Russia were now recognised as being significant. There was little the Germans could do about the Gulf and Siberia convoys, but they could tackle those to Murmansk and Archangel, and Hitler himself called for this supply line to be cut, believing that renewed Russian counter-attacks were made possible by the supplies being carried by the convoys. In 1942, work, abandoned because of Luftwaffe/Kriegsmarine rivalry, on the aircraft carrier *Graf Zeppelin*, was ordered to restart, while the Hipper-class cruiser *Seydlitz* was prepared for conversion to an aircraft carrier and the liners *Potsdam*, *Europa* and *Gneisenau*, which presumably would have had to be renamed to avoid confusion with the battlecruiser, considered for conversion to auxiliary carriers. With *Seydltz*, work progressed as far as having her superstructure removed and the hull taken to Konigsberg, but the order was rescinded early in 1943 and later the hull was scuttled, which seems an incredible waste of valuable scrap metal. Meanwhile, the U-boats and the Luftwaffe were to take the burden of countering the Arctic convoys.

It would have taken more than six months for the *Graf Zeppelin* to be completed, more than a year for *Seydltz* and the three liners to be converted, depending on the resources that Germany could commit. The aircraft could have been made available, but without any prior experience or expertise, landing high performance Messerschmitt Bf109s on the carriers would have been a painful and costly lesson, although prototypes of the carrier variant, the Bf109T, were completed. The Junkers Ju87 Stuka dive-bombers, of which the carrier version was the Ju87C, would have been easier and could have made an excellent carrier strike aircraft, although by this time it was slower than the latest naval aircraft being supplied by the United States. Learning lessons about carrier operations would have been best done during the closing years of peace.

There were some interesting features of the planned German

naval aircraft. The Ju87C, for example, not only was equipped for catapult operations, but also the fixed landing gear could be jettisoned for an emergency landing in the sea. British experience with aircraft with fixed landing gear, on aircraft such as the Fairey Swordfish, was that ditching the aircraft required careful flying, but it was possible to do it safely providing that the tailplane was kept low, otherwise the aircraft would somersault.

After plans for conversion of the cruiser and the liners were abandoned early in 1943, the *Graf Zeppelin* was finally cancelled, remaining afloat but without fitting out she was unserviceable. Her catapults were stripped out and sent to Italy for use in the planned Italian aircraft carrier, *Aquila*, converted from the passenger liner *Roma*, but she too was never completed. While policy had swung in favour of aircraft carriers again, it had been but briefly, before being reversed. Given the shortage of materials and the impact on production of Allied bombing, the stop-start nature of these decisions and the change in policy was wasteful.

The truth was that Germany was no longer in command of events.

Notes
1 Bundesarchiv Lichterfelde Branch.
2 Tooze, Adam, *The Wages of Destruction*, Allen Lane, London, 2006

CHAPTER ELEVEN

Battles with Plan Z

Speculating on how Plan Z may have changed the outcome of the Second World War, or changed the way in which events unfolded at sea, is difficult. This is not just because everything assumes that war did indeed break out after 1943, or even that one has to take into account the changes in the strength of both the Royal Navy and the French Navy in the intervening years, but there is the question about just how much the German naval planners understood about the integration of a more balanced fleet and the way in which it could be used in operations.

For a start, Dönitz had rightly assumed that naval air power would have to be not only under naval control, but those wielding it would have had to be members of the Kriegsmarine. In this he was undoubtedly right, as the British Admiralty had not simply discovered, but had agitated for control of its own aviation for some years. What is strange is that despite the interest in naval aviation, seldom did the Germans coordinate maritime-reconnaissance with the deployment and operation of the U-boat hunting packs.

The problem was that in Germany, Hitler's close associate Hermann Goering was Air Minister, and used his influence to maintain control of all German service aviation. Even the small naval air arm, restricted to the role of providing reconnaissance and gunnery observation from battleships, battlecruisers, *Panzerschiffe* and cruisers, was transferred to the Luftwaffe shortly after war broke out. A similar situation existed in Italy, but not in Japan, interestingly enough. Indeed, by contrast, the Japanese did not have an autonomous air force as such, but instead divided all service aviation between the Imperial Japanese Navy and the Imperial Japanese Army. This policy in turn was far from ideal as it led to overlap and duplication.

Goering's supremacy over service aviation did not mean that he developed a truly autonomous air service capable of exercising strategic air power. The opposite was the case. The Luftwaffe was tied to the tactical needs of supporting ground forces while also providing maritime-reconnaissance and anti-shipping strikes for the Kriegsmarine. This worked wonderfully when the Germans struck east into Poland, and again when they seized Denmark and even when they launched the amphibious and air-landed invasion of Norway, and again worked well in the invasion of Luxembourg, the Low Countries and France. It was far less successful when the Battle of Britain started, and again failed in the Blitz on British towns and cities. This problem was known to senior officers, and while resources had been concentrated in light and medium bombers before the war, in October 1938, when optimist plans were laid for expansion of the armaments programme, a strategic heavy bomber force was planned. When the Heinkel He177 heavy bomber finally did enter service, there were too few of them and too late, and the aircraft was chronically unreliable.

It can be argued, with much justification, that the Battle of Britain failed because the attack on British airfields ended too soon, allowing RAF Fighter Command to recover. There is a lot of truth in this. Nevertheless, the German fighter pilots once they reached the skies of Southern England that summer of 1940 were at a profound disadvantage compared to their RAF counterparts, they were short of fuel. While the Allies struggled in the early years of the strategic bombing campaign because of the lack of long-range escort fighters, the Germans would not have needed such a long range in 1940 flying from their bases in France across the English Channel, but they still did not have the range. They left their bomber formations with less protection than necessary. True, many German bomber pilots accused their fighter escorts of preferring to dog fight with the RAF than protect them, but the RAF had a two-prong strategy, whenever possible leaving the bombers to the Hurricane squadrons and the fighters to the Spitfires, and had the Messerschmitt Bf109 pilots tried to stick with the bombers, they would have suffered even higher casualties – when combat was offered, they had no choice.

It can also be argued that the Blitz ended too soon because the Luftwaffe was diverted from the operations against British cities and eastwards towards the Soviet Union. This was true, and not just for Great Britain, but for Malta as well. Nevertheless, at no stage could the Luftwaffe bring the maximum force to bear on the raids, and this was simply because they lacked a strategic heavy bomber. The bomb loads carried by individual Luftwaffe aircraft seldom exceeded 4,000-lbs, while the RAF routinely had loads of 8,000-lbs or more. The 8,000-lb 'Double Cookie' was more effective than two 4,000-lb bombs. Ignore the 14,000-lb Tallboy and 22,000-lb Grand Slam for the purposes of this argument, for effective though these were, these were for special operations, it was the ability to send bombers with heavy loads night after night, and over a short period send more than a thousand of these for several nights, that proved so devastating. Aerial photographs of air raid damage to German cities show far worse destruction than visited on British cities. Even the Heinkel He111, Dornier Do17s and Junkers Ju88s did not appear in large enough numbers or sufficient concentration of force compared to the RAF. When the Heinkel He177 finally did arrive, it was in insufficient numbers to affect the outcome. And when the United States Army Air Force joined in, the end was obvious.

When Operation Barbarossa started, the lack of true strategic air power once again affected the outcome. While Stalin famously ignored warnings about the pending German assault, the Soviet Union had nevertheless moved much of its heavy industry east of the Urals, where almost all of it was beyond the reach of German bombers. It was not just that Hitler was fighting wars on two fronts in defiance of his own policies and of military theory, it was that the Germans were as ill-prepared for this campaign as they were for the campaign at sea. On the ground, German troops lacked adequate equipment for winter operations and the Luftwaffe lacked the right kind of bombs, with many shattering on the frozen ground in winter, but even before this, supply lines were dangerously over-stretched and aircraft did not have the range to cripple Soviet industry and communications.

The Eastern Front was a front too far. Yet Germany had little choice, for without the food, fuel and raw materials it could provide, the war machine would grind to a halt. Yet, with this additional burden, Germany was increasingly vulnerable and her forces over-stretched.

What would have happened firstly, if war had not broken out when it did with the United Kingdom and France again offering appeasement, allowing time for at least part of Plan Z to be implemented? What would have happened if the balanced fleet that Plan Z had offered had been available at the major naval engagements between the Kriegsmarine and the Royal Navy?

APPEASEMENT AGAIN

If September 1939 had started with frantic diplomatic exchanges between London and Paris, and with Berlin, perhaps with the realisation amongst the European Allies that United States support could not be guaranteed, appeasement may well have been an option. The surveys of public opinion by Mass Observation at the time of Munich showed that appeasement was not unpopular with a public that dreaded a repeat of the First World War. On the eve of the war, it also found that the public then, as now, believed Britain's armed forces to be stronger and in better shape than was in fact the case. In the early twenty-first century, such attitudes spring from indifference and a failure to recognise a threat, while in 1939, these attitudes were the result of jingoism and a firm belief on the invincibility of the British Empire.

The remaining years of peace had not been wasted by the British government, which had reluctantly come to recognise the growing threat from Germany and Italy, while Japanese ambitions were also increasingly understood. Two First World War allies were now aligned against Britain and France. Neither Italy nor Japan had played a significant part in the First World War, although Italy had engaged Austro-Hungarian forces and Japan had sent destroyers to reinforce the British Mediterranean Fleet. Nevertheless, both countries deployed powerful forces and in their respective theatres of war, were far stronger than the British forces that could be deployed against them, even taking into account the French presence in the Mediterranean and those of Australia, New Zealand and India in the Far East and the Pacific.

The Royal Navy in 1939 still had one of the world's largest fleets of aircraft carriers, but the original ships were obsolete and in reserve. *Furious* and *Argus* were conversions, showing their age, but suitable for training, or as aircraft transports, and could also be used for escort work. The first aircraft carrier designed as such, *Hermes*, was too small and too slow, although again, she could have been a useful escort, but under wartime pressures, she was pushed into the frontline searching for German commerce raiders and was off Ceylon when the Japanese Navy Air Force found her in 1942. *Courageous* and *Glorious*, which had both started life as sister ships of *Furious* before conversion from battlecruisers, were limited and really due for withdrawal once the generation of new aircraft carriers entered service, but again were retained under wartime pressures. They didn't last long, with *Courageous* being torpedoed and sunk just two weeks after the outbreak of war, and *Glorious* being sunk by the twin battlecruisers, *Scharnhorst* and *Gneisenau*, during the withdrawal from Norway.

Nevertheless, six aircraft carriers that were larger, faster and heavily armoured were on order, as was a depot or support ship that was designed to operate as an aircraft carrier if necessary, HMS *Unicorn*. The first six ships, of the Illustrious and Implacable-classes, were described by many as the best aircraft carriers of the Second World War, but *Unicorn* was also useful and during the war mostly served as an aircraft carrier. These ships, with the last pre-war carrier, *Ark Royal*, which had an impressive aircraft capacity but a weak flight deck, already more than matched the planned four large aircraft carriers and four smaller ships incorporated in the final years of Plan Z.

No less impressively, the Admiralty before the war had already started to worry about not having enough flight decks and was looking at merchant ships for conversion, including the new fast Cunard liners, *Queen Mary* and *Queen Elizabeth*, but these were considered to be of greater use as troopships. By 1941, before Hitler's promised date for the commencement of hostilities with the British Empire, the Admiralty was already ready to order aircraft carriers that could be produced quickly and easily in yards accustomed to merchant shipbuilding. In between, the merchant aircraft carriers or MAC-ships and the escort carriers, not all of which came from the United States, were ordered.

Meanwhile, France would have been able to complete the *Joffre* and the *Painleve*, and possibly add two more ships of this design to the Marine Nationale had war been delayed.

In fact, the two Allies, and the Royal Navy in particular, showed a greater ability to act and improvise, and make the best of what they had got, than was the case with the Germans. Obsolete 'C'-class cruisers from the First World War were converted by the Royal Navy into anti-aircraft cruisers, ideal for convoy escort and recognising the fact that they would be hopelessly outclassed in a fleet action. Meanwhile, the impressive Town-class cruisers, classed as 'heavy' despite having 6-in main armament, doubtless because they had up to twelve guns in four turrets, were entering service. The new class of battleship, the King George V-class, were useful, although the main armament was reduced to 14-in due to a pre-war decision to reduce the maximum calibre of guns aboard battleships, but more of a reminder that even in this field, the Germans would find that the Royal Navy had progressed, as would have had the French, completing the *Jean Bart*.

Of course, the question arises, would the British and French electorates have objected to continuing high levels of defence expenditure without a war being fought? Undoubtedly, appeasement would have encouraged Hitler to continue to take risks and advance the boundaries of the Reich ever eastward and also southward. Poland was a relatively new ally of the British, but modern Greece was another area of British influence. There were also links with Yugoslavia through the royal houses of both countries. An attack by Hitler on the Soviet Union would have had Communists and fellow travellers in both the Allied countries pressing for war.

Nevertheless, while it was the case that Germany could not afford the war economy in peacetime, and could only do so in wartime if the territory that she gained yielded prizes in the form of industrial capacity, raw materials, food and fuel, the British and French economies were in a condition that was not so different. It has long been said that in 1939, British politicians and their advisers knew that the country could only win a long war, but could only afford a short one. The level of rearmament in both countries in 1938 and 1939 was exceeding the capacity of both the British and the French economies to absorb the costs. When war came, it was funded not just by heavy taxation and borrowing from the British public, not just by Lend-Lease from the United States, but by heavy borrowing from the wealthier members of the British Empire and the use of their sterling balances.

It is possible; therefore, that only those warships ordered in 1938 and 1939 would have entered service, and that, without going to war, defence expenditure would have begun to be cut back by 1940, or, *would have had* to be cut back. Certainly, the mobilisation of reservists would have had to be reversed under pressure from industry and, no doubt, their families, as well as the need to retain export markets. The last-mentioned has been a factor already mentioned in the case of Germany, but it was so important that even at the height of the Second World War, Britain continued to export a wide variety of goods, and especially consumer goods. Whisky still crossed the North Atlantic, and naval personnel going for a 'run ashore' in places such as Cape Town in South Africa, would find in the shops, freely on sale, items that were unobtainable at home. One member of the Fleet Air Arm rejoiced in being able to buy his mother and sisters knicker elastic.

141

BATTLE OF THE RIVER PLATE REVISITED

The first naval engagement of the Second World War was the Battle of the River Plate, which saw three cruisers, HMS *Ajax*, her Royal New Zealand Navy-manned sister *Achilles*, and the heavy cruiser *Exeter*, so damage the *Panzerschiff Graf Spee* that she was eventually scuttled by her commanding officer in the estuary of the River Plate. This was a brilliant action, and while minor in terms of the numbers of ships involved, was a much-needed fillip to British morale. The icing on the cake came the following year in Norwegian waters with the *Altmark* incident, when the Royal Navy rescued the Merchant Navy personnel who had been taken prisoners-of-war by the *Graf Spee*.

Had the *Graf Spee* been operating with even a small carrier with an air group embarked, the outcome could have been different. First, she would have been even more successful in her commerce raiding, finding merchant shipping along the sea lanes linking the United Kingdom with the Argentine and Uruguay, both major sources of beef for British consumers. Second, had good well-planned reconnaissance missions been flown, it is unlikely that the three cruisers would have come within firing range. They could even have become victims themselves.

On the other hand, would a *Panzerschiff*, after all only a 'pocket battleship', been allocated an aircraft carrier. Plan Z only specified four aircraft carriers in the early years, with four smaller ships following in the mid-1940s. The addition of an aircraft carrier would have required extra supply ships, which would in turn have had to be protected during their long passage between Germany and the South Atlantic. At first, some of these might have masqueraded as ordinary merchantmen, but their cover would have been blown sooner or later.

In fact, it is unlikely that the outcome of the Battle of the River Plate would have been any different. Aircraft carrier protection would have been most unlikely. Even if merchant ships had been converted to provide auxiliary carriers, these would have been unlikely to have kept up with the fast-moving *Graf Spee*, and might not have had her long range.

On the other hand, had some of the ideas of the U-boat enthusiasts at the *Marineleitung* been fulfilled before war broke out, the presence of long-range submarines and supply submarines might well have changed the outcome. First, there might not have been the battle at all, and the three cruisers would have been vulnerable confronting a submarine. Operating submarines at such extreme range from a base would have been difficult, but it could have changed the pattern of the war completely. Indeed, what needed to be recognised was that the day of the surface vessel as a commerce raider had ended. As the war progressed, the German auxiliary cruisers, all of which intended to act as commerce raiders rather than as convoy escorts, in contrast to Royal Navy practice, were soon put out of action by British and American warships.

HAMPERING THE WITHDRAWAL FROM NORWAY

There can be no doubt that the German invasion of Norway showed considerable skill and planning with excellent use of the resources available, just as the armed forces were preparing for the launch of the offensive in the west. Amphibious warfare was in its infancy, with little progress over the means used at Gallipoli. While they lost the troop transport *Bhicker*, carrying the main headquarters staff, at Oslo, to Norwegian fire, the lack of an aircraft carrier was not a serious problem at first. It might have made the entire operation easier and completion faster, especially since good airfields ashore were few and far between. This was also a problem for the Allies, and had the Royal Navy had high performance fighters aboard its carriers deployed at short notice to Norway, the outcome might just have been different.

At the outset of the campaign, however, there was one naval engagement that might have had a different outcome had the Germans had an aircraft carrier operating with the two battle-cruisers *Scharnhorst* and *Gneisenau*. On 9 April 1940, the battlecruiser HMS *Renown* was off northern Norway accompanied by nine destroyers when the two German ships were sighted. At 04.05, at nine miles, *Renown* opened fire, and shortly afterwards she hit *Gneisenau* and put the German ship's main armament out of action. The Germans withdrew, but *Renown* gave chase at 29 knots despite a rising sea and snow squalls. Her destroyer escort, unable to maintain high speed in the prevailing conditions, were diverted to cover the entrance to the Vestfjord. *Renown* scored further hits on *Gneisenau* before contact was lost at 06.30 in appalling conditions.

This action was inconclusive as no losses were incurred, but the much older and lightly protected *Renown*, originally commissioned in 1916, faced an enemy force that was in many ways superior, for while she had 15-in guns against the 11-in of the German ships, there were two of them and 11-in shells could have penetrated her light armour. On the other hand, had an aircraft carrier been with the German ships, before the weather closed in, they could have detected *Renown*, denied her the chance of surprise, and even mounted a successful attack.

The need to withdraw from Norway to reinforce British and French troops fighting in France came so late and took so long that the Dunkirk evacuation was completed as the last troops withdrew from Norway. The withdrawal was marred by the loss of the British aircraft carrier *Glorious* on 8 June to gunfire from *Scharnhorst* and *Gneisenau*. *Glorious* was completely unprepared for the engagement, having her aircraft struck down into the hangar deck, no reconnaissance sorties being flown and not even the crow's nest manned by a lookout, while she had no radar. She was sunk despite a courageous and sacrificial attack on the German battlecruisers by the carrier's destroyer escorts, *Acasta* and *Ardent*.

Again, a carrier hunting with the two German battlecruisers could have struck at *Glorious* before she could have mounted a defence. Even more important, the other aircraft carrier engaged in the evacuation from Norway was the new *Ark Royal*, fast but with a fatal weakness, a thin and weak flight deck through which bombs would have penetrated without difficulty. Both ships could have been sunk by naval air power.

THE BISMARCK ENGAGEMENT

If any German warship justified being paired with an aircraft carrier, it was the battleship *Bismarck*, the pride of the Kriegsmarine when she entered service. *Bismarck* had an official net displacement of 46,000 tonnes and a full load displacement of 50,955 tonnes, although a post-war USN assessment put the latter figure at closer to 53,000 tonnes. Her reconnaissance aircraft were four single-engined Arado Ar196 monoplane floatplanes, capable of flying at almost 200mph. *Bismarck* had a complement of 2,200 men. Her value to the Germans can be judged by the fact that she was escorted by the heavy cruiser, *Prinz Eugen*.

On 18 May 1941, the two ships left the German port of Gotenhafen for a commerce raiding operation under the command of Captain Lindemann with Admiral Gunther Lutjens in overall charge, for a commerce-raiding mission, code-named 'Operation Rhine Exercise'. *Bismarck*'s fuel tanks were not completely full since a hose had given way and interrupted fuelling and even when she called at Korsfjord in Norway, no more fuel was taken on, possibly because it was not available. After leaving Norway, the German ships were shadowed by two heavy cruisers, *Suffolk* and *Norfolk*, and using radar these managed to track the Germans in heavy seas. Vice-Admiral Holland took the battlecruiser *Hood*, and the new battleship *Prince of Wales*, planning to bring the Germans to battle. On 24 May, the four ships met in the Denmark Strait for a classic naval engagement. Only minutes into the battle, *Hood* blew up, generally believed to have been caused by a shell from *Prinz Eugen* penetrating one of her magazines, with the loss of 1,500 men, leaving just three survivors. *Prince of Wales*, still not fully worked up, was forced to retire after taking several hits from the German ships. The engagement was not completely one-sided as *Bismarck* was hit three times, breaking the connections to the engine rooms from the forward fuel tanks. Lutjens was forced to break company with the *Prinz Eugen* and head for St Nazaire, in occupied France.

Norfolk and *Suffolk* had continued to track *Bismarck*. At 21.30 GMT, 22.30 British Summer Time, nine Fairey Swordfish from HMS *Victorious* found the *Bismarck* and launched a torpedo attack. A torpedo dropped at close range hit the armour belt at the waterline amidships, doing little damage but killing a warrant officer and injuring six engineers. The attack was followed by a brief gunnery exchange with the *Prince of Wales* before nightfall.

On 25 May, Force H left Gibraltar under the command of Vice-Admiral Sir James Somerville, with the aircraft carrier *Ark Royal*, the battlecruiser *Renown* and two cruisers. Contact with the *Bismarck* was lost early on 26 May, until an RAF Consolidated Catalina flying-boat rediscovered the ship. Early in the afternoon, in rough weather, fifteen Swordfish took off from the *Ark Royal*, but attacked *Sheffield* by mistake. Meanwhile, closing in on the *Bismarck* was Admiral Tovey, commander-in-chief of the Royal Navy's Home Fleet, with the battleships *King George V* and *Rodney* accompanied by a destroyer escort. At 19.15, again in low cloud and poor visibility, a further strike by fifteen Swordfish was launched from *Ark Royal*. This time two torpedoes struck the ship, one immediately after the other, jamming the rudder and sending the ship into a continuous turn.

A night torpedo attack on the *Bismarck* by destroyers caused little further damage. On the morning of 27 May, *King George V* and *Rodney* engaged the *Bismarck* in a final gunnery duel, hitting the *Bismarck* several times and after ninety minutes she was burning fiercely. Two cruisers then torpedoed the stricken ship, after which Captain Lindemann gave the order to abandon her.

Once again, the presence of naval aircraft could have changed the outcome as decisively for the Germans as they did for the British. The two heavy cruisers, *Norfolk* and *Suffolk*, could have found that they were being tracked and even attacked. This would have made it more difficult for *Prince of Wales* and *Hood* to find the *Bismarck*, but not necessarily made it impossible. Would a classic naval engagement have developed, or would the German carrier-borne aircraft have attempted a torpedo attack on the two British ships? One possible scenario would have been that the engagement that did develop could have been a forerunner of the Battle of the Coral Sea, with strikes flown by carrier-borne aircraft from, say, the *Graf Zeppelin* and the *Ark Royal*. In such conditions, the Junkers Ju87 Stuka would have been superior to the Fairey Swordfish. Whether or not the Messerschmitt Bf109 would have proved a good carrier fighter is open to doubt, as the aircraft had a weak tail section and would have found the arduous conditions of carrier landings diffi-cult to sustain. On the other hand, *Ark Royal* had a thin flight deck, which on one occasion was breached when a 20-lb practice bomb fell off the wing of an aircraft, killing personnel in the hangar below. The Admiralty was fully aware that this ship was vulnerable to air attack. Certainly, she could not have survived an attack such as that endured by *Illustrious* off Malta in January 1941.

THE INVASION OF CRETE
The German airborne invasion of Crete started on 20 May 1941, led for the first time in history by the Luftwaffe rather than by seaborne troops. The initial assault was by paratroops and air-landed troops, many of whom arrived by glider but, as airfields were taken, the ubiquitous Junkers Ju52/3 trimotor transports also ferried in men and supplies. The rationale behind awarding the operation to the Luftwaffe was sound. Discovering that most of the British and Greek forces defending the island were deployed on the coast, expecting a seaborne invasion, Goering had persuaded Hitler that the Luftwaffe, which included Germany's paratroops, could mount the invasion, leaving the German army and navy to support it. In the event, despite the defenders losing their heavy weaponry and communications equipment in Greece, the invasion proved so costly for Germany that for a time Hitler forbade any further airborne assaults. The loss of paratroops and glider-landed

146

troops was bad enough, but the Royal Navy seriously disrupted the convoys bringing troops and heavy equipment by sea, wiping out one major convoy and sinking the heavily laden but unwieldy caiques. Typical of the fate suffered by the seaborne force was the action on the night of 21/22 May, when the cruisers *Ajax*, *Dido* and *Orion* with four destroyers completely destroyed one convoy carrying troops and munitions. The Luftwaffe responded on 22 May with another crippling attack on the Mediterranean Fleet, sinking the cruisers *Fiji* and *Gloucester* and a destroyer, and badly damaging *Warspite* and the cruisers *Carlisle* and *Naiad*. Cunningham sent the battleships *Queen Elizabeth* and *Barham* with nine destroyers to attack Axis airfields in the Dodecanese, with attacks by aircraft from *Formidable*, but by this time the carrier's air power was seriously limited due to a shortage of aircraft, and she could do little to defend herself when the Luftwaffe turned its attentions to her, causing serious damage.

Could the Germans have used aircraft carriers for a more effective assault on Crete? Undoubtedly additional air power would have been welcome, and could have reduced the loss of German surface forces in the invasion. On the other hand, would such ships have been able to reach Crete? Even if they managed to pass the British Isles and cross the Bay of Biscay without interference from the Royal Navy or the Royal Air Force, they would have had to clear the Straits of Gibraltar and then pass between Malta and either Sicily or Libya. At the very least, Malta would have had to be invaded or neutralised first before making such a passage in wartime. Once past Malta, the aircraft carrier or carriers would have been vulnerable to attack by both shore-based aircraft from Egypt and from HMS *Formidable*. Even the latter suffered grievously in the Battle for Crete, and for the second time during the war in the Mediterranean, a British aircraft carrier was damaged beyond local repair and *Formidable* had to be sent away.

It is difficult to believe that even had aircraft carriers been available, that such a valuable fleet asset would have been risked by the Germans even for a target as tempting as Crete. The ultimate goal, of course, was to make life for British forces in Egypt as difficult as possible with the Suez Canal being the real prize, and always with the tempting possibility that, by changing the balance of power in the Near East, Turkey might have been persuaded to enter the war. With Turkey as an ally, the invasion of the Soviet Union, Operation Barbarossa, would have had an even greater chance of success – indeed, it may even have been that this was the missing but vital link in ensuring success given the forces available to Hitler at the time and the limited amount of time available for achieving the objectives of the invasion. The other vital link in ensuring a successful invasion of the Soviet Union would have been to damage the supply lines through what was then Persia to the USSR. Perhaps these would have been the best target for the aircraft carrier, with ships and long-range maritime-reconnaissance aircraft based on Madagascar hitting at the Allied convoys in the Indian Ocean heading for the Persian Gulf.

THE CHANNEL DASH

Despite the absence of an aircraft carrier, the fast battlecruisers *Scharnhorst* and *Gneisenau* still posed a major threat to British shipping in the Atlantic and the Bay of Biscay. In 1940, they had accounted for twenty-two ships, totalling 116,000 tons. The Royal Navy had forced them to take refuge at Brest, in occupied France, along with the heavy cruiser *Prinz Eugen*, where the RAF had repeatedly bombed them, causing some damage but unable to ensure their destruction with the bombs available at the time. Hitler decided to return the three ships to northern waters where they would be safer, and could be used against the Arctic convoys, but instead of taking the long route around the west of Ireland, on the Fuhrer's orders, on 12 February 1942, the ships were sent through the Straits of Dover. Delays in detecting the ships and communications difficulties over mounting an attack meant that a force of just six Swordfish from No 825 Naval Air Squadron was all that was available to attack the three ships, which were escorted by a combat air patrol of thirty Luftwaffe fighters.

In the gloom of a late winter afternoon, Lt Cdr Eugene Esmonde took his six aircraft into the air, but instead of the escort of sixty Spitfire fighters that he had been promised, just ten Spitfires turned up. In poor light, they found the three warships and their escort of ten destroyers. The lumbering Swordfish were caught in a hail of fire from the fighters above and the warships below, but they pressed home a torpedo attack. His aircraft badly damaged as pieces were knocked off it in the heavy fire, Esmonde managed to keep the aircraft airborne long enough to launch its torpedo before it crashed into the sea. His target, the *Prinz Eugen*, managed to avoid the torpedo. All six Swordfish were shot down, with the loss of Esmonde and twelve others out of the eighteen naval airmen involved in the attack. Esmonde was awarded a posthumous VC.

Had the two battlecruisers been accompanied by an aircraft carrier, operating with them from their base in France, undoubtedly their operations against British merchant shipping would have been far more effective. On the other hand, the large expanse of flight deck on the carrier would have meant that it would have been more vulnerable to the RAF's bombing than the armoured decks and gun turrets of the battlecruisers. This is an important point as the value of the French bases to the Germans cannot be underestimated. As far as the Channel Dash itself was concerned, the carrier's aircraft would have made little difference as the Luftwaffe managed to maintain a substantial level of fighter cover above the three ships as they approached and then swept through the Straits of Dover.

THE INVASION OF MADAGASCAR

The large French island colony of Madagascar, off the coast of East Africa, was governed by Vichy after the fall of France in 1940. It offered a base for naval and air forces from which they could spread out over the Indian Ocean and attack shipping heading for the Suez Canal, which by 1942 was being used as a roundabout means of supplying British forces in Egypt rather than as a short cut for shipping between Great Britain and the Gulf, India and Australia and New Zealand.

Initially, German commerce raiders used the island as a base, but the difficulty of reaching Madagascar from Germany or Italy, or even from Japan, meant that the Axis powers failed to make full use of the island. Nevertheless, with an aircraft carrier providing air cover, the Kriegsmarine could have deployed surface raiders to the island. Had aircraft been shipped to the island by sea, they could have operated from the shore bases. Possibly, Japanese support could have been provided, but Japanese warships rarely operated west of southern India and Ceylon, the empire having stretched itself to its limits by spring 1942.

As it was, the Allies were sufficiently concerned about Madagascar becoming a base for Axis forces, and unsure about the attitude of the Vichy French, that on 5 May 1942, they mounted Operation Ironclad. The forces deployed by the British were insignificant, but included two modern fast armoured aircraft carriers, *Illustrious* and *Indomitable*, as well as the elderly battleship *Ramillies*, two cruisers and eleven destroyers. By 8 May, the island was firmly secured. The only counter-attack of any

149

significance was by Japanese midget submarines on 30 May, which put *Ramillies* out of action for several months.

It is inconceivable that Axis forces on Madagascar would have been allowed to stay by the Allies, but the resources deployed would have been far heavier had there been a significant Axis naval and air presence on the island. While it might be an exaggeration to suggest that Madagascar could have played as effective a role in interrupting Allied supplies as Malta did in disrupting the supply lines between Italy and North Africa, it certainly would have been a thorn in the Allied flesh for as long as armed forces managed to stay on the island.

BATTLE OF THE BARENTS SEA

This was a battle that should have been an easy victory for the Germans, with two heavy cruisers and six destroyers attacking a convoy with just five destroyers and five other minor warships as the escort. On 22 December 1942, Convoy JW51B left Loch Ewe for Russia, with fourteen ships carrying 200 tanks, 2,000 vehicles and 120 warplanes, as well as other cargo. The escort was led by Captain Robert Sherbrooke, aged 42 years, in *Onslow*, accompanied by *Obedient*, *Orwell*, *Obdurate* and *Achates*, with five other ships including minesweepers. The convoy was spotted by a U-boat that reported it to the heavy cruiser *Admiral Hipper*. The *Panzerschiff* (although by this time reclassified as a heavy cruiser) *Lutzow*, and heavy cruiser *Admiral Hipper* and six destroyers sailed from the Altenfjord on 31 December to intercept. Sherbrooke sent the merchantmen at full speed away from the convoy and led his destroyers straight at the enemy as if to make a torpedo attack. Four times the Germans attempted to attack the convoy, but on each occasion they were forced to withdraw under cover of a smoke-screen as the destroyers raced in, driving the Germans beyond range of the convoy and towards a British covering force of two cruisers. This series of actions lasted about two hours. After Sherbrooke was badly wounded, Lt Cdr Kinloch in *Obedient* took over, mounting a fifth feint towards the enemy, finally turning the heavy cruiser *Admiral Hipper* away, but not before she had hit *Achates* and killed her commanding officer. Then the cruisers *Sheffield* and *Jamaica* arrived and their shells started hitting *Hipper*. The German destroyer *Friedrich Eckholdt* raced towards *Hipper* but was sunk by *Sheffield*.

A lack of determination on the part of the Germans led Hitler to demand that the German surface fleet be scrapped, and the German Navy's C-in-C, Raeder, was forced to resign. That the British destroyers could have been fought off can be judged by the different outcome when HMS *Acasta* and *Ardent* were sunk in a hopeless bid to defend the British aircraft carrier, *Glorious*.

Had an aircraft carrier been present, attacks could have been mounted on the British cruisers and on the merchantmen in the convoy, although naval aircraft would have found fast-moving destroyers difficult to hit either with torpedoes or bombs. On the other hand, would the carrier have become a victim? After all, the German heavy cruisers should have been able to strike at the British destroyers before they got within torpedo range. This was a classic example from the British side of the boldest moves being the safest.

BATTLE OF THE NORTH CAPE

One major battle of the Second World War without any aircraft carrier being involved was the Battle of the North Cape. Had the Germans had a carrier available, it could have made a significant difference, although operations could have been curtailed by the severe weather encountered and which naturally enough affected both sides.

The sequence of events that led to the battle started in late December 1943, when the British Admiralty heard from Ultra intelligence that the battlecruiser *Scharnhorst* was on short notice for steam. *Scharnhorst* was reputed to be Hitler's favourite ship. In 1940, during the withdrawal from Norway, *Scharnhorst*, and her sister *Gneisnau*, had sunk the aircraft carrier *Glorious*.

On 21 December 1943, Admiral Sir Bruce Fraser, Commander-in-Chief Home Fleet, was aboard his flagship, the battleship *Duke of York* as she entered Akureyri Fjord in Iceland, escorted by the cruiser *Jamaica* and four destroyers. On receiving the news about the *Scharnhorst*, he assembled his captains for a conference. His plan was that once refuelled, his squadron, now to be known as Force Two, should head north at 15 knots to conserve fuel, and if they did encounter the *Scharnhorst*, *Jamaica* was to remain with the flagship while the destroyers were to divide into two divisions and mount a torpedo attack. *Duke of York* would open fire at a range of seven miles, initially using star shells.

The bait for the *Scharnhorst* was Convoy JW55B, while home-bound RA55A was leaving Kola with an escort consisting of eight

151

destroyers, three corvettes and a minesweeper. The two convoys were due to cross off Bear Island on Christmas Day. JW55B had a mixed Royal Navy and Royal Canadian Navy escort. Rear Admiral Burnett commanded Force One, the cruiser support for the two convoys, with *Belfast*, *Norfolk* and *Sheffield*.

Fraser took Force Two to sea at 23.00 on 23 December. Ultra decrypts had warned him that U-boats had been ordered to attack JW55B, while *Scharnhorst* was on three hours' notice to sail. The Germans had discovered JW55B almost by accident, as the aircraft that spotted them was on weather reconnaissance. Two U-boats, *U-601* and *U-716* made contact with the convoy on 24 December, but were driven off by the escorts.

Aboard the *Scharnhorst*, her usual commander, *Vizeadmiral* Kummetz, was ill and on Christmas Day was replaced by *Konteradmiral* (Rear Admiral) 'Achmed' Bey, an experienced destroyer commander rather than a big ship man. Bey objected to the plans to send the battlecruiser to sea, preferring instead to make the maximum use of destroyers, his weapon of choice despite the poor weather conditions. His orders were not to hazard the *Scharnhorst*, and he was also free to use destroyers only if he felt that the conditions were right. His orders from Dönitz were that he must 'disengage if a superior enemy force is encountered'.

Both convoys had their courses altered by Fraser, so that they were heading away from the Norwegian coast and towards the ice, but the change was almost impossible to make because of the bad weather. *U-601* continued to track the progress of the convoy, but the Germans remained unaware of the presence of Force Two. Signals between Fraser and the two convoys had been intercepted, but had been misunderstood, while the Germans expected the heavy units to be kept well to the west of the convoy.

Just before 19.00 on Christmas Day, Bey had his flag captain, *Kapitan zur See* Hintze, prepare to sail, and the German 4th Destroyer Flotilla had the order passed on to it. The five destroyers preceded the battlecruiser as the force steamed out of the Altenfjord, and set off west at 25 knots. In an exchange of communications, Bey was assured that no significant surface force was within 50 miles of JW55B, although the intelligence was out of date, and he informed naval HQ at Kiel that the weather would inhibit the operational efficiency of his destroyers, rolling wildly in the severe weather and high sea state.

Even aboard the *Duke of York*, slightly larger than the

Scharnhorst, at 35,000 tons to 31,800 tons, the motion of the ship was uncomfortable. Despite having the heaviest armour plating of any contemporary battleship, the ship was far from immune to the weather because of her low hull lines, intended to allow her 'A' turret to fire forwards. Oerlikon anti-aircraft cannon were swept off the foredeck by the crashing waves coming over the bows, despite the slow speed being made, and cold sea water poured through the rivet holes into the messdecks below. The most forward of the gun turrets, 'A' turret, also suffered water ingression, some of it finding its way to the shell room below. Once again, it was the destroyers that suffered the most, and as with the German ships, they would find high speed action impossible unless the sea conditions eased.

Both ships were a compromise. *Duke of York* had been limited to 35,000 tons by the Washington Naval Treaty of 1922. Originally intended to have 16-in guns, a further treaty limited the calibre to 14-in. *Scharnhorst* was originally intended to have 15-in guns, but had to make do with 11-in, and although it was always the intention to upgrade her weaponry at a refit, the opportunity never arose.

Very early on 26 December, at 01.30, a signal from the Admiralty based on an Ultra decrypt informed Fraser that a codeword had been flashed to the commanding officer of a battle group, suggesting that an operation was about to begin. The intelligence was ten hours old. Confirmation was not long in coming, for at 02.17 came the signal: 'Emergency SCHARNHORST probably sailed 1800/25 December.' A further signal followed almost immediately advising that a German patrol vessel had been warned at 17.15 that the battle-cruiser would soon pass outward bound. Then at 04.00, Fraser was told that the 'Admiralty appreciate that SCHARNHORST is now at sea.'

Fraser was less inclined to keep radio silence than his contemporaries in the Royal Navy, believing that knowledge of the disposition of other fleet units and warning of impending events was far more important. The risk was that signals traffic betrayed both position and intention. Nevertheless, on balance he was almost certainly right bearing in mind the number of occasions when the absence of communication had resulted in failure. Now, unaware that the convoy had been unable to turn west, he was concerned that he was still too far away to help the convoy. He ordered speed increased to 24 knots, then signalled Force One and the convoy to report their positions, even though this meant revealing his own. There was no risk as the Germans either did not intercept the signals or ignored them.

It was only after Fraser had made the signal that he discovered that the convoy was fifty miles south of Bear Island, with Force One 150 miles from the convoy but planning to be within thirty miles of it by 08.17. Force Two was 350 miles from the convoy, and too far away to save it, although it would be able to stop the Germans from returning to their base. Now understanding that the convoy had not turned round, Fraser ordered it to turn north. While the order was received, it took some time to retransmit this to all of the ships in the convoy, and it was not until around 06.00 that the change of course could be made. Bey, meanwhile, was heading due north 100 miles from the convoy, but just 90 miles from Force One. His plan was to attack the convoy as it cleared the North Cape.

The relatively narrow stretch of water between the edge of the Polar ice cap and the enemy-held shoreline forced a further compromise. At 06.28, Fraser ordered JW55B to take a revised course, heading north-east to avoid being caught between the ice and the Germans.

Bey, meanwhile, who had informed Dönitz of the difficulties suffered by his destroyers, was surprised to receive a signal from the *Grossadmiral* telling him to leave the destroyers behind if they could not keep station, and attack the convoy with the battlecruiser alone. This was contrary to the *Konteradmiral*'s own instincts and experience.

Two U-boats, *U-601* and *U-716* were now tailing the convoy, and had failed to notice the turn to the north. Thus it happened that, as the *Scharnhorst* approached the expected position of the convoy, and *Kapitan sur See* Hintze broadcast the message from Dönitz that a successful attack would relieve the situation on the Eastern Front before sending the men to action stations, there was a massive anticlimax as nothing was found. Frustrated, Bey turned his force south-west and spread his destroyers at five mile intervals. At around 09.40, the northernmost destroyer passed the southernmost escort of the convoy at a distance of around fifteen miles, both completely unaware of the other's presence in the poor visibility. As the weather worsened, and the destroyers suffered as ice built up on their decks and superstructure, with frost and snow covering the optical gunnery control instruments, Bey was forced to order speed reduced first to 12 knots and then to 10 knots. This put the battlecruiser at risk of attack by Allied submarines, so he took the ship on a zig-zag course astern of the destroyers.

Force One had gone to action stations shortly before dawn, at around 08.30, and shortly afterwards, *Norfolk* picked up radar echoes of a single ship seventeen miles to the west-north-west. *Belfast*, Burnett's flagship, then picked up the same echoes. At 09.21, the lookouts on the third cruiser, *Sheffield*, spotted a large ship on the horizon seven miles to port. Immediately, *Belfast* opened fire with star shell, but these fell short. At 09.29, Burnett ordered the three ships to open fire with their main armament, 6-in for *Belfast* and *Sheffield*, 8-in for *Norfolk*. Force One turned to port to close the range, but this gave difficulties and all three cruisers could not bring their guns to bear fully on the German ship. Using radar control, however, *Norfolk* succeeded in sending six broadsides towards the *Scharnhorst*, with three 8-in shells exploding on the battlecruiser, destroying her main radar scanner and her port high angle (anti-aircraft) gunnery director, while a fourth shell went through the upper deck but failed to explode.

One of the German destroyers was off course, and the others assumed that this meant that the enemy was approaching. Their leader signalled *Scharnhorst*, only to receive a reply that she was being engaged by British cruisers.

As the shells exploded aboard *Scharnhorst*, Bey had her turn south-east and make smoke while speed increased to 30 knots. At 09.40, Force One ceased fire and gave chase, but as the distance between the hunters and the hunted widened, Burnett realised that they had no chance of catching the battlecruiser in such weather as her greater size meant that she could cope with a heavier sea than any of the cruisers. Force One turned back towards the convoy.

The Germans were not running away, but simply playing for time. Bey intended to attack the convoy from the north, with the destroyers attacking from the south. The destroyers' 5.9-in guns were almost a match for those of *Belfast* and *Sheffield*, while torpedo attack would also threaten the cruisers, leaving *Scharnhorst* free to savage the convoy.

Fraser again ordered the convoy onto a northerly course and had the four destroyers from the homebound convoy RA55A diverted to reinforce the screen around Force One's cruisers. At the same time, *Belfast* found the *Scharnhorst* on her radar again. Burnett's concern for the convoy was well founded, as the battlecruiser had steamed in an arc and reappeared forty miles to the north. At 12.20, the battlecruiser came into sight and Burnett ordered his cruisers to open fire and his destroyers to mount a torpedo attack.

Fearing a torpedo attack, *Kapitan sur See* Hintze opened fire and started to take evasive action to avoid the destroyers. The range shortened to four-and-a-half miles, while his gunnery direction officers concentrated fire on *Norfolk*, whose 8-in guns were not using flashless cordite and so allowed her range to be established easily. The heavy cruiser was soon taking fire, with an 11-in shell knocking out 'X' turret aft, and her radio sets were also disabled. *Sheffield* was showered in shell splinters. In return, just one shell from the British cruisers hit the German ship, landing on the quarterdeck and failing to explode. Then, disappearing at 12.41 almost as quickly as she had appeared, *Scharnhorst* raced off to the south-east. The high seas had meant that the destroyers had been unable to get into position for a torpedo attack before the battle-cruiser disappeared from sight. This time the cruisers gave chase at 28 knots, using radar to maintain contact, while the destroyers did their best to keep up. By 14.00, the battlecruiser, instead of homing in on the convoy was some thirty miles ahead of it, desperately seeking to return to the Altenfjord. Force One was now in the happy position of driving the German ship towards the 14-in guns of *Duke of York*.

Meanwhile, those aboard the British battleship had been through moments of despair, feeling at first that their prey had evaded the cruisers, then Force Two was spotted by a Blohm und Voss Bv138 flying boat, which could not have failed to notice the significance of the ships. They were not to know that the aircraft simply reported 'one big and several smaller ships', which aroused no suspicions at all. He signalled that unless contact could be regained by Force One, he had no chance of finding *Scharnhorst*. At the back of Fraser's mind was the real possibility that the battlecruiser was not in fact interested in the convoy, but instead was seeking to break out into the wider Atlantic, packed with convoys and the large fast passenger liners now acting as troopships bringing American and Canadian troops for the forthcoming invasion of Europe. He turned Force Two to west-south-west. His change of course caused a ripple of disappointment to run through his squadron, as it was clear that their high hopes of catching the German ship were to come to nothing. The mood changed almost as abruptly, as Fraser received news of the fresh contact, and ordered Force Two to turn back to its previous course.

Meanwhile, the German destroyers had found that the convoy was not where it had been expected, thanks to the changes of course taken and misleading reports from the U-boats. At 14.18, when he had finally decided to return to the Altenfjord, Bey also signalled to his destroyers to return.

Aboard the ships of Force Two, at 15.30 everyone went to action stations and they closed up for combat, closing all armoured hatches and watertight doors. They had not too long to wait. At 16.18, the trace of the *Scharnhorst* appeared on the *Duke of York*'s radar, and soon afterwards a cluster of smaller traces showed Force One still on the chase. At 16.32, the battlecruiser appeared on the fire control radar at a distance of eleven miles, but Fraser decided to hold fire until the distance closed further, although he ordered his destroyers to prepare for a torpedo attack, but to await the go-ahead.

Force Two and the *Scharnhorst* were less than seven miles apart at 16.50, when Fraser changed course to allow all of his guns and those of the cruiser *Jamaica* to come to bear on the battlecruiser. The secondary armament of 5.25-in guns aboard the *Duke of York* fired four star-shells which exploded above and behind the *Scharnhorst*, illuminating her against the dark night and showing that she was completely unprepared for action with her guns aligned fore and aft. Fraser ordered a full broadside, with all ten 14-in guns firing at once, with the 6-in guns of *Jamaica* following. The radar-controlled guns were spot on target, and the green glows of shell hits could be seen, having taken just 15 seconds to travel the 6.8 miles separating the opposing ships. The German's 'A' turret forward was wrecked. *Kapitan sur See* Hintze swung his ship away to the north, only to find himself facing the pursuing cruisers of Force One, although *Sheffield* was dropping back. The other two cruisers opened fire, causing Bey to order a turn eastwards.

Scharnhorst was now outpacing Force One, although her actual progress was reduced by Hintze swinging the ship from time to time to allow her 'B' turret to return fire. At 17.00, Force Two's destroyers were still attempting to overhaul the German so that they mount a torpedo attack, a penalty for Fraser's refusal to allow them to start earlier. Two shells from the German battlecruiser passed harmlessly through the British battleship's tripod mast. At 17.13, the destroyers were ordered to launch their torpedoes, but while they could still hang on to the battleship, they were in no position to launch as they pitched and rolled in the heavy seas. *Jamaica* was also falling behind, and it looked as if the faster German battle-cruiser would also outrun the British battleship. It now looked like a gunnery duel between the two ships, with the 14-in guns of *Duke of York* capable of hitting a target at eighteen miles. Unfortunately, the massive broadsides had wrecked the gunnery radar, and visual gunnery was being made difficult by smoke being made by the *Scharnhorst*.

Once again, events on the German side at first unknown to the British were to change the position. One of the 14-in shells had penetrated the starboard boiler room and the *Scharnhorst*'s speed fell to 10 knots, although fast work in appalling conditions by her engine room personnel saw the steam supply reconnected and speed increased again to 22 knots, and the range opened up to eleven miles. While this was happening, the British destroyers had closed on the battlecruiser, and while two on the *Scharnhorst*'s port quarter attracted the fire of her secondary armament, the star-shell from the destroyers also hid the approach of two more on the starboard side until they were two miles away. *Scharnhorst* turned abruptly to starboard to comb the tracks of any torpedoes, but the two destroyers *Scorpion* and *Stord* fired sixteen torpedoes at 18.52, and one of them struck home. The change of course gave the destroyers *Saumarez* and *Savage* their chance, and a dozen torpedoes were fired at the battlecruiser, with one of them wrecking a second boiler room and another distorting a propeller shaft. The speed of the wounded ship again fell to 10 knots.

While the four destroyers withdrew, having attacked under fire and taken damage and casualties, the *Duke of York*'s gunnery radar had been repaired, while *Jamaica* was catching up as the German ship had changed course. Force Two now opened fire, with both ships quickly finding their range, steaming past the battlecruiser and repeatedly hitting her with armour-piercing shells. The *Jamaica* detached to give the *Scharnhorst* another torpedo attack as she slowed and her guns fell silent. Then Force One appeared, with *Belfast* and *Norfolk* ready for torpedo attack, which came at 19.18, while Force One's destroyers were also sent into action, with two of their torpedoes striking on the port side where the bilges were already exposed. Damaged voice pipes meant that the torpedo crews aboard the destroyer *Matchless* missed the order to fire, but *Musketeer*'s torpedoes struck home. The German ship was now listing heavily to port with her crew mustered on deck ready to abandon ship. *Kapitan sur See* Hintze ordered them to slide into the water on the port side and not to forget to inflate their lifejackets.

Yet, no one on the British side saw the end of this great ship, as smoke hanging over the scene obscured their view, and even when a radar operator reported that the blip was fading, he was told to retune it. More than half an hour passed before *Belfast* was able to confirm that the *Scharnhorst* had indeed been sunk. A single raft contained frozen survivors. The destroyer *Scorpion* picked up just thirty survivors, while *Matchless* picked up a further six, but 1,767 officers and men had lost their lives, including the *Konteradmiral* and the *Kapitan sur See*. The loss of so many suggests that her final moments must have seen a traumatic capsizing that trapped many of those on the port side as she rolled over, but, of course, the freezing seas would have accounted for many within minutes, especially the lightly clad men from below decks.

The shadowing U-boats who were hoping to attack were sent on a fruitless search for survivors from the *Scharnhorst*.

Had the Germans had an aircraft carrier to operate with the *Scharnhorst*, the outcome could have been different. It would have been far more difficult for the British cruisers to have tailed the German battlecruiser while under attack from torpedo-carrying aircraft and dive-bombers, and even the heavily armed and armoured *Duke of York* would have been threatened by aerial attack. Perhaps most important of all, however, would have been the intelligence available to Bey and Hintze if good aerial reconnaissance patterns had been flown. Here again, it becomes a question of experience and having sufficient aircraft, and fuel, available to fly the correct reconnaissance patterns. Even the Japanese, with all of their carrier experience, failed to fly thorough reconnaissance patterns before the Battle of Midway, and as a result missed the American carriers, with the result that they lost four of their own in just one day.

CHAPTER TWELVE

The Convoy War

The first three years of the Second World War were characterised by Allied weakness in the North Atlantic, where there existed what was variously known as the 'Atlantic Gap' or the 'Black Gap', a stretch of sea amounting to some 850 miles, over which air cover was not available. The advent of the merchant aircraft carrier, or MAC-ship, and then the escort carrier, ended the Atlantic Gap, and the work was completed with the advent of ever longer-range maritime-reconnaissance aircraft, and most notably the Consolidated Liberator, the longest-range bomber of the war years. Aircraft fitted with radar could hunt down submarines and force them to remain submerged, making it difficult for them to track convoys effectively and virtually impossible for them to get into position ahead of a convoy.

An aircraft carrier operating in the North Atlantic would have made it far more difficult to close the 'Gap'. The MAC-ships would have been vulnerable as they were unable to carry any fighter aircraft to provide air cover, and even the escort carriers had such limited capacity that their fighter strength was usually small and, of course, always at the expense of a corresponding number of anti-submarine aircraft.

As in the Battle of the North Cape, the other important role of the aircraft carrier would have been improved reconnaissance and intelligence. When convoy commodores ordered a change of course to avoid the U-boat packs, carrier-borne aircraft offered the chance to detect such changes and relay them to the U-boat commanders.

At the same time, there would have been a risk of a 'blue on blue' or friendly fire incident. Aircraft carriers such as the *Graf Zeppelin*, would have looked similar to the British *Courageous* and *Glorious* until these were sunk.

Supporting an aircraft carrier in the open sea would not have been an easy task, and the support vessels would also have needed protection. German plans were for four aircraft carriers initially, to be joined by four smaller ships later. The smaller ships would no doubt have been engaged in protecting the supply lines for the larger ships. A German aircraft carrier loose in the Atlantic would have been such a threat that it is likely that a carrier to carrier battle on the lines of the Battle of the Coral Sea or the Battle of Midway would have resulted. If Hitler's promises that war would not break out until 1943 or 1944 had been fulfilled, it would not have been a case of elderly British ships or the vulnerable *Ark Royal* with her thin flight deck engaging the German ships, but of a fast armoured carrier such as *Illustrious* and her sisters engaging the German ship, which, we must bear in mind, was of dated design. The big question would have been whether, without the bitter experience of the early years of war, the Royal Navy would have procured high performance fighters for their ships.

Basing the German carrier would have been another problem. The French ports used by the German battlecruisers would have ideal for operations in the Bay of Biscay and out into the mid-Atlantic, but vulnerable to British bombing. The Norwegian fjords offered far better protection, but again, we are comparing battle-cruisers and battleships with aircraft carriers. Would a German aircraft carrier have been as safe in a Norwegian fjord as the *Tirpitz*? The answer is probably not, as the bombs that bounced off the *Tirpitz* would have damaged a carrier's flight deck.

On the other hand, a carrier operating out of Norway would have made the Arctic convoys to Russia even more difficult than was in fact the case. Changing course to the west to minimise the chance of attack by the Luftwaffe would have been of little value with a carrier waiting out to sea. The Germans could even have practised shuttle bombing, with aircraft flying from the carrier to shore bases and then back again, mounting an attack in each direction. Nevertheless, the reaction by the Royal Navy would have been to make use of the fleet carrier in the distant escort to counter the threat from the German carrier.

What would have been the fate of some of the more famous, or perhaps notorious is a better description, of the Arctic convoys?

CONVOY PQ17

PQ17, the convoy to the Soviet Union, sailed from Reykjavik on 27 June 1942. This was both the most famous and infamous of all the many convoys fought through the long and hazardous passage from Scotland and Iceland, on which the weather was as much a threat as the Germans. At the time, the British strategic assessment was that the situation was entirely in Germany's favour, with naval forces operating close to their bases and supported by land-based aircraft and with a screen of U-boats. While the weather could be expected to be more benign in June than for much of the rest of the year, the long summer days and short Arctic summer nights meant that German attack could be constant.

In the event of the Germans deploying their major surface units, the Home Fleet plan was for the unfortunate convoy to sail to the west to a position 10 degrees east, hopefully to lure the Germans on to the guns of the Home Fleet, sitting beyond any effective German aerial attack. In command of the Home Fleet, Admiral Sir John Tovey hoped that the Germans would give chase, but realised that they might well suspect a trap and return to harbour, or instead opt to hang around off the coast waiting for the convoy to return to its course, during which time they could be prey for the Allied submarines off the Norwegian coast.

The Admiralty did not agree with Tovey's logic, and instead proposed that in such circumstances any convoy should scatter. The logic was that many ships spread across the ocean would be far more difficult for the Germans to track down than a concentrated group of ships. Tovey's view was that this would be 'sheer bloody murder', not least because in keeping together there was a degree of unity that boosted strength, since the merchantmen had shown themselves increasingly competent at contributing to the convoys' AA defences, and also improved morale. In the end, a compromise was agreed. The Home Fleet would give its usual distant or heavy cover, while the cruiser squadron would provide a supplementary escort as far as 10 degrees east, but would be allowed to proceed beyond Bear Island to a point no further east than 25 degrees east if the convoy was threatened by 'the presence of a force which the cruiser force could fight.' In other words, the cruisers could face German cruisers and destroyers, but not battleships or battlecruisers, or what the British press termed 'pocket battleships', officially known at the outset of the war as a *Panzerschiff*, armoured ship, but which the Germans had by this time reclassified as heavy cruisers. Tovey's alternative suggestion that the convoy should be split in two was also rejected, largely because the Admiralty was caught between American irritation that supplies were building up in the UK and

USA, and Soviet anger that their demands were not being met.

There were other problems. Some of the merchant ships waiting in Iceland for the next convoy had been troubled by indiscipline. The rapid expansion of the merchant fleets created by the war, and the loss of so many experienced men to the navies as reservists were called up, had meant that many of those manning the ships lacked experience of life at sea, while others saw no reason why they should risk life and limb for what they saw as a British war. Idleness contributes greatly to indiscipline, and life for the merchant seamen was a dreary round of visits to unattractive locations, with too much time spent cooped up in ships that were overcrowded, given the presence of the AA gunners for which the merchantmen had not been designed, and in between there was the stress and strain of fighting the convoys through, and if they were not fighting the Germans or waiting for them to attack, it was usually because the weather was so bad! Even the Royal Navy was not immune to problems of discipline, with those men assigned to the convoys more likely than usual to be late back from leave, often taking the view that even a spell in the cells at a detention centre was better than life with the convoys.

The Admiralty had already lost two cruisers, HMS *Trinidad* and *Edinburgh* in Arctic waters. But the presence of such ships had a deterrent effect on the Germans and a comfort factor for those with the convoys.

For PQ17, a larger than usual escort was planned and rescue ships would be provided as well as a dummy convoy. Quite how a dummy convoy could be provided given the shortage of merchant ships is another question, but in fact the 'dummy' turned out to be more of a dummy raiding force than a convoy. The distant cover would include the United States Navy's Task Force 99 under Rear Admiral Griffen, while Rear Admiral Louis 'Turtle' Hamilton would command the First Cruiser Squadron sailing with PQ17. Tovey would also have his new second-in-command, Vice-Admiral Sir Bruce Fraser. Hamilton was an advocate of naval air power, and one of those who shared the view of the United States Navy, that air power should be used to keep the seas open rather than bombing German cities.

The dummy convoy was known as Operation ES, and consisted of minelayers and four colliers escorted by two cruisers, *Curacao* and *Sirius*, five destroyers and a number of armed trawlers. Doubtless colliers were chosen as such ships were more likely to have been available given that the normal heavy British coastal traffic along the east coast was largely suspended after the fall of the Low Countries as it was too exposed to attack by German aircraft and light forces. ES sailed from Scapa Flow two days after PQ17 and headed towards the Norwegian Sea to give the impression that it was making for southern Norway on a raiding or mine laying mission. It remained undetected by German reconnaissance, even when repeated a week later, and was nothing more than a waste of time and fuel, keeping scarce ships away from more productive duties.

Meanwhile, a telex message from German naval headquarters to the local commander at Narvik on 14 June had been intercepted by Swedish intelligence and the information passed to the British Naval Attaché in Stockholm, Captain Henry Denham. This revealed details of operation *Rosselsprung*, otherwise 'The Knight's Move', which comprised the German plans to destroy the next convoy. Aerial reconnaissance was to locate the convoy before it reached Jan Mayen Island, so that air attacks could be mounted from bases in northern Norway. The heavy cruisers and six destroyers would move to Altenfjord while *Tirpitz* and *Admiral Hipper* would move to Narvik, and warships would commence operations once the convoy reached 5 degrees east. Once the convoy reached the meridian of Bear Island, there would be coordinated attacks by aircraft, surface vessels and U-boats. In short, the complete and devastating destruction of an entire convoy, using surface vessels that could achieve as much in a few hours as a U-boat wolfpack could achieve in as many days. The more adventurous and confident approach being planned could have owed much to the replacement of *Vizeadmiral* Otto Ciliax, who was unwell, aboard the *Tirpitz* by *Vizeadmiral* Otto Schniewind, who was anxious that his battle group should conduct offensive operations. A further sign of the change in attitude was the allocation of 15,000 tons of scarce bunker oil. The Germans had also built-up their air strength in Norway, and while this included additional He115 seaplane torpedo-bombers, the real significance lay in additional He111s and Ju88s, and thirty Ju87 Stuka dive-bombers, while reconnaissance strength was also boosted.

The one advantage that the Royal Navy held was its possession of naval air power, and even the limited capabilities of the British naval aircraft of the day had undermined confidence to a degree perhaps not appreciated outside Germany. Obsolescent Swordfish biplanes had not only crippled the Italian battle fleet at Taranto, they had contributed to the loss of the *Bismarck*, sister ship to *Tirpitz*, the previous year. Even earlier, Blackburn Skua fighter/ dive-bombers had sunk the cruiser *Konigsberg* during the Norwegian campaign of 1940. Even the fighters, the slow and lumbering Fairey Fulmar, had had an impact. The head of the German Navy, *Grossadmiral*, Grand Admiral, Erich Raeder, was keen to show what his service could do and win the Fuhrer's favour, but he hesitated to send his ships to sea without strong assurances of support from the Luftwaffe. The two heavy cruisers, or ex- 'pocket battleships', *Lutzow* and *Scheer*, with a maximum speed of just 28 knots, were regarded as being especially vulnerable, for, after all, their sister, *Graf Spee*, had been destroyed by just a heavy cruiser and two light cruisers.

Three U-boats were sent to patrol off Iceland, keeping watch for Allied shipping movements. During the period 15–23 June, eight U-boats were despatched to a patrol area off Jan Mayen Island to wait for the next convoy.

Nevertheless, caution was still the watchword, even at the very top. Raeder approached Hitler with his plans for the Knight's Move, seeking full Luftwaffe support, since only the Fuhrer himself could ensure that this would happen. Hitler agreed, but on condition that the major fleet units were not to venture out to sea until any aircraft carrier had been dealt with by the Luftwaffe. Disappointed, Raeder did at least manage to persuade Hitler that the ships could go to sea if carrier-borne aircraft were out of range. Hitler reluctantly agreed, but the plan could still only go ahead subject to his approval. Once again, the Fuhrer system was stifling initiative, while locally communications between operational units of the two armed services involved remained patchy. In both world wars, it was also the case that Germany's battleships were regarded as so important that their use was limited by fears about their safety.

Tovey took the Home Fleet to sea to provide the distant or heavy escort, flying his flag in the battleship *Duke of York*. His deputy Vice-Admiral Fraser was aboard the aircraft carrier *Victorious*, with Rear Admiral Burrough aboard the cruiser *Nigeria*, joined by the heavy cruiser *Cumberland*, while Rear Admiral Griffin was aboard the battleship USS *Washington*. An anti-submarine screen of a dozen British and American destroyers completed the force.

After the Home Fleet wasted time and fuel steaming eastwards as if it was covering the decoy convoy ES, Tovey could take his force to patrol an area where it could offer some support to the convoy. Amongst Tovey's problems, the First Sea Lord, the ailing Dudley Pound, was interfering in his decisions, using the fact that the Admiralty could have more up-to-date information due to the Ultra decrypts to reserve much of the decision-making to himself. It was clear that the Admiralty expected to control the convoy from a distance.

PQ17 consisted of thirty-six merchantmen, most of them American, under the command of Commodore Dowding in the *River Afton*, but it also had two fleet oilers, one of them comprising Force Q with its own escorting destroyer. The convoy carried 150,000 tons of stores and general cargo, as well as 594 tanks, 4,246 military vehicles and 297 aircraft.

On 2 July, PQ17 and the reciprocal convoy QP13 passed, and Force Q, the oiler and destroyer, switched from PQ17 to QP13. The following day, three of the destroyers were detached on direct orders from the Admiralty to conduct a sweep looking for the *Tirpitz*, known to be missing from her moorings. The following day, QP13 was divided, again on Admiralty orders, with nineteen ships, including the *Empire Selwyn* with Commodore Gale aboard, directed to Loch Ewe in Scotland, while the remaining sixteen, mainly American, maintained their course for Hvalfjordur with Captain J. Hiss, master of the *American Robin*, as commodore.

PQ17 meanwhile had been reduced to thirty-five ships when an American ship ran aground off Iceland, and despite a trawler and a tug being sent to her aid, the ship was left behind. Most of PQ17's ships were intended for Archangel, with just eight for Murmansk as the latter port had been bombed so heavily that it had had to suspend operations for a period. The ice cap had receded further than usual for the time of year, allowing the convoy to keep well to the west and pass north of Bear Island. Nevertheless, while still in the Denmark Strait heavy ice was encountered and another American ship was too badly damaged to continue, and her repeated radioed requests for help doubtless helped to provide the Germans with the position of the convoy. Next, one of the naval auxiliaries, the oiler *Grey Ranger*, intended to act as a fuel ship in Russia, also struck an iceberg that split her bows wide open so that she too would have to turn back. It was decided that she should swap places with the *Aldersdale*, the other fleet oiler, and that her fuel should be used to top up the escort vessels.

On 30 June the ocean escort arrived. This was led by Commander

J.E. Broome in the destroyer *Keppel*, one of eight destroyers and three corvettes, two anti-aircraft ships converted from fruit carriers, and two submarines, escorting the convoy, while another destroyer and the tanker *Aldersdale* comprised Force Q. There was also a solitary CAM-ship, *Empire Tide*. This was the only air cover available to PQ17.

Rear Admiral Louis 'Turtle' Hamilton had been present when Broome had briefed the convoy masters at Hvalfjordur. His four cruisers, led by his flagship *London*, were to provide heavy support for the convoy. The other cruisers were *Norfolk* and the American ships *Tuscaloosa* and *Wichita*, supported by one British and two American destroyers. While the masters had been briefed on what to do in the event of air attack, Hamilton's naval commanding officers knew that while the primary objective was to get PQ17 to the Soviet Union, a subsidiary objective was to try to draw out the heavy units of the Kriegsmarine, not for the cruisers to engage these, but instead to shadow them and report their position to the Home Fleet.

The cruiser squadron was the last to leave Iceland, sailing on 1 July, their superior speed making it easy for them to catch the slow moving convoy, proceeding at just eight knots. The weather at the outset was good, and on 1 July while the Allied Cruiser Squadron was catching up, the escorts took the opportunity to refuel. At midday, the first U-boats were sighted and chased off, but this caused radio silence to be broken and confirmed to the Germans once again the convoy's position. Two U-boats, *U-255* and *U-408* now maintained contact with the convoy's progress, while *U-334* and *U-456* were directed to join them. Another six U-boats were directed further east to form a wolfpack or patrol line. The U-boats were assisted by a Blohm und Voss Bv138 reconnaissance flying-boat which arrived at 14.00 and started to transmit homing signals for the U-boats. Alarm spread through the convoy when capital ships were spotted silhouetted against the horizon, but on investigation by a trawler these proved to be the Home Fleet.

The number of German aircraft keeping PQ17 under observation rose to three. Later that afternoon, the convoy was forced to wheel to avoid torpedoes believed to have come from *U-456*, which was counter-attacked by three destroyers and a corvette, but without success. At 18.00, the USS *Rowan*, an American destroyer escorting the Allied cruisers, approached the convoy to refuel from the *Aldersdale*, and as she did so nine He115 seaplanes made a half-hearted torpedo attack on the anti-aircraft ship *Pozarica*, until confronted by her heavy AA fire to which *Rowan* also made a contribution, shooting down one of the aircraft, which crash-landed in the water. The Germans were not without nerve, however, as one of the other aircraft landed and rescued the crew from the downed aircraft! Mercifully, fog then descended and the convoy was able to change course to the east, towards Bear Island, evading the Luftwaffe.

The following day started with a number of U-boat scares, which kept the escorts busy as the convoy passed in and out of fog banks. While tracking down U-boats doubtless kept them at bay, it also meant that fuel and in some cases depth charges were being used at a considerable rate. With Hamilton and his cruisers steering a parallel course some forty miles to the north, the convoy continued to be kept under close observation by a Walrus, at this time from HMS *London*. At this time Hamilton believed that *Tirpitz* and *Hipper* would be sent after QP13 in an attempt to draw the Home Fleet away, leaving PQ17 for *Lutzow* and *Scheer*. Doubtless with the Battle of the River Plate in mind, Hamilton believed that his orders gave him scope to engage these two German ships. There was an exchange of fire between the Walrus and a Bv138 later when the former landed close to *Keppel* with a message from Hamilton for Broome, advising the SO(E) that the ice-edge had receded considerably to the north and also advising that the convoy should change course northwards increasing the distance between it and the Luftwaffe base at Banak, but Broome, the SO(E), didn't take the convoy as far north as Hamilton suggested, anxious to continue pressing eastwards.

The situation was complicated at this time by poor weather over Norway that prevented effective aerial reconnaissance. No one on the British side was aware that the *Lutzow*, *Scheer* and six destroyers had left their base at Narvik under the command of *Vizeadmiral* Oskar Kummetz, but they were convinced that *Vizeadmiral* Otto Schniewind had taken *Tirpitz* from Trondheim with the *Hipper*, four destroyers and two large ocean-going torpedo-boats. Nevertheless, the more northerly of these two forces, that from Narvik, soon ran into trouble, with the *Lutzow* running aground as she emerged from the Ofotfjord in fog, while further south three of Schniewind's destroyers hit uncharted rocks, although two replacements were with him when he took the *Tirpitz* and *Hipper* into the Altenfjord.

Aware of the movements of the *Tirpitz* group, Hamilton was then shadowed by German aircraft and sent his Walrus off on a reconnaissance sortie, but the aircraft hit fog and then ran out of fuel, having to make a forced landing and be taken in tow by a trawler. Meanwhile, the fog that had made life so difficult for the Walrus closed in over the convoy so that the German reconnaissance aircraft lost track of it, and when it did begin to lift, the fog then settled at a convenient mast height – poor for aerial reconnaissance, but reassuring for station-keeping.

Once again information came from intelligence sources in Sweden about German intentions, which were that the convoy would be attacked between longitudes 15 and 30 east, and this was passed on by the Admiralty early on 4 July when the convoy was almost exactly midway between these two points. With the movement of the German ships, it seemed that a combined heavy force was preparing to attack the convoy.

PQ17 was by this time some sixty miles north of Bear Island, when a lookout aboard the anti-aircraft ship *Palomares*, heard the sound of aircraft engines overhead, and as the fog thinned those aboard saw a Heinkel He111 diving to launch its torpedo. Too late, the ship's AA defences opened up while six blasts were given on her siren to warn those around the ship that she was about to take evasive action. The torpedo missed *Palomares*, but continued and hit the American merchantman, *Christopher Newport*, a Liberty ship carrying 10,000 tons of munitions, despite one of the gunners aboard calmly taking aim and striking the torpedo with his .30 machine guns. Exploding in the engine room, the torpedo killed an engineer and two greasers, while the ship lost power and started to swing round out of control, forcing the rest of the convoy to have to change course to steer around her. Unwelcome fireworks with which to celebrate Independence Day! The rescue ship *Zamalek* was soon alongside and took aboard forty-seven survivors, many of whom had time to dress in their best clothes and bring with them small arms and personal possessions. Broome ordered the submarine *P614* to torpedo the *Christopher Newport*, but two torpedoes from the submarine and then depth charges from the corvette *Dianella* failed to deliver the desired *coup de grace*, leaving the job to *U-457* later.

Set against this loss was the signal from the Admiralty to Hamilton allowing him the discretion of taking his cruisers beyond 25 degrees east. Unaware of the full picture, Tovey later signalled

Hamilton warning him not to enter the Barents Sea unless he could be certain that he would not encounter the *Tirpitz*. Hamilton decided to take his cruisers further south, only then did he discover that the convoy was thirty miles further south than he had expected it to be, as a result of Broome's decision to press on to the east. He eventually took his ships to a position twelve miles ahead of the convoy and at 16.45 ordered Broome to change course to the northeast. The convoy obeyed, but meantime it was under observation by both the Luftwaffe, who had decided that the anti-submarine aircraft flown from the USS *Wichita* had come from an aircraft carrier, and the commanding officer of *U-457*, shadowing the convoy, who reported that the cruiser squadron included a battleship: combined these two reports misled the Germans into believing that the Home Fleet was much closer than was the case, when in fact it was 350 miles away from the convoy. The result was that the German surface ships would not sail because Hitler had insisted on any aircraft carrier being put out of action first. Meanwhile, the other U-boats were homing in on *U-457* and PQ17.

The first of the assembled U-boats to attack was *U-88*, which had lain low and quiet while the first escorts steamed by, and then risen to periscope depth amidst the convoy and fired salvoes of torpedoes from bow and stern tubes, none of which found a target. A formation of He115s also headed for the convoy, but failed to get beyond the convoy's air defences. Despite the increased threat, the cruiser squadron's destroyer screen started to fall back towards the convoy to refuel from the *Aldersdale* in a flat calm sea. At 19.30, the American *Wainwright* was preparing to start replenishment when a stick of bombs exploded on her port bow, persuading her commanding officer, Captain D. P. Moon to postpone refuelling and position his ship abeam of *Keppel* ready for the expected air attack.

Radar returns were good in the calm conditions, and at 20.20 the duty radar operators aboard the *Palomares* detected a low level attack, always giving shorter warning than a high level attack, and upwards of twenty-five He111s of KG26 and a number of torpedo-carrying Ju88s of KG30 flew straight into the convoy, attacking from astern. The *Wainwright*, which had complete freedom of action at this time, turned to starboard and raced past the convoy towards the German aircraft, turning beam on to give the largest number of AA weapons a chance to bear on the attackers, and opened fire giving an effective long-range barrage that effectively turned back the first wave when one He111 was shot down. The second wave was more determined. The leading He111 dropped a bomb on the surfaced *P614*, and despite being on fire from the intense AA barrage, released its torpedo to sink the British merchantman *Navarino*, whose lifeboats were lowered so hurriedly that they slipped in the falls and tipped their unfortunate occupants into the cold water where they were nearly mown down by the ship that followed. The aircraft then struck the water and those aboard a passing merchantman could see the crew being burnt alive as the aircraft sank. Then the aircraft that followed dropped a torpedo that struck the American merchantman *William Hooper*, and exploded the boiler. The cruisers then arrived to lend their contribution to the AA barrage, but the attack then faltered, although the British destroyer *Offa* claimed a Heinkel. Several ships narrowly missed torpedoes, while shots from the American *Hoosier* detonated a torpedo warhead. Less fortunate was the Soviet tanker *Azerbaijan* which was hit by a torpedo and exploded in a sheet of flame, but survived largely because she was carrying linseed oil rather than fuel oil. Also unfortunate were those aboard the *Empire Tide* and *Ironclad*, which suffered damage from AA gunners forgetting the injunction to be careful about hitting other convoy ships when firing at low flying aircraft.

In the aftermath of the attack, the rescue ships moved in and the escorts were ordered to set about sinking both the *Navarino* and the *William Hooper*, which they failed to do before moving on, but the *Azerbaijan* astonished everybody as with her largely female crew she steamed on at nine knots. Surprisingly, despite at least seven U-boats being present, they had not intervened, missing the rare opportunity to attack the convoy when everyone was pre-occupied with the air attack.

Aircraft were in the air from the cruisers, with the Walrus from *Norfolk* looking for icebergs while the Vought Kingfisher from *Tuscaloosa* was looking for U-boats, but the Admiralty was now warning that heavy surface units were at sea. Broome ordered the Hurricane from *Empire Tide* to be launched to shoot down the Bv138 shadowing the convoy. He also contacted the two accompanying submarines, one of which signalled back that if heavy enemy surface units attacked, he intended to remain on the surface, receiving the reply from Broome, 'So do I.' A further line of defence was from the Allied submarines, with six Soviet boats watching the Norwegian coast between Vanna and the North Cape, and eight British boats and one Free French further out to sea, augmented by the two submarines that had accompanied the convoy.

At 21.11 on 4 July, the Admiralty signalled both Hamilton and Tovey: 'Cruiser force to withdraw to westward at high speed.' The clear impression was given, following early warnings about the proximity of enemy surface units, that *Tirpitz* was at sea. The next signal, at 21.23, was addressed to both officers and also to Broome: 'Owing to threat from surface ships convoy is to disperse and proceed to Russian ports.' Then at 21.36, to the same three recipients, added emphasis was given to the previous signal with the unambiguous signal: 'Convoy is to scatter.'

The Admiralty was convinced that the *Tirpitz* was at sea, despite a member of the naval staff maintaining that there was no indication that the ship was at sea. A complete communications silence from the Germans could not be enforced once major fleet units had gone to sea as the U-boat commanders would have had to be warned that friendly surface vessels were at sea.

The problem was that the Admiralty believed that it alone had possession of all the facts, and to be fair, the First Sea Lord, Pound, also felt that it would be unfair to place the full burden of absolute responsibility on the shoulders of Commander Broome once Hamilton had left with his cruisers. Dispersal was Pound's solution, his second-in-command, the Vice-Chief of the Naval Staff, Vice-Admiral Sir Henry Moore, believed that this would take too long, and that the quicker the ships scattered, the safer they would be, and when Pound stated that by 'dispersal', he meant 'scatter', the further signal was sent to ensure that this was understood.

While everyone involved at the Admiralty was acting with the best of intentions, albeit that they placed a higher value on their own major ships than on the merchantmen in the convoy, they were seemingly unaware of the nature of running a convoy through to northern Russia. As the convoys proceeded, they were channelled into an increasingly narrow funnel between the southern edge of the Arctic ice-cap and the Norwegian coast, so that the final stages became the most hazardous, caught between proximity to German airfields and the ice, a northern Scylla and Charybis. It was also the case that the merchantmen in a convoy were always ordered to keep station, not to straggle and that survival lay in operating as a unit, for mutual protection and, if the worst came to the worst, rescue.

The signal gave both Hamilton and Broome problems. Hamilton

had no option but to set course westwards, but he delayed for thirty minutes in the hope that *Norfolk* would be able to recover her Walrus, but without success, so he turned the cruiser squadron round and onto a westward course, which had the embarrassing result that the merchantmen and close escort could see the heaviest ships available deserting them, racing past the convoy at high speed.

Broome also hesitated, but for a different reason, since he knew that the merchantmen would be vulnerable on their own. At 22.15, he ordered the hoisting of the signal to scatter. This meant that the convoy had to separate fanwise, with each column steering a course outwards at 10 degrees more than its inner neighbour. Individual ships then steered away from their closest neighbour and increased to best speed, the maximum speed of which the individual ship was capable given the weather conditions. While this was happening, the ships in the centre column maintained station, then finally they too scattered, with the odd-numbers moving out to starboard, the even numbers to port. Heading the centre column was the *River Afton*, with the convoy commodore, who signalled that he didn't understand the order, forcing Broome to take his destroyer, HMS *Keppel*, alongside to repeat the order through a megaphone, then apologising for having to leave the convoy. As for the destroyers, Broome decided that his destroyers should come together as a cohesive fighting force, while the other warships made their own way to Russian ports.

The scatter signal caught some of the ships at an awkward moment, with the destroyer *Somali* in the middle of refuelling from *Aldersdale*, and having to stop abruptly so as to rejoin Hamilton's squadron, fortunately heading in the destroyer's direction.

Tovey believed that scattering the convoy would result in 'sheer bloody murder', while Broome expected 'a shambles', and a 'bloody business'. Both were to be proved right. Worse was to follow when they heard from the Admiralty early the following morning that enemy ships were simply presumed to be north of Tromso, but that it wasn't certain that they were at sea.

U-456 was the first to report the withdrawal of the cruisers, and later this was one of several U-boats to report merchant ships heading in unexpected directions, which was soon confirmed by aerial reconnaissance. Early on 5 July, *U-334* had tried to torpedo the *Navarino*, but the ship had sunk before the torpedoes could reach it, and had then disposed of the *William Hooper*. No matter, *Konteradmiral* (Rear Admiral) Hubert Schmundt, 'Admiral Arctic', lost no time in ordering his U-boats into action against the merchant vessels, while KG30's He111s were getting ready at Banak. Elsewhere, on learning of the convoy scattering, senior officers pressed for the *Rosselsprung* operation to be activated, but Raeder refused. When aerial reconnaissance showed the Home Fleet heading north-east, the major surface units were ordered to be ready to go to sea while Raeder approached Hitler for his approval, which was given. A battle group led by the *Tirpitz* with *Hipper* and *Scheer* slipped out to sea with a screen of seven destroyers and two ocean-going torpedo-boats. Shortly after leaving Norway, the Soviet submarine *K-21* spotted *Tirpitz*, every Allied submarine commander's dream, and fired her torpedoes, but without success. For his part, Raeder then sent a signal to Schniewind implying caution by stating that 'partial success' would be more important than 'total victory involving major expenditure of time'. The battle group was spotted by the British submarine *Unshaken* and then by an RAF Catalina flying boat before the Germans eventually lost their nerve and recalled the ships to port, to the dismay of those aboard who felt embarrassed at sitting in port while the rest of the armed forces were involved in increasingly intensive warfare. When *Vizeadmiral* Oskar Kummetz proposed that *Scheer* should return to sea on her own, he was refused.

It was left to *Kapitan zur See* Wagner, Chief of Naval Operations, to sum up the situation: 'Every operation by our surface forces has been hampered by the Fuhrer's desire to avoid losses and reverses at all costs.'

The presence of a German aircraft carrier would not only have provided earlier notice of the convoy being scattered, the merchantmen would have been vulnerable to aerial torpedo attack. As it was, a number of ships finally managed to reach their destination. There could have been some justification for the Germans congratulating themselves on virtually wiping out an entire convoy, and it was not until *U-88*'s commanding officer, Heino Bohmann, who had been present at so much of the destruction, injected some realism into the debate over how many ships had been sunk that they realised that many ships had passed either undetected or had survived attack.

It is also possible that the presence of a German aircraft carrier would have made the Germans, and by this one means both Raeder and Hitler, more confident in sending their major surface units to sea. These would have posed a challenge for the Home Fleet and while a carrier versus carrier battle could have occurred, it would also have left the German heavy cruisers free to engage the convoys.

PQ18

It was clear that the convoys did not get the cover they needed from the presence of an aircraft carrier with the distant escort, but that they needed their own air cover. In the wake of the disaster that was PQ17, a number of measures were immediately put in hand. Some of these were more or less routine, such as the despatch of four destroyers to Archangel loaded with ammunition and replacement anti-aircraft gun barrels, as well as interpreters in an attempt to improve liaison with the Russians, all of which arrived on 24 July 1942. Then on 13 August, the American cruiser *Tuscaloosa* sailed escorted by two American and one British destroyer, carrying RAF ground crew and equipment, as well as spares, for two squadrons of Hampden bombers destined to be based in northern Russia, along with photo-reconnaissance Spitfires and a squadron of Coastal Command Catalina flying boats. Also included in the cargo carried by the second group of warships was a demountable medical centre and hospital unit, with appropriate medical supplies, but while the Soviets took the medical supplies, they rejected the hospital that would have done so much to improve the lot of Allied seamen in need of attention on reaching a Russian port.

Several of the Hampden bombers, already obsolescent at this stage of the war, were shot down in transit by the Germans and, by mistake, by the Russians. One of those shot down by the Germans came down over Norway, and as bad luck would have it, contained details of the defence of the next pair of convoys, PQ18 and QP14. Doubtless because PQ18 was to have an escort carrier, plans were laid to attack the convoy with a combination of Luftwaffe bombing and U-boats, but QP14, not so fortunate, was to be the target for the *Scheer*, with the cruisers *Hipper* and *Koln*, and a supporting screen of destroyers. The German surface force moved to the Altenfjord on 1 September.

PQ18 was the first Arctic convoy to have an escort carrier, with the US-built HMS *Avenger*. The carrier had three radar-equipped Swordfish from 825 Squadron for anti-submarine duties as well as six Sea Hurricanes, with another six dismantled and stowed beneath the hangar deck in a hold, for fighter defence. The fighter aircraft were drawn from 802 and 883 squadrons. Another Sea Hurricane was aboard the CAM-ship, *Empire Morn*. The convoy escort also included the cruiser *Scylla*, two destroyers, two anti-aircraft ships converted from merchant vessels, four corvettes, four anti-submarine trawlers, three minesweepers and two submarines. Once again there was a rescue ship, but just one as three minesweepers being delivered to the Soviet Union also acted in this role.

While the convoy had gained an escort carrier, the Home Fleet had lost its fleet carrier, *Victorious*, which needed a refit after suffering damage while escorting the convoy Operation Pedestal to Malta in August. Also missing were the American ships, transferred to the Pacific. Tovey also made other changes to the distant escort. This time he would remain aboard *King George V* at Scapa Flow where he could have constant telephone communication with the Admiralty, while his deputy, Vice-Admiral Sir Bruce Fraser went to sea in the battleship *Anson*. The strong destroyer escort afforded PQ16 would be repeated to protect both PQ18 and QP14. This meant allowing the destroyers to leave the close escort to the corvettes, trawlers, anti-aircraft ships and minesweepers if the situation warranted it, with freedom of action to make a sweep looking for U-boats or German surface units. Nevertheless, to save fuel, the officer in command of the destroyers, Rear Admiral Robert Burnett, aboard the light cruiser *Scylla*, ordered that no U-boat hunt by the destroyers was to exceed ninety minutes. Not only would the convoy have the support of Force Q with its fleet oiler, but this time there would be two of them, while Force P, with two tankers and four destroyers was deployed ahead of the convoy to Spitzbergen, while a resupply operation for the Norwegian garrison on Spitzbergen was also linked with these forces.

Once again, Iceland was the main rendezvous. Even getting to Iceland was difficult. Seas were so rough that a Sea Hurricane was swept off *Avenger*'s deck, and the steel ropes securing aircraft in the hangar failed to stop the aircraft breaking loose, crashing into one another and into the sides of the hangar. Fused 500-lb bombs stored in the lift well broke loose, and had to be captured by laying down duffle coats with rope ties, to be quickly tied up as soon as a bomb rolled on to the coats! The ship suffered engine problems due to fuel contamination. Even remote Iceland was still not completely safe, for here the carrier was discovered and bombed by a Focke-Wulf Fw200 Condor long-range maritime-reconnaissance aircraft, which dropped a stick of bombs close to the ship, but without inflicting any damage.

The engine problems aboard *Avenger* meant that the convoy, already spotted by a U-boat whilst on passage to Iceland from

Scotland, had to sail without the carrier, and on 8 September, the convoy was discovered by another Condor. Low overcast then protected the convoy from German aircraft until 12 September, when a Blohm und Voss Bv138 flying-boat dropped through the clouds. By this time *Avenger* had caught up with the convoy and was able to launch a flight of four Sea Hurricanes, but not in time to catch the German aircraft before it disappeared.

The Swordfish were extremely vulnerable on the Artic convoys. This meant that the fighters were not simply concerned with protecting the ships from aerial attack, they also had to cover the Swordfish, which could have fallen prey to many German aircraft. At 04.00 on 9 September, the Sea Hurricanes were scrambled after Swordfish on anti-submarine patrol were discovered by another two Luftwaffe aircraft, a Bv138 flying-boat and a Junkers Ju88 reconnaissance aircraft, but again, these disappeared into the low cloud before the fighters could reach them. Another role of the Swordfish was to see exactly what the Luftwaffe was up to, and on one occasion, PQ18's Swordfish reported that Bv138s were dropping mines ahead of the ships.

PQ18 was repeatedly attacked from the air, requiring the ships to make massed turns and to put up heavy AA fire, all of which made life for the returning Swordfish crews very interesting. Ditching in the sea was never anything to be considered lightly, but in Arctic waters, survival time could be very short indeed. The Sea Hurricanes attempted to keep a constant combat air patrol, CAP, over the convoy, eventually with each aircraft spending twenty-five minutes in the air before landing to refuel, and in such circumstances, keeping a constant watch over the Swordfish as well was almost impossible.

On 14 September, the first Swordfish of the day found *U-589* on the surface, but she dived leaving the Swordfish to mark the spot with a smoke flare. Alerted by the Swordfish, the destroyer *Onslow* raced to the scene, attacked with depth charges and destroyed her. This led the Germans, so far not accustomed to a convoy having its own air cover and aerial reconnaissance, to change their tactics. Reconnaissance Bv138s and Ju88s were sent to intimidate the Swordfish, forcing them back onto the convoy, until the Germans were driven away by heavy AA fire. The Swordfish would then venture out, only to be found and driven back again.

The next day, the remaining Sea Hurricanes and the Swordfish were again in the air, with the former breaking up further attacks. It was not until 16 September, that the Swordfish were relieved of their patrolling by shore-based RAF Consolidated Catalina flying-boats of No210 Squadron operating from Russia. The break was short-lived. Later that day, the convoy passed the homeward convoy, QP14, with the survivors of the ill-fated PQ17, and *Avenger*, with her aircraft and some of the other escorts transferred to this convoy. The interval had been used by the ship's air engineering team to assemble five Sea Hurricanes, more than replacing the four lost on the outward convoy. All in all, the Sea Hurricanes had accounted for a total of five enemy aircraft and damaged seventeen others out of a total of forty-four enemy aircraft shot down. It was fortunate that the three Fairey Swordfish remained serviceable as no replacement aircraft were carried.

During the convoy, *Avenger*'s commanding officer, Commander Colthurst, changed the operational pattern for the Sea Hurricanes in an attempt to get the maximum benefit from his small force, having a single aircraft in the air most of the time rather than having all of his aircraft, or none of them, airborne at the same time.

Clearly, even an escort carrier with a mix of fighters and Swordfish was hard pressed to provide adequate air cover. Indeed, such a convoy could have done with two or more escort carriers, or one of the larger ships such as *Nairana* or *Vindex*, with up to fourteen Swordfish and six Wildcat fighters, a much better aircraft than the Sea Hurricane. As PQ18 approached its destination, there was no sign of the promised Red Air Force air support. The problem was that while the escort carrier had proved itself beyond any doubt, these did not become more generally available until 1943, so there were to be many more convoys without any real attempt at air cover.

The escort carrier and its aircraft would have offered little resistance to a German aircraft carrier with a decent mix of Messerschmitt Bf109 fighters and Junkers Ju87 Stuka dive-bombers, which could also have used torpedoes. The existing German aerial superiority over the convoy would have been strengthened, and HMS *Avenger* would have been vulnerable, not least because of her lack of armour protection and relatively low speed. The Sea Hurricanes and the Hurricane launched from the CAM-ship would have been no match for the Bf109s, although the heavy seas often found on the Arctic convoys would have made landing a Bf109 aboard a carrier difficult because of the aircraft's weak tail section.

CHAPTER THIRTEEN

Conclusion

Plan Z was a dream, perhaps even just one man's dream, Karl Dönitz. Yet, as with so much else, it had its origins in the days before the First World War. One should not be surprised by this. Governments and even systems of government may change, and even national boundaries, nations often do not. Just as Russia always wanted to extend its frontiers and gain a warm water port, regardless of whether the Tsar or the Communists held power, Germany wanted to be not just a continental power, but a maritime power, so that she could become a world power, regardless of whether the Kaiser or the Fuhrer ruled. There is no substitute, even with air power, for boots on the ground or hulls in the water, but while boots on the ground can give continental power, the hulls in the water are essential to world power, and most of all, to power projection.

Nevertheless, plans can be laid, but without the financial means and the industrial capacity to implement them, they are just so much scrap paper. There also has to be the political will to implement them. This was probably the greatest weakness in German naval planning during the Hitler era. Hitler knew first hand about armies, albeit from the viewpoint of a very junior and non-commissioned member of the Kaiser's armies. He was seduced by air power and influenced by his friend Hermann Goering. On one occasion, after the invasion of Poland, he was treated to a private air show with wonderful aircraft and weapons, all ready to enter production. That was so much rot. The Germans lacked the means to put their ideas into production, so apart from a few significant developments such as the Messerschmitt Me262 jet fighter and Me163 rocket-powered interceptor, they had to make do with updates of aircraft which for the most part had been in service in 1939. To meet demand and avoid wasting materials, strict standardisation was enforced. Even the new technology for the U-boats came too late and in insufficient quantities.

179

Had a measured and balanced programme of expansion of the armed forces been started in 1933 or 1934, the German Navy would have been stronger in 1939 than was in fact the case. Nevertheless, it would still not have been the Plan Z Navy. Such progress would also have meant a smaller army and air force than did in fact exist in 1939 and 1940. After all, measured and balanced also means that other demands on the economy would not have been neglected, and indeed, the economy itself would have been a priority for the governing party at a time when the world economy itself was fragile.

That would also have meant resisting demands for territory and avoiding upsetting the neighbours, or at least deferring aggressive and unrealistic demands until, perhaps, the mid or even late 1940s.

Such policies would have been sane and practical, but Hitler was neither of these things. Even before the war, and long before the Third Reich found itself under threat and facing inevitable defeat, he refused to listen to his advisers. Policy was made almost on the trot, switching one way and then another. He was satisfied with the Sudetenland in October 1938, but wanted the rest of Czechoslovakia the following March. In January 1939, he authorised the massive programme of naval construction that was Plan Z, even denying the Army the materials it needed for its own expansion plans, and in September, Plan Z was scrapped. Sometimes, as with the balance between exports and the programme of military expansion, it was one message one day, and the direct opposite a week or two later.

This was a regime that worked on hatred. In its policies towards the Jewish population, it denied itself talent and even patriotism, for many had been Germans for generations. It even wasted scarce resources and manpower in the so-called final solution.

Had Plan Z been stripped of the inessentials and instead a programme of mainly U-boat construction proceeded with, Germany could have entered the war with a more potent and dangerous fleet than was in fact the case, but could the U-boats alone have delivered all that was expected of the Kriegsmarine? As the war progressed, increasingly it became the case that they could not. Raeder was unduly pessimistic about the value of asdic and its impact on submarine operations, but Dönitz was equally over-optimistic. As elsewhere in 1930s Germany, objectivity was lacking.

In fact, the real surprise must be that efforts were not made earlier to seize the French fleet, or encourage or bribe senior French naval officers to join the war against the British Empire. This is not so far-fetched. After all, Darlan was known for his anti-British attitudes, a true Anglophobe, and there were those in France who wanted the country to change sides and ally with Germany. What was it? Suspicion about French intentions, racial superiority or even a determination to go it alone and to hell with the consequences that made Hitler reject French approaches. Certainly, they wanted the French to understand that they had been defeated, and here again the resentments of the First World War defeat probably carried more weight than reason. France as an ally might have been unreliable, as many Frenchmen wanted no truck with the Germans, but she would have offered a substantial fleet and a worldwide network of bases, second only to those offered by the British Empire.

If this seems to have been a missed opportunity, one must also take into account that at no time did anyone try to make the Axis a truly significant and workable alliance. Mussolini did as he wished, as did the Japanese, but so too did the Germans, concluding a secret pact with the Soviet Union on the eve of war, even though this was bound to anger and alienate the Japanese.

Comparison of Commissioned Ranks Reichsmarine/Kriegsmarine and Royal Navy

Normally, new appointments were announced during the summer and appointments or reorganisations took effect on 1 October each year when a new *Rangliste* or rank list was published, but given the upheavals of the 1920s, sometimes this was not possible.

German	British
Grossadmiral – Grand Admiral	Admiral of the Fleet
Generaladmiral – General Admiral	no equivalent
Admiral – Admiral	Admiral
Vizeadmiral – Vice-Admiral	Vice-Admiral
Konteradmiral – Rear Admiral	Rear Admiral
Kommodore – Commodore*	Commodore
Kapitan zur See – Captain (Senior)	Captain
Fregattenkapitan – Captain (Junior)**	no equivalent
Korvettenkapitan – Corvette Captain	Commander
Kapitanleutnant – Captain Lieutenant	Lieutenant-Commander
Oberleutnant zur See – Lieutenant (Senior)	Lieutenant
Leutnant zur See – Lieutenant (Junior)	no equivalent, but one ring
Oberfahnrich zur See – Senior Midshipman	Sub-Lieutenant
Fahnrich zur See – Midshipman (Senior)	Midshipman
Kadett – Cadet or Midshipman (Junior)	no equivalent
Matrose (Offiiziersanwarter) – Seaman (Officer Candidate)	no equiv.

* In the German Navy, a commodore was normally a *Kapitan zur See* 'acting up' as a rear admiral.
** Whether senior or junior, captains still had the same four rings.

These ranks would have been suffixed with the following specialist designations:

Deck or Navigating Officer	. . . . .nothing
Engineering Officer	. . . .*Ingenieur*, usually abbreviated to *Ing*
Administrative Officer	. . . .*Verwaltungsoffizier*, abbreviated as V
Weapons Officer	. . . .*Waffenoffizier*, abbreviated as W

Different titles were used for doctors.

Chronology of the Reichsmarine/Kriegsmarine

It is clear that even at the moment of defeat and the armistice, elements in the Imperial German Navy were planning its resurrection, and planning for a new service was in hand even during the days of the Weimar Republic.

The term 'total war' was an accurate description of the war at sea. There has been much written since about what the British called the 'phoney war', and the Germans called the *Sitzkrieg* or 'sitting war' between the outbreak of war in September 1939 and the German invasion of Denmark and Norway in April 1940, but at sea there was no such period, with the first loss being on the first day of war, the British liner *Athena*. In just a fortnight of war being declared, the first major warship to be lost was the aircraft carrier HMS *Courageous*, torpedoed by *U-29* in the Western Approaches.

1918
11 November – an armistice ends the First World War.
21 November – all remaining German warships surrendered.
> As a last act on abdication, the Kaiser awards all men who served in the light cruiser *Emden*, which had an exemplary war record, the right to add the name of the ship to their surname, even though he was not legally entitled to do this at the time.

1919
31 March – Admiral Adolf von Trotha appointed Supreme Commander-in-Chief of the *Kaiserliche Marine* or Imperial Navy.
21 June – Seventy ships of the German fleet interned at Scapa Flow in Orkney with skeleton maintenance crews aboard scuttled.

1920

8 August – Foundation of the National Socialists' Workers Party
(*Nationalsozialistische Deutsche Arbeiter Partei, NSDAP*),
which became known as the Nazis because the Socialists were
nicknamed Sozis.

30 August – Admiral Paul Behncke appointed Supreme
Commander-in-Chief of the *Kaiserliche Marine*.

1921

1 January – Imperial Navy, *Kaiserliche Marine*, is renamed State
Navy, *Reichsmarine*.

11 April – *Reichsmarine* standard hoisted for the first time.

21 July – Senior United States Navy officers angered when the
United States Army Air Corps sinks the former German battleship *Ostfriesland* using just six bombs dropped from an
aircraft.

13 December – The Washington Naval Treaty is signed and takes
effect in 1922.

31 December – Imperial Navy ensign lowered for the last time, but
hoisted annually on 31 May to commemorate those who died
in the First World War.

1924

January – Light cruiser *Berlin*, commanded by *Fregattenkapitan*
Paul Wolfgang von Ditten, left Kiel for a two month cruise to
the Azores, Madeira, Canaries and Spain – the first post-war
cadet training cruise to go beyond the Baltic.

October – Admiral Hans Zenker appointed Supreme Commander-
in-Chief of the *Reichsmarine*.

Squadron of battleships visits Spain while *Berlin* embarks on her
second cruise in Atlantic waters.

1925

7 January – Light cruiser *Emden* launched in Wilhelmshaven
– Germany's first major warship built after the First World
War.

April – Admiral Konrad Mommsen appointed as Fleet Commander,
a position left vacant since the end of the First World War.

- Survey ship *Meteor* commanded by *Fregattenkapitan* Fritz Spiess
left on South Atlantic survey that lasted until May 1927.

26 April – General Paul von Hindenburg, victor against the Russians

at Tannenberg in 1914 and a former Supreme Commander-in-Chief of the General Army Staff, elected President. He wanted to restore the Kaiser.

August – Light cruiser *Hamburg*, commanded by *Fregattenkapitan* Groos departed Wilhelmshaven for first German post-war circumnavigation.

September – Light cruiser *Berlin* under *Kapitan zur See* Ernst Junkermann departed on a cadet training cruise around South America.

1926

14 November – The new light cruiser *Emden* under command of *Kapitan zur See* Richard Foerster departed Wilhelmshaven for a world tour cadet training cruise.

1927

December – Light cruiser *Berlin* commanded by *Kapitan zur See* Carl Kolbe departed for a training cruise to the Far East and Australia.

1928

1 October – Admiral Erich Raeder appointed Supreme Commander-in-Chief of the *Reichsmarine*.

December – Light cruiser *Emden*, commanded by Kapitan zur See Lothar von Arnauld de la Periere departs for world cadet training cruise.

1929

13 May – Light cruiser *Emden* returns from world cruise and entire company of cadets is transferred to the new light cruiser, *Karlsruhe, Kapitan zur See* Eugen Landau, for shakedown cruise through Mediterranean and then around Africa.

1930

December – Light cruiser *Emden*, commanded by *Fregattenkapitan* Robert Witthoeft-Emden, departed for cruise to Africa and Far East.

1931

31 May – *Panzerschiff* ('pocket battleship') *Deutschland* launched.

November – New light cruiser *Karlsruhe*, commanded by *Kapitan zur See* Erwin Wassner, departs on cadet training cruise to South America and Alaska.

1933

January – German embassies in London, Paris and Washington have naval attaches for the first time since the end of the First World War.

30 January – Hindenburg appoints Hitler as Chancellor.

14 March – Black, red and gold striped jack inset in the naval ensign removed by order of Reich President Hindenburg.

1934

3 June – *Panzerschiff Admiral Graf Spee* launched.

1935

16 March – Hitler rejects treaty of Versailles and reintroduces conscription.

21 May – Reichsmarine renamed Kriegsmarine.

18 June – Anglo-German Naval Agreement signed in London. Also known as London Naval Agreement.

29 June – *U-1*, the first new submarine since the end of the First World War, commissioned.

27 September – Karl Dönitz appointed chief of the First U-Boat Flotilla with effect from 1 October. Flotilla named after First World War U-boat commander Otto Weddigen.

7 November – New naval ensign incorporating swastika hoisted officially for the first time.

1936

7 March – Rhineland reoccupied by the German Army.

30 May – First phase of the Naval Memorial at Laboe, near Kiel, completed and officially opened by Adolf Hitler, who laid the first wreath in the Hall of Commemoration.

18 July – Spanish Civil War begins.

3 October – Battlecruiser *Scharnhorst* launched.

1937

6 February – Heavy cruiser *Admiral Hipper* launched.

8 June – Heavy cruiser *Blucher* launched.

1938

4 February – Hitler appoints himself Supreme Commander-in-Chief of all of the armed forces, and servicemen of all ranks swear an oath of allegiance to him personally.

13 March – Austria incorporated into the Reich.

28 March – Spanish Civil War ends with victory for the Nationalists.

21 May – Battlecruiser *Gneisenau* launched.

22 August – Heavy cruiser *Prinz Eugen* launched.

September – Plan Z formulated.

29 September – Munich Agreement signed allowing Germany to incorporate the Czechoslovak territory of the Sudetenland into the Reich. British Prime Minister Neville Chamberlain returns home proclaiming 'Peace in our time.'

8 December – Aircraft carrier *Graf Zeppelin* launched.

1939

27 January – Hitler formally approves Plan Z.

14 February – Battleship *Bismarck* launched.

15 March – German troops march into Czechoslovak regions of Bohemia and Moravia.

1 April – Battleship *Tirpitz* launched.

- Erich Raeder promoted to *Grossadmiral* (Grand Admiral or Admiral of the Fleet), the first officer to hold this rank since the end of the First World War.

28 April – Hitler renounces Anglo-German Naval Agreement.

22 May – Treaty of mutual military support signed by Germany and Italy.

18 August – German Naval High Command orders emergency war programme to begin.

19 August – First U-boats leave German ports to take up wartime stations in the North Atlantic.

21 August – *Panzerschiff Graf Spee* leaves Germany to take up her position in the South Atlantic.

22 August – A mutual non-aggression pact signed between Germany and the Soviet Union – the von Ribbentrop-Stalin Pact.

24 August – *Panzerschiff Deutschland* leaves Germany to take up war position in North Atlantic.

1 September – German troops reoccupy Polish territories that had been removed from Germany and granted to the new Polish Republic by the Treaty of Versailles.

3 September – Britain and France declare war on Germany after an ultimatum expires.

13 September – U-boat badge reintroduced with up-dated design with the old imperial crown replaced by the swastika.

17 September – Aircraft carrier *Courageous* torpedoed by *U-29* and sunk.

- Soviet forces invade the eastern regions of Poland without opposition from Great Britain or France.

26 September – Dornier Do18 flying-boat shot down by Blackburn Skua from *Ark Royal*, the first German aircraft to be shot down in the war.

14 October – Battleship *Royal Oak* torpedoed by *U-47* at Scapa Flow and sunk.

November – *Panzerschiff Deutschland* renamed *Lutzow* on orders from Hitler, fearing the effect on morale if she is sunk.

23 November – Armed merchant cruiser *Rawalpindi* sunk by German battlecruisers *Gneisenau* and *Scharnhorst* while protecting convoy off Iceland.

13 December – Battle of the River Plate in which cruisers *Ajax*, *Achilles* and *Exeter* inflict serious damage on the 'pocket' battleship *Admiral Graf Spee*, which seeks refuge in Montevideo, but returns to sea and is scuttled on 17 December.

1940

14 February – Destroyer *Cossack* sends boarding party onto German supply ship *Altmark* within Norwegian territorial waters and releases 303 British prisoners from merchant ships sunk by the *Graf Spee*.

31 March – First German auxiliary cruiser *Atlantis*, converted merchantman, commanded by *Kapitan zur See* Bernhard Rogge, leaves Germany for the longest cruise of the war, 622 days.

6 April – Second auxiliary cruiser, *Orion*, commanded by *Kapitan zur See* Kurt Weyher, leaves German waters.

8 April – Britain begins to mine Norwegian waters.

9 April – Germany occupies Denmark and begins invasion of Norway.

- British submarine *Truant* torpedoes and sinks light cruiser *Karlsruhe* off Norway, while heavy cruiser *Blucher* sunk in Oslo Fjord by Norwegian artillery.

- British battlecruiser *Renown* inflicts serious damage on *Gneisenau* putting main armament put out of action.
Mid-April – British and French troops land in Norway, *Furious* covers the landings and afterwards acts as an aircraft transport, *Ark Royal* joins her. *Glorious* recalled from Mediterranean.
10 April – Luftwaffe attacks Home Fleet south-west of Bergen, sinking a destroyer and causing minor damage to the battleship *Rodney* and the cruisers *Devonshire*, *Glasgow* and *Southampton*.
- First destroyer action in Narvik Fjord, with British destroyers sinking two German destroyers and several merchantmen, but two British destroyers are sunk.
- Skuas of Nos 800 and 803 Naval Air Squadrons flying from *Sparrowhawk*, RNAS Hatston on Orkney attack and sink the German light cruiser *Konigsberg* at Bergen, the first operational major warship to be sunk by naval aircraft.
11 April – Submarine *Spearfish* torpedoes *Panzerschiff Lutzow* but fails to sink her.
13 April – Second destroyer action at Narvik, often referred to as the 'Second Battle of Narvik', with the battleship *Warspite* and nine destroyers sinking the remaining eight German destroyers.
10 May – Germany invades Luxembourg, the Netherlands, Belgium and France.
15 May – Dutch forces surrender.
26 May – Operation Dynamo, the evacuation of the British Expeditionary Force from Dunkirk, begins under the command of Admiral Ramsay at Dover, continues to 4 June..
4 June – War Badge for German destroyers introduced.
8 June – Aircraft carrier *Glorious* caught and shelled by *Gneisenau* and *Scharnhorst* during withdrawal from Norway. Carrier and two escorting destroyers *Acasta* and *Ardent* sunk, although *Acasta* scores torpedo hit on *Scharnhorst*.
10 June – Italy declares war on France and the United Kingdom.
- Great Britain completes withdrawal from Norway.
13 June – Aircraft from *Ark Royal* attack *Scharnhorst* at Trondheim, but only one bomb hits the ship and this fails to explode.
17 June – French seek armistice, meaning that the Royal Navy is on its own in the Mediterranean.
- First U-boats refuelled in French ports.

22 June – Armistice signed by France.

27 June – Great Britain announces blockade of continental Europe.

30 June – Germany begins occupation of the Channel Islands.

3 July – Battle of Mers El-Kebir, attacking Vichy French warships near Oran after French admiral refuses to surrender. French battleship *Bretagne* blows up, while battleship *Provence* and battlecruiser *Dunkerque* crippled.

8 July – Aircraft from *Hermes* accompanied by two heavy cruisers attack Vichy French fleet at Dakar, damaging the battleship *Richelieu*.

19 July – U-boat sunk by 830 Squadron aircraft.

August – Great Britain allows USN use of Caribbean bases in exchange for fifty First World War-vintage US destroyers, commissioned into Royal Navy as the Town-class.

17 August – Germany announces blockade of the British Isles with unrestricted U-boat warfare.

24 August – Battleship *Bismarck* commissioned.

30 August – Plans for invasion of Southern England postponed.

31 August – War Badge introduced for German minesweepers, submarine hunters and naval security forces.

23–25 September – Second attack on Dakar, with heavy damage suffered by both navies. Submarines *Persee* and *Ajax* sunk by British, and destroyer *Audacieux* put out of action by cruiser HMAS *Australia*, but submarine *Beveziers* torpedoes *Resolution* while battleship *Barham* and cruiser *Cumberland* both damaged by shellfire, as are two destroyers.

17–20 October – Nine U-boats attack convoys SC7 and HX79 with a total of 79 ships, and this develops into a four day battle in which 32 ships are lost without any losses by the U-boats, who simply expend all of their torpedoes.

5 November – Armed merchant cruiser *Jervis Bay* sunk by heavy cruiser *Admiral Scheer*, but her sacrifice limits the losses in the convoy she is escorting to five ships, and earns her CO, Capt E. S. F. Fergen, RN, a posthumous VC.

11/12 November – Twenty-one aircraft fly from *Illustrious* to attack the Italian fleet at Taranto, putting three battleships out of action and damaging several other ships and shore installations for the loss of two aircraft. Hitler is reputedly furious at such losses without a naval battle.

1941

10 January – *Illustrious* attacked by Luftwaffe and badly damaged during Operation Excess, the handover of a convoy from Gibraltar to Alexandria off Malta. Ship puts into Malta for emergency repairs.

11 January – Luftwaffe attacks cruisers *Gloucester* and *Southampton* escorting four merchantmen, with *Southampton* having to be abandoned.

16 January – *Illustrious* provokes an intensified blitz during her stay in Malta for emergency repairs, reaching a peak on this day.

8–11 February – Convoy battle off Cape St Vincent after *U-37* sinks two ships in convoy HG53 and also alerts the Luftwaffe, which sends five aircraft which each sink a ship. *U-37* then sinks another ship, and guides in the cruiser *Hipper* to sink a number of stragglers before moving on to convoy SLS64 and sinking seven ships.

25 February – Battleship *Tirpitz* commissioned.

17 March – *U-99* and *U-100* sunk by British destroyers after being detected by radar, the first engagement in which radar played a vital role.

1 April – Germans introduce war badge for blockade breakers.

6/7 April – German troops attack both Yugoslavia and Greece, while the Luftwaffe bombs Piraeus blowing up a British ammunition ship that takes ten other ships with her and damages many more, putting the port out of action.

13 April – British submarine *Spearfish* cripples German *Panzerschiff Lutzow* (ex-*Deutschland*) in the Baltic.

23 April – Greek Army surrenders, and British Mediterranean Fleet helps in the evacuation of British forces to Crete.

24 April – Germans introduce war badge for auxiliary cruisers.

30 April – Auxiliary cruiser *Thir*, *Kapitan zur See* Otto Kahler, returns to Hamburg after a successful cruise lasting 329 days.

- Fleet war badge introduced.

8 May – HMS *Cornwall* sinks armed merchant or auxiliary cruiser *Pinguin*, the German auxiliary cruiser that sank or captured most British shipping.

9 May – *U-110* captured by Royal Navy with its Enigma code-machine and books intact, giving the British access to German signals traffic.

18–27 May – Battleship *Bismarck* escorted by the heavy cruiser *Prinz Eugen* makes her maiden sortie, causing the battlecruiser *Hood* and the new battleship *Prince of Wales* to intercept. They are soon followed by the battleship *King George V*, the battle-cruiser *Repulse* and the aircraft carrier *Victorious*. The cruisers *Suffolk* and *Norfolk* sight the German ships and proceed to track them on radar. *Hood* and *Prince of Wales* engage the German ships, but after five minutes *Hood* blows up. *Prince of Wales* is badly damaged and breaks off the fight, but *Bismarck* is also damaged with a fuel leak and has to divert to Brest. Late on 24 May, Swordfish from *Victorious* attack *Bismarck*. On 25 May, Force H with *Renown, Ark Royal* and two cruisers leaves Gibraltar. The following day, Swordfish from *Ark Royal* score two torpedo hits, while that night destroyers make an unsuccessful torpedo attack. The next day, *King George V* and *Rodney* plus two cruisers engage *Bismarck*, and after ninety minutes she is dead in the water and on fire, later sinking.

20 May – German airborne landings on Crete leaves the Royal Navy to disrupt the follow-up seaborne invasion.

21/22 May – The cruisers *Ajax, Dido* and *Orion* with four destroyers destroys a German convoy carrying troops and munitions to Crete.

22 May – Luftwaffe attacks Mediterranean Fleet, sinking cruisers *Fiji* and *Gloucester* as well as a destroyer, damaging *Warspite* and cruisers *Carlisle* and *Naiad*.

26 May – Battleships *Queen Elizabeth* and *Barham* with carrier *Formidable* and nine destroyers attack Axis airfields in the Dodecanese, but shortage of aircraft limits the effect and the Luftwaffe seriously damages the carrier. This leaves the Royal Navy with the task of evacuating 17,000 British, Commonwealth and Greek troops from Crete.

30 May – Motor torpedo boat war badge introduced.

4 June – Kaiser Wilhelm II dies in the Netherlands.

22 June – Germany invades the Soviet Union in Operation Barbarossa.

24 June – Naval artillery war badge introduced.

22–25 July – To help the USSR, invaded by Germany in June, aircraft from *Victorious* and *Furious* attack Petsamo and Kirkenes north of the Arctic Circle with little success, losing fifteen aircraft.

23 August – Auxiliary cruiser *Orion*, commanded by *Kapitan zur See* Kurt Weyer, docks in France after a successful war cruise of 511 days.

28 August – *U-570, Kapitanleutnant* Hans Rahmlow, surrenders to an aircraft in mid-Atlantic.

September – The United States Navy starts to escort convoys as far as the mid-ocean meeting point, easing the pressure on the Royal Navy.

October – Axis losing more than 60 per cent of supplies sent from Italy to North Africa. Two light cruisers and two destroyers based at Malta as Force K.

November – Axis Mediterranean convoy losses reaches 77 per cent.

9 November – Force K from Malta, two cruisers and two destroyers, follows aerial reconnaissance report of an Italian convoy and using radar makes a surprise attack, sinking all seven merchantmen in the convoy and one out of the six escorting destroyers. By this time, the flow of men and materiel between Italy and North Africa is effectively stopped.

13 November – *U-81* torpedoes *Ark Royal*, crippling the ship and she sinks the following day.

15 November – First purpose-built supply U-boat, *U-459*, *Korvettenkapitan* George von Wilamowitz-Mollendorf, enters service.

22 November – *Devonshire* sinks German armed merchant cruiser *Atlantis, Kapitan zur See* Bernhard Rogge, which has been at sea for 622 days.

25 November – *U-331* torpedoes *Barham* off the coast of Libya, and as she rolls over and sinks, the battleship blows up.

29 November – HMAS *Sydney* sinks German armed merchant cruiser *Kormoran, Kapitan zur See* Theodor Detmers, which has been at sea for 350 days.

30 November – Auxiliary cruiser *Komet, Konteradmiral* Robert Eyssen, returns to Hamburg after 516 days at sea.

7 December – Aircraft from the Japanese carriers *Akagi, Kaga, Shokaku, Zuikaku, Hiryu* and *Soryu* send 353 aircraft in two waves to attack the US Pacific Fleet in its forward base at Pearl Harbour in Hawaii, bringing the United States into the war.

10 December – Battleship *Prince of Wales* and battlecruiser *Repulse*, with four destroyers, attacked by Japanese aircraft as they steam for Singapore, with both ships sunk.

11 December – Germany declares war against the United States.

14–23 December – A convoy battle develops off Portugal as convoy HG76 on passage from Gibraltar to the UK is attacked by twelve U-boats. The thirty-two merchantmen have Britain's first escort carrier, *Audacity*, three destroyers and nine smaller warships, but the carrier's aircraft and the escorts together manage to sink five U-boats for the cost of three merchantmen, a destroyer and the carrier herself.

1942

14 January – Auxiliary cruiser *Thor* leaves the Gironde estuary in France on her second war cruise.

7–15 February – Japanese forces take Singapore with its major naval base.

12/13 February – *Gneisenau*, *Scharnhorst* and *Prinz Eugen* leave Brest for the 'Channel Dash', but are detected by the British too late due to technical and organisational failures. Attacks by MTBs and destroyers are beaten off, while all six Swordfish sent to attack are shot down, for which Lt-Cdr Eugene Esmonde receives the Fleet Air Arm's first VC posthumously.

23 February – Submarine *Trident* torpedoes *Prinz Eugene*, putting out of service for the rest of the year.

26/27 February – battlecruiser *Gneisenau* put out of action by bombing while at Kiel.

6 March – German attempt to attack convoy PQ12 to the USSR using the battleship *Tirpitz* and three destroyers is foiled by bad weather. Later, an attack by aircraft from *Victorious* is beaten off.

13/14 March – Auxiliary cruiser *Michel* successfully breaks through English Channel on the start of her first war cruise.

27 March – British commando raid on St Nazaire puts out of action the only dry dock in France capable of accommodating German battleships.

April – Heavy attacks by the Luftwaffe throughout the month see three destroyers and three submarines sunk, as well as a number of smaller vessels.

8 April – The cruiser *Penelope* escapes from Malta to receive repairs – she has been so badly damaged by shrapnel that she is nick-named ' Pepperpot'.

20 April – USS Wasp flies off forty-eight Spitfires to Malta, of which forty-seven arrive, but twenty destroyed and twelve badly damaged by air attack within minutes of landing.

- Motor torpedo boats given their own autonomous command under *Kapitan zur See* Rudolf Petersen.

5–8 May – British forces invade Madagascar with an initial landing at Diego Suarez, supported by the battleship *Ramillies*, aircraft carriers *Illustrious* and *Indomitable*, cruisers and eleven destroyers, finding weak opposition.

9 May – *Eagle* and USS *Wasp* fly off sixty-four Spitfires to Malta, of which sixty-one arrive.

- Auxiliary cruiser *Stier* leaves Germany on war cruise.

11 May – The Luftwaffe sinks three out of four destroyers attempting to attack an Axis convoy from Italy to Benghazi.

12–16 June – Convoy Operations Harpoon and Vigorous attempt to lift the siege on Malta, sailing from Gibraltar and Alexandria respectively. Heavy attacks are mounted by E-boats, U-boats and aircraft, so that after the loss of two merchantmen the Alexandria convoy is recalled. Four out of the six merchantmen on the Gibraltar convoy are sunk, but two get through to Malta at a cost of the cruiser *Hermione* and five destroyers, while another three cruisers are damaged. The Italians lose a cruiser, *Trento*, and the battleship *Littorio* is hit by bombs and torpedoes.

2–13 July – Convoy PQ17 to the Soviet Union includes thirty-four merchantmen, thirteen escorts and three rescue ships, plus a close support force of four cruisers and three destroyers, while the Home Fleet is at some distance on long-range protection with two battleships, an aircraft carrier, two cruisers and four-teen destroyers. After a Luftwaffe attack sinks three ships on 2 July, the Admiralty learns that the North Sea Combat Group with the *Tirpitz* and the cruisers *Hipper*, *Lutzow* and *Scheer* is at sea and orders the convoy to scatter. The Home Fleet prepares to intervene, but the German ships turn back. Over the next few days, heavy submarine and air attack develops, with twenty-three merchantmen and one rescue ship lost for five aircraft.

10–15 August – Convoy Operation Pedestal sees a fourteen ship convoy from Gibraltar to Malta with a heavy escort including the aircraft carriers *Eagle*, *Furious*, *Indomitable* and *Victorious* and the battleships *Nelson* and *Rodney*, seven cruisers and twenty-seven destroyers. Shortage of fuel keeps the Italian fleet in harbour, but E-boats, U-boats and the Luftwaffe attack continuously. *Eagle* is sunk by *U-73*, while the cruisers *Manchester* and *Cairo* and a destroyer are also lost, along with nine merchantmen. The cruisers *Nigeria* and *Kenya* are badly damaged. The convoy effectively lifts the siege of Malta.

12 September – *U-156*, *Korvettenkapitan* Werner Jartenstein, sinks the troopship *Laconia*, but discovers that Italian prisoners of war are on board so a rescue operation is launched.

12–18 September – Convoy PQ18 to the Soviet Union is the first Arctic convoy to have an escort carrier, *Avenger*, with another twenty warships, to escort forty-one merchantmen. Ten merchantmen are lost to aerial attack, another three to U-boats, but the Germans lose three U-boats and forty aircraft.

27 September – Auxiliary cruiser *Stier* scuttled after being damaged by the US auxiliary cruiser *Stephen Hopkins*.

4 November – Axis defeat at El Alamein marks end of German and Italian advance in North African.

8 November – Operation Torch, the Allied landings in North Africa, supported by the United States Navy and Royal Navy. Overall command of naval forces is with Admiral Sir Andrew Cunningham, and the Royal Navy covers two of the three task forces. Centre Task Force has two escort carriers, three cruisers and thirteen destroyers, while Eastern Task Force has the carrier *Argus*, an escort carrier, three cruisers and sixteen destroyers. The eastern flank of the invasion forces is covered by a reinforced Force H which is deployed in the western Mediterranean with the battleships *Duke of York*, *Nelson* and *Rodney*, the aircraft carriers *Formidable*, *Furious* and *Victorious*, plus three cruisers and seventeen destroyers.

31 December – Action off Bear Island as German heavy cruiser *Hipper* and *Panzerschiff* (now reclassified as heavy cruiser) *Lutzow*, each with an escort of three destroyers, attacks Arctic convoy JW51B, escorted by five destroyers and five other Royal Navy vessels. The escorting destroyers mount a determined resistance until reinforced by cruisers *Jamaica* and *Sheffield*, forcing the Germans to break off. *Hipper* hit three times and both navies lose a destroyer each.

1943

January – Hitler proposes scrapping the Kriegsmarine's surface fleet following successive defeats.

30 January – *Grossadmiral* Erich Raeder resigns and is succeeded as Supreme Commander in Chief of the *Kriesgmarine* by Karl Dönitz.

1 February – Fast minelayer *Welshman* lost off Tobruk with half of her ship's company.

2 February – Battle of Stalingrad ends with the surrender of the final pocket of German resistance, but surrender by Field Marshal Friedrich Paulus had been on 31 January.

March – For the sixth successive month in succession, the Kriegsmarine had more than a hundred U-boats in the North Atlantic.

16–20 March – Atlantic convoys HX229 and SC122, with more than ninety ships between them, become involved in a the largest convoy battle of the war with forty U-boats. Over four days, twenty-one ships are lost for the cost of one U-boat.

23 March – 8 April – Eastbound Convoy HX231 crosses Atlantic from Canada without a single loss fighting off every attempted attack by U-boats. The 'Atlantic Gap', the distance without air cover, is still some 500 miles wide.

May – In this month, more than forty U-boats are lost, although Dönitz refuses to recognise it as anything more than a temporary setback.

- re-supply of Axis forces in North Africa has become impossible, forcing them to surrender shortly afterwards.

10 July – Operation Husky, the Allied landings in Sicily, with Admiral Sir Andrew Cunningham once again in command of the naval forces. The USN provides the Western Naval Task Force, the RN the Eastern. No less than 580 warships and 2,000 landing craft are used, covered by Force H and the Mediterranean Fleet with the battleships *King George V, Howe, Nelson, Rodney, Warspite* and *Valiant*, the carriers *Formidable* and *Indomitable*, six cruisers and twenty-four destroyers. Naval firepower breaks up a German armoured division making a counter-attack.

25 July – Mussolini deposed in Italy.

3 September – Allied forces cross the Straits of Messina to land at Calabria.

8 September – Italy surrenders and changes sides to fight with the Allies.

9 September – Operation Avalanche, the Allied landings at Salerno, is covered by Force H with the battleships *Nelson* and *Rodney* and the carriers *Formidable* and *Illustrious*, while Force V under the command of Rear Admiral Sir Philip Vian with *Unicorn* and four escort carriers, *Attacker, Battler, Hunter* and *Stalker* covering ground forces ashore.

- Following Italian surrender, the Italian fleet sails for Malta and are escorted by the battleships *Howe, King George V, Valiant* and *Warspite*, which also cover a landing at the major Italian naval base of Taranto. German air attack sees *Warspite* and the cruiser *Uganda* damaged, as well as two American cruisers.

22 September – British midget submarines, X-craft, attack *Tirpitz* in the Alternfjord and put her out of action for six months.

4 October – British carrier-borne aircraft attack German convoys around Narvik, sinking 40,000 tons of shipping.

17 October – *Michel*, the last surviving operational auxiliary cruiser, sunk by US submarine *Tarpon*.

26 December – Battle of the North Cape occurs after battlecruiser *Scharnhorst* with five destroyers attempts to attack Arctic convoy JW55B, escorted by fourteen destroyers but with a close support cruiser squadron including *Belfast, Norfolk* and *Sheffield*, while a long-range protection group includes the battleship *Duke of York* with the cruiser *Jamaica* and four destroyers. The convoy is missed in bad weather which also separates *Scharnhorst* from her escorts, after which the German ship is confronted by the British cruisers, and after a second attempt a 20-minute battle breaks out with each side scoring two hits, after which *Scharnhorst* attempts to withdraw but runs into the *Duke of York* and *Jamaica*, ending up bracketed by the two British support groups. After *Duke of York* scores several hits, British destroyers mount a torpedo attack, after which British gunfire resumes as the battlecruiser loses way and eventually capsizes.

1944

22 January – Operation Shingle, Allied landing at Anzio, involves four cruisers and a number of destroyers. Cruiser *Spartan* sunk by air attack on 29 January, the cruiser *Penelope* is torpedoed by a U-boat and sunk on 18 February.

3 April – Operation Tungsten, carrier-borne bombers from *Furious* and *Victorious* and three escort carriers, *Emperor, Pursuer* and *Searcher*, attack *Tirpitz* and put her out of action for a further three months.

11 May – Clasp for the Roll of Honour of the German Navy instituted.

15 May – U-boat Clasp instituted.

6 June – Operation Overlord, the Allied invasion of Normandy, sees naval forces commanded by Admiral Ramsay, and in addition

to manning many of the landing craft, the Royal Navy provides a bombardment group with the battleships *Warspite* and *Ramillies*, twelve cruisers and twenty destroyers, with a reserve force including *Nelson* and *Rodney* and three cruisers. Attacks by German destroyers and E-boats see a British destroyer sunk as well as two German ships. Other Allied destroyers were sunk by mines, as were a number of landing craft.

11 June – *U-490*, the last surviving supply submarine, sunk.

12 June – *U-2321*, Type XXIII, the first electro-submarine, commissioned.

27 June – *U-2501*, Type XXI, the first large electro-submarine, commissioned.

July – Experimental command established under Admiral Helmuth Heye within the Kriegsmarine to develop midget submarines.

15 August – Operation Dragoon, the Allied landing in south of France, with battleship *Ramiliies* amongst the five Allied battleships providing covering fire. Fleet of nine escort carriers includes five British ships, *Attacker*, *Emperor*, *Khedive*, *Searcher* and *Stalker*.

September/October – British naval forces enter the Aegean, with seven escort carriers, seven cruisers, nineteen destroyers and frigates, to attack the German evacuation from Greece and destroy the remaining German naval units in the area.

12 November – Aircraft from 617 Squadron RAF bomb *Tirpitz* and capsize the ship with hundreds of her crew trapped below.

13 November – War Badge for Midget weapons introduced with seven grades.

1945

30 January – Passenger liner *Wilhelm Gustoff* sunk in Baltic by Soviet submarine, with more than 5,000 German refugees, fleeing from the advancing Soviet armies, killed.

10 February – Passenger liner *General von Steuben* sunk in Baltic by Soviet submarine, with more than 2,700 German refugees killed.

1 April – British Pacific Fleet reinforces the US Fifth Fleet at the landings on Okinawa, providing the aircraft carriers *Indomitable*, *Victorious*, *Illustrious* and *Indefatigable* with 220 aircraft and the battleships *King George V* and *Howe*, with five cruisers. The ships hit are *Formidable*, *Victorious* and *Indefatigable*.

16 April – Passenger liner *Goya* sunk in Baltic by Soviet submarine

with the loss of more than 6,000 German refugees – the worst loss of life at sea in a single ship in maritime history.

30 April – Hitler commits suicide in his command bunker in Berlin, and *Grossadmiral* Karl Dönitz becomes Head of State. Originally, Goering was to fulfil this role, but he was in disgrace during the final months of the Third Reich.

3 May – Passenger liner *Cap Arkona* sunk in Baltic with the loss of several thousand lives, with other merchant ships also lost around this time adding to the mounting death toll.

4 May – At 18.30, German delegation signs Instrument of Surrender at Field Marshal Montgomery's headquarters to the south of Hamburg.

5 May – At 08.00, all hostilities by German forces come into effect.

Bibliography

Angolia, John R. and Schlicht, Adolph, *Die Kriegsmarine*, (2 vols), San Jose, 1991.

Bekker, Cajus, *Das Grosse Bilduch der Deutschen Kriegsmarine 1939–1945*, Stalling, Hamburg, 1973.

Hitler's Naval War, London, 1974

Blundel, W.D.G., *German Navy Warships 1929–1945*, Almark Publishing, New Malden, 1972.

Cunningham of Hyndhope, Admiral of the Fleet Viscount, RN, *A Sailor's Odyssey*, Hutchinson, London, 1951.

Davis, Brian Leigh, *Badges and Insignia of the Third Reich 1933–1945*, Blandford, Poole, 1983.

Dönitz, Karl, *Deutshce Strategie zur See im Zweiten Weltkrieg*, Bernard & Graefe, Frankfurt, 1972.

Mein wechselvolles Leben, Musterschmidt, Gottingen, 1968.

Ten Years and Twenty Days, Weidenfeld & Nicolson, London, 1959.

Ireland, Bernard, *Jane's Naval History of World War II*, HarperCollins, London, 1998.

Elfrath, Ulrich, *Die Deutsche Kriegsmarine 1935–1945*, Podzun Pallas, Friedberg, 1985.

Keegan, John, *The Price of Admiralty*, Hutchinson, London, 1988.

Kennedy, Ludovic, *Menace: The Life and Death of the Tirpitz*, Sidgwick & Jackson, London, 1979.

Lohmann, W., and Hildebrand, H.H., *Die Deutsche Kriegsmarine, 1939–1945*, (several vols) Podzun, Dorheim, 1956–1964.

Mallman Showell, Jak P., *The German Navy Handbook 1939–1945*, Sutton, Stroud, 1999.

Overy, Richard, *Why the Allies Won*, Jonathan Cape, London, 1995

Padfield, Peter, *Dönitz The Last Fuhrer, Portrait of a Nazi War Leader*, Victor Gollancz, London, 1984

Poolman, Kenneth, *The Sea Hunters: Escort Carriers v U-boats 1941–1945*, Arms & Armour Press, London, 1982.,

Armed Merchant Cruisers, Leo Cooper in association with Secker & Warburg, London

Preston, Antony, *The History of the Royal Navy in the 20th Century*, Bison Books, London, 1987.

U-boats, Arms & Armour Press, London, 1973.

Raeder, Erich, *Struggle for the Sea*, William Kimber, London, 1959.

My Life, United States Naval Institute, 1960.

Roskill, Captain, S W, *The Navy at War, 1939–45*, O, London, 1960.

The War at Sea, 1939–45, Vols I-III, O, London, 1976.

Rossler, E., *The U-boat*, Arms & Armour Press, London, 1981

Sainsbury, Capt A B, & Phillips, Lt-Cdr F L, *The Royal Navy Day by Day*, Sutton, Stroud, 2005

Thompson, Julian, *Imperial War Museum Book of the War at Sea, 1939–45: The Royal Navy in the Second World War*, IWM/Sigwick & Jackson, London, 1996.

Tooze, Adam, *The Wages of Destruction – The Making and Breaking of the Nazi Economy*, Allen Lane, London, 2006.

Van der Vat, Dan, *Standard of Power – The Royal Navy in the Twentieth Century*, Hutchinson, London, 2000.

Vian, Admiral Sir Philip, *Action This Day*, Muller, London, 1960.

Woodman, Richard, *Artic Convoys*, John Murray, London, 1974.

Wragg, David, *Sacrifice for Stalin*, Pen & Sword, Barnsley, 2005

Second World War Carrier Campaigns, Pen & Sword, Barnsley, 2004.

Carrier Combat, Sutton, Stroud, 1997.

Wings Over The Sea: A History of Naval Aviation, David & Charles, Newton Abbot and London, 1979.

Index

Abyssinia, 58, 100/101, 118, 121;
Abwehr, 38;
'Admiral Arctic', 173;
Admiralty, 20, 55, 100/101, 136, 140, 146, 162–179;
Adriatic, 19, 21/22, 66, 120;
Aegean, 22;
Aerial-reconnaissance, 63;
Aircraft carriers, 133–135, 160/161, 161;
Akureyri Fjord, 151;
Albania, 18, 66, 118;
Aldersdale, RFA, 166/167, 170, 173;
Alexandria, 101, 112;
Algeria, 21;
Allied Control Commission, 30, 39/40;
Allies (WWI), 43;
Allies (WWII), 85, 137;
Alsace, 2, 41, 110;
Altenfjord, 168, 175;
Altmark, 142;
Ammunition, 87;
Andrea Doria-class, 120;
Anglo-French-Soviet Alliance, 86;
Anschluss, 64/65, 81;
Appeasement, 66, 139;
Arado, Ar196, 144;
Archangel, 134, 166–179;
Arctic, 148, 160–179;
Argentine, 142;
Armistice, 28, 40;
Armoured warships, 42;
Asdic, 58, 68, 74, 104;
Atlantic, 20, 23–25, 71/72, 76, 123, 148, 160–179;
Atlantic Fleet, British, 100/101;
'Atlantic Gap', 160;
Austria, 12, 18, 43, 64/65, 78, 81;
Austrian Succession, War of, 1;
Austro-Hungarian Empire, 2, 17, 18–20, 24, 41, 93, 121, 139;
Axis, 99, 123;
Azerbaijan, 171;
Azores, 71;

Balkans, 18, 121;
Baltic, 13, 24, 38, 41, 75, 93, 101;
Baltic Fleet, 35;
Banak, 168, 174;
Barbary pirates, 50;
Battenberg, Admiral Prince Louis, 13;
Battles: Barents Sea, 150/151; Britain, 137; Coral Sea, 146; Midway, 159; North Cape, 151–159; River Plate, 142–144;
Bear Island, 166, 169;
Bebel, August, 16;
Beck, General Ludwig, 91;
Beit, Alfred, 12;
Belgian Congo, 3;
Belgium, 3, 17, 106;
Bergen, 27;
Berlin, 14, 51, 93;
Berlin, University of, 5;
Berliner Tagblatt, 40;
Bey, *Konteradmiral* 'Achmed', 152–159;
Biscay, Bay of, 67, 72, 147/148, 161;
Bismarck, Prince Otto von, 2, 62;
Black Sea, 23, 101;
Blackburn Skua, 165;
Blitzkrieg, 92;
Blockade, Naval, of Germany, 28;
Blohm und Voss Bv138, 156, 167/168, 171, 177;
Blomberg, General, 53, 64;
Boer War, 10;
Bohman, Heino, 174;
Bolshevik groups, 32, Revolution, 28, 39;
Bone, 21;
Bothnia, Gulf of, 57, 93;
Brauchitsch, General Werner von, 91/92;
Bremen, 133;
Brest, 67, 148;
Brindisi, 20;
Broome, Commander J.E., RN, 167–175;
Bruening, Heinrich, 43;
Bulow, Bernhard von, 6;
Bundestag, 6, 18;
Burnett, Rear Admiral, RN, 152–159, 176;

Burney, Vice-Admiral Sir Cecil, RN, 18;
Burrough, Rear Admiral, RN, 165;

C-class, 140;
CAM-ship, 167, 178;
Canada, 71;
Canaris, Wilhelm, Admiral, 38, 41, 51;
Cape Bon, 52;
Cape Town, 71;
Cape Wrath, 24;
Captured warships, 112;
Caribbean, 50;
Carls, Admiral, 68;
Carol, King of Romania, 95;
Case A, 46;
Case White, 74–77;
Catholic Centre Party, 44;
Cavagnari, Admiral Domenico, 122;
Ceylon, 139,149;
Channel Dash, 148/149;
Childers, Erskine, 12;
China, 58, 84;
Christopher Newport, 169;
Churchill, Winston, 24;
Ciliax, *Vizeadmiral* Otto, 164;
Coastal Command, RAF, 175;
Colonisation, 49;
Colthurst, Commander, RN, 178;
Communists, 40, 45, 47/48, 58/59, 81;
Condor Legion, 59;
Consolidated Catalina, 145, 174/175, 178;
Constantinople, 21, 27;
Continental System, 1;
Contre-torpilleur, 107/108, 114/115;
Convoys: JW51B, 150; JW55B, 151–154;
    Operation Pedestal, 176; PQ16, 176;
    PQ17, 161–175; PQ18, 175–178;
    QP13, 166; QP14, 175/176; RA55A,
    151–154; War, 160–178;
Copenhagen, 6;
Corfu, 18;
Coronel, Battle of, 24;
Corsair submarine, 68, 108;
Crete, 120, 146–148;
Crimean War, 8;
Cruiser U-boats, 67/68, 72;
Cunningham, Admiral Sir Andrew, RN,
    119, 147;
Czechoslovakia, 64–66, 79, 83, 87, 101;

Dakar, 114;
Danzig, 36;
Dardanelles, 23/24;
Darlan, Admiral, 112, 114, 181;
Dartmouth, 16;
'death ride', 28, 31;
Denham, Captain Henry, RN; 164;
Denmark, 2, 67, 94, 137;

Denmark Strait, 145, 166;
Deutsch-Osterreich, 65;
Deutsche Luft Hansa, 49;
Dodecanese, 120, 147;
Donitz, Karl; 15–17, 27, 30, 32, 35–38,
    40/41, 48, 51–53, 56, 60, *et al*;
Dornier Do17, 138;
Dover, Straits of, 148149;
Dowding, Commodore, RN, 166;
Dreadnought-type, 11, 13–15, 29, 97;
Dreyse, Friedrich, 80;
Dumas, Captain Philip, RN, 10/11, 13–15;
Dunkerque-class, 55;
Dunkirk, 28;

E-boats, 35, 98;
East Africa, 24, 112;
East Prussia, 36;
Eastern Europe, 49;
Eastern Fleet, British, 102;
Eastern Front, 93;
Edward VII, HM King, 11/12;
Elbe, River, 25;
Empire Morn, 175;
Empire Selwyn, 166;
Empire Tide, 167, 171;
Enabling Law, 44;
Entente Cordiale, 12, 17;
Entente Powers. 20;
Esmonde, Lieutenant-Commander, Eugene,
    RN, 148/149;
Ethiopia, 58, 100;
Europa, 134;
Exports, 81/82

Fairey Swordfish, 135, 145/146, 148,
    164/165, 177–179;
Falklands, Battle of, 24;
Far East, 51;
Fascists, 59;
Finland, 41;
First Cruiser squadron, 163;
First World War, 13, 21 *et al*;
Fisher, Admiral Sir (later Lord) John
    'Jacky', RN, 6, 8–13, 24, 28, 61, 100;
Fleet Air Arm, 70, 94, 100/101;
Fliegerkorps X, 122, 124;
Focke-Wulf Fw200 Condor, 176/177;
Foerster, Admiral, 58, 61;
Forbes, Admiral Sir Charles, RN, 101;
Force H, 114, 123,145/146;
Force One, 152–159;
Force P, 176;
Force Q, 166/167, 176;
Force Two, 151–159
Force Z, 102;
France, 2/3, 8/9, 13/14, 17–19, 21, 43, 46,
    48, 50, 54, 60, 63 *et al*;

O-class, 68;
Ofotfjord, 168;
'One Power Standard', 98;
Operation: Barbarossa, 123, 138; ES,
    163–166; Felix, 124; Ironclad,
    149–150; Pedestal, 176; Rhine
    Exercise, 144–146; *Rosselsprung*,
    164–175;
Orkney, 28, 89, 101;
Osborne, 16;
Oslo, 144;
Ostend, 28;

P-class, 69;
Palomares, 169/170;
Panzer, 91, 131, 132;
Panzerschiff(e), 42, 56, 59, 68, 76, 107,
    136, 142, 150, 162;
Paris, 15;
Paris Air Agreement, 41, 99;
Patzig, *Oberleutnant zur See* Helmut, 33;
Pearl Harbour, 129;
Pelopponese, 23;
Petain, Marshal, 112;
Pfeiffer, Rear Admiral Adolph, 38;
Phoebus, 40;
Pilsudski, Marshal, 105;
Piraeus, 23;
Plan X, 68;
Plan Y, 68;
Plan Z, 60, *et al*;
Plate, River, 71;
Pola, 19;
Poland, 36, 39, 46, 48, 54, 60, 64, 66,
    74–79, 83–85, 88–92, 105, 118,
    132/133, 137, 141;
'Polish Corridor', 36;
Portugal, 72;
Potsdam, 134;
Pound, Admiral of the Fleet, Sir Dudley,
    RN, 166, 172;
Prussia, 1–3, 7, 15, 78;

Q-ships, 24;
Queen Elizabeth, 140;
Queen Mary, 140;
Queenstown, 27;

Raeder, Rear (later Grand) Admiral, 37,
    41, 51, 54–58, 62–64, 66/67, 74–77,
    88, 151, 165, 174;
RAF Squadrons: No.210, 178;
Rathlin Island, 27;
Regia Navale, 104, 118–124;
Reich, 6, 45, 56, 64/65;
Reich Defence Council, 129;
Reichsmarine, 31 *et al*;
Reichsbank, 37, 39, 78–96, 129;

Reichsmark, 78–96;
Reichstag, 6/7, 18, 38, 40, 43/44;
Reparations, 43;
Reugen, 129;
Reykjavik, 161;
Rhineland, 49;
Ribbentrop, von, 64, 83–86;
Richthofen, 6;
Riddle of the Sands, The, 12;
River Afton, 166, 173;
Roberts, General Lord, 14/15;
Roma, 135;
Romania, 43, 86, 95;
Roosevelt, President Franklin, 84;
Rosenberg, Admiral von, 35;
Rosyth, 28, 101/102;
Rote Marine, 38;
Rotterdam, 34, 38, 40, 40/41;
Royal Air Force, 70/71, 87, 99/100,
    137/138, 147/148, 174–179;
Royal Naval Air Service, 99;
Royal Navy, 4, 6, 12, 17 *et al*;
Rufiji River, 24;
Ruhr, 36;
Russia, 2/3, 14, 17–19, 23, 150, 161–179;

SA, 51, 53;
Saarland, 56;
Salisbury, Lord, 8;
Sardinia, 120;
Scapa Flow, 28–31, 89, 101/102, 164, 176;
Schacht, Horace, 62, 80;
Scheer, Admiral von, 26, 32;
Schleswig-Holstein, 2, 6;
Schmundt, *Konteradmiral*, Hubert, 173;
Schniewind, *Vizeadmiral* Otto, 164, 168;
Scutari, 18;
Second World War, 50 *et al*;
Seetransport, 40
Serbia, 19;
Sheerness, 14;
Sheffield, 30;
Sherbrooke, Captain Robert, RN, 150;
Sicily, 120, 124;
Silesia, 1;
Siluro a Lenta Corsa, 121;
Simon, Sir John, 55;
Skagerrak, 12, 94;
Slovakia, 66;
Somerville, Vice-Admiral Sir James, RN,
    145;
Souchon, Admiral, 20–23, 29;
South Atlantic, 72;
South Tyrol, 78;
Southampton, 30;
Soviet Union, 34, 39, 53/54, 60, 76, 83–85,
    93–96, 105, 123, 130, 137, 141;
Spahkeuzer-class, 68;